P9-DTY-033

SON
OF
GROUCHO

Also by the Author

SON
OF
GROUCHO

Arthur Marx

David McKay Company, Inc.
New York

B
MARX

SON OF GROUCHO

COPYRIGHT © 1972 BY ARTHUR MARX

All rights reserved, including the right to reproduce
this book, or parts thereof, in any form, except for
the inclusion of brief quotations in a review.

LIBRARY OF CONGRESS CATALOG CARD NUMBER: 72-86964

MANUFACTURED IN THE UNITED STATES OF AMERICA

To Lois

FOREWORD

"What's it like being Groucho's son?"

"Is he as funny at home as he is in the movies?"

"I'll bet he's more laughs than a barrel of monkeys."

I thought I laid most of those questions and speculations to rest when I wrote *Life with Groucho*. And perhaps I did—temporarily.

But twenty years have passed since I published that book, and much has happened to the Marx family in the interim, not the least of which is the sudden new popularity of old Marx Brothers films. In fact, such a cult of Marx Brothers fans has sprung up in recent years—especially among the under-thirty group of film-goers—that I find I'm being asked more questions about my father and his brothers than ever before.

Even Dean Martin, Jr., who's nineteen and hip and should have a pretty good idea of what life spent in the proximity of a celebrity is all about, said to me one day, when we were sitting around the Beverly Hills Tennis Club:

"What's it like having Groucho for a father?"

"Don't you know?" I replied. "Your father's a celebrity, too."

"But your father's one of the *Marx Brothers*!" exclaimed young Dino.

I was surprised at such awe. I figured we more or less had the same problems. But to paraphrase Tolstoy, I guess every celebrity's family is different in different ways. ("And a prophet's without honor in his own home," as my father used to complain when my sister, Miriam, and I didn't laugh at one of his jokes.)

At any rate, it was Dino's interest in the subject that rekindled mine and caused me to take this glance backwards at my life as Groucho's son.

However, *Son of Groucho* isn't so much a book about Arthur Marx as it is about a circumstance—the circumstance of living life in the shadow of a world-famous gentleman. And although I can safely say that there have been times when it hasn't been quite as much fun as "a barrel of monkeys," I still wouldn't trade places with any other son in the world.

CONTENTS

SON
OF
GROUCHO

CHAPTER 1

WHO
AM I?

YOUNG people of today's so called "hip generation" are constantly striving to find out who they are. At least, that's *their* excuse for behaving the way they do.

Well, I have news for them. All my life I've had an identity problem that I'll stack up against the most paranoid of today's kids: after fifty years I'm still not sure whether my name is Arthur Marx or Son of Groucho.

I was named "Arthur" (after my Uncle Harpo, whose real name was Arthur) but I didn't have to be out in the world very long before I discovered that to the general public I was probably always going to be known as Groucho's son.

It's the first reality you must learn to accept when you spring

1

from the loins of a famous parent. No matter what you set out to achieve on your own, there's a strong likelihood, even if you achieve it, that the specter of your old man will always be hovering over you. It stands to reason. He had a head start by at least twenty years—in my case, thirty. And it was his name first. Besides, looking at it from a purely statistical point of view, greatness or genius, or whatever you want to call the spark that makes one person stand out so far above the crowd in the field of his choosing, rarely strikes twice in succeeding generations. With luck, the second generation may be blessed with some talent. But genius—well, you can count those cases on the fingers of one hand.

Thus, Peter Fonda will always be known as Henry's son; Liza Minelli as you-know-who's daughter; and Dick Zanuck as Darryl's son (no matter how many millions *Hello Dolly* lost as a film).

If you let it bug you, living in the shadow of a famous parent can drive you to drink or drugs, or into a shell and complete obscurity. Or it can have the opposite effect, and give you the incentive to accomplish something on your own.

In my own case, the latter has been true. Although I have to admit there have been times in my life when having Groucho for a father has caused me to get pretty damn drunk, paradoxically, the resulting hangover has always turned out to be further incentive not to give up.

I've been a nationally ranked tennis player. I've written a number of books, magazine articles and television shows. And I've co-authored several plays, including *The Impossible Years*, which was a two-year hit on Broadway, and, when turned into a film, became one of the few money-makers to come out of Hollywood in recent years.

So, since I don't know any playwright who can beat me at tennis (including Neil Simon), or any tennis player who's written a Broadway hit (including Rod Laver), I believe I own one distinction no other person can lay claim to: I am the world's Number One ranking Playwright-Tennis Player.

Still the "Son of Groucho" label persists, and as I have traveled along through life, I have found it harder to get rid of than a summer cold.

Although I was fifty years old on my last birthday, hosts and hostesses still, on occasion, introduce me to their friends by saying, "You know Groucho's son," and leave my own name out of the introduction entirely.

When I was playing serious tennis, the headline on the sports page following a victory would often read:

SON OF GROUCHO
COPS TENNIS TITLE

Somewhere in the body of the story I might find that someone named Arthur Marx actually swung the racket.

I remember the first time I went away from home to play the grass court tennis circuit in the Pacific Northwest.

I was only seventeen, but I'd already had a couple of important victories in local Southern California tournaments and I was eager to make a name for myself and show my father that I, too, could do something to make the world take notice. A few more wins along the tournament trail, and I was sure Groucho would soon be known as "Arthur Marx's Father."

But after running myself ragged for six days in the broiling Washington sun, my picture appeared in the sports section of *The Tacoma Herald* with the following caption:

ART GROUX
ADVANCES TO SEMIS

The linotype operator had apparently become so excited that anyone even related to a Hollywood celebrity would be visiting his town that when he read "Groucho" in the story which was ostensibly about me, he completely lost his cool and ran both our names together.

From that point on, I was known to my fellow tennis players (who have a strange sense of humor, anyway) as Art Groux. People thought I was a Frenchman, and again I'd lost my identity.

When my first novel, *The Ordeal of Willie Brown*, was published in 1951, I was confident that my identity problem was finally at an end. I'd soon be known to the world as "novelist Arthur Marx," without the "Son of Groucho" trademark.

Some indication that this was a goal never to be attained came at my first book & author luncheon, in a banquet hall filled with Helen

Hokinson ladies at the Huntington Hotel in Pasadena. As I sat down on the rostrum to dig into my baked salmon loaf, I noticed a slight misprint in my billing on the program card at my place:

THE ORDEAL OF GROUCHO MARX
by Willie Brown

Over the years my sense of humor has been put to the supreme test by having my name always linked to Groucho's, either accidentally or deliberately. But I would be lying if I didn't confess that sometimes I can't laugh about it. I don't know where they get the idea, but most people of humble beginnings believe that if you have a famous father you automatically have it made in the career of your choosing.

To their naive way of thinking, I never could have won a tennis tournament, or written a successful book or play without my famous father exerting influence and pressure somewhere along the line. Like, all he had to do was pick up a phone, call some person of importance, and say, "This is Groucho Marx. Publish my son's book."

Or produce his play.

Or see that he gets a good draw in a tennis tournament.

Or give him a cushy job.

In actuality, quite the opposite is true: my father once *stopped* me from getting a job, and another time tried to *stop* the publication of one of my books.

I'm not saying that having Groucho for a father was always a hindrance to my career. There were times when his name helped me get my foot in doors that would have been closed to others. So in that respect I must admit our relationship has yielded positive as well as negative results.

My first job in show business came as a direct result of Father's influence.

It was 1942, I was fresh out of USC with about eight months to kill before going into the service, and I had no job except to sit in my bedroom day after day, pounding a typewriter under the delusion that I was writing the great American novel.

My future had never looked bleaker, and Father wasn't too sanguine about it, either—especially after I brought him my first few chapters to look over one morning when he was sitting in his book-lined study, browsing through *The Los Angeles Times.*

After solemnly studying my manuscript for about an hour—while I watched with bated breath—Father finally dropped it on the floor beside his leather chair, peered at me over the rims of his pince-nez and exclaimed, "Amateur night!"

It wasn't exactly what I'd hoped to hear. But I did respect his judgment and candor, besides being in awe of the fact that he was the author of a number of *published* books and magazine articles himself.

"Okay, I'll try again," I said, not wishing to show my disappointment at his suggestion that I toss my book into the nearest incinerator.

"Better still you should get a job," he said.

"A job!" A suggestion like that could put a young man in shock.

"Yes. Why do you want to write books?" he said. "Most novelists starve to death."

"You have to start somewhere," I said, a retort which didn't exactly bowl over the world's foremost comedian.

"You've lain around the house long enough," he said, giving me a critical look. "You're going to work!"

As I was wondering who'd hire a neophyte like me, he picked up the phone, dialed The J. Walter Thompson Advertising Agency, and asked to speak to Mannie Manheim, the head writer of the Milton Berle radio show.

"Hello, fat boy," began Father in his usual complimentary fashion, "this is Groucho. My son Arthur wants to be a writer, and I'm sick of supporting him. How about giving him a chance on that turkey you're working for? He's pretty good with a joke."

With Groucho acting as my agent—and a suave approach like that—I was confident that I'd never have to worry about going to work. But I'd forgotten that Father had given Mannie Manheim his first job in radio, and that the man was anxious to return the favor.

After completing the call, Father turned to me and said, "Okay, Big Feet"—Big Feet was his favorite term of endearment—"Mannie's putting you on as a gag writer for fifty bucks a week. The rest is up to you."

If my father's name had been Harry Grama, and he had been a plumbing contractor instead of one of the world's most respected comedians, I'm sure I wouldn't have landed a job on a network radio show with so little experience.

For that opportunity, I've always been grateful.

But that was the first and last job I ever got because my father's name was Groucho.

However, I can remember jobs I *lost* or wasn't offered because of it.

After World War II my agent got me a week-to-week job writing a "B" picture, one of the "Dagwood and Blondie" series, at Columbia Studios.

It was my first venture into screen writing, but somehow I managed to come up with a story idea that the producer liked, and he gave me the green light to start on the screenplay. I was half through the screenplay and my pages seemed to be pleasing my boss when I heard from a friend who had been privy to a conversation between Harry Cohn and my producer, that I was going to be bounced.

It seems that Harry Cohn, Columbia's owner, hadn't been aware that "Groucho's son" was working on the lot until my producer happened to mention it to him one day when they were having lunch in the Executive's Dining Room. Upon hearing the news, Cohn went white with rage, and shouted out in front of all the other executives, "Fire Groucho's son!"

"Why?" asked my producer. "He wrote a good yarn."

"I don't care if he wrote *Gone with the Wind*," roared the choleric Mr. Cohn. "That son of a bitch father of his won't give us permission to imitate the Marx Brothers in the Rita Hayworth musical."

My producer convinced Cohn that it would be cheaper to let me finish my assignment than to hire a new writer, so I stayed on until I'd written the final fade out. But I never worked at Columbia again while Cohn was alive, even though the studio was pleased with the film I'd written.

I didn't work anywhere for a long while. In the late forties, Hollywood suddenly found itself in the throes of its first post-war depression, and most writers of my lowly standing in the community couldn't get work. Since I had a pregnant wife to support by then, and my father had cut off my allowance because I had married without his permission, I was pretty desperate for funds.

Finally, I fired my agent, and decided to get my own job. I phoned Bill Perlberg, at Twentieth Century–Fox, and asked if I could have an appointment with him at the studio.

Besides being a good friend of Father's, Perlberg was an important producer in the industry at the time, and one of the few executives who wasn't running scared. His most recent picture, *Miracle on 42nd Street*, had won an Academy Award, so I figured if anyone could give me a job he could.

When I finished telling Perlberg why I had come to see him, he shook his head lugubriously and said he was sorry but there just weren't any writing assignments around.

"Okay, then give me any kind of a job," I pleaded out of desperation. "I'll even be a can boy. But I need something." I knew if I could just get my foot in the door, I could prove my worth in the studio.

But Perlberg just looked at me dispassionately, and remarked with all the warmth and understanding of a rattlesnake, "Aw, kid, you don't have to work. Your old man's loaded!"

As I've just shown, another one of the fringe drawbacks of having Groucho for a father is that people automatically assume that if he's rich, so must be his son.

Well, purely as a matter of self-defense, I'd like to scotch this myth immediately. Please believe me, future employers, there is no share-the-wealth plan in Marxville—at least not Groucho Marxville. There isn't even a basic minimum salary for being Groucho's son. Not that there should be. I just want to set the record straight.

When I was seventeen, I had a tennis ranking in Southern California that entitled me to expense money from the Tennis Association for my travels East to compete in the important junior tournaments. As most boys who are anxious to accomplish something on their own would be, I was proud of the fact that I would no longer have to ask my father to foot my tennis-travel bills.

However, when I applied for expense money, Perry Jones, the then reigning czar of Southern California tennis, turned me down flat. Why?

"Your father's Groucho," he explained with a fatuous smile. "You don't need any money from us."

It mattered not that I was entitled to it because of my tennis ability.

Women who approach me for charitable donations apparently think I'm loaded, too.

If I don't scribble out a large enough check, or if I candidly admit that five hundred dollars a plate might be too steep for me—no matter how worthy the cause—they look at me as if I'm the second coming of Silas Marner.

One eager fund raiser said to me just recently when I turned her down for a thousand-dollar-a-plate charity dinner, "Oh, come now, Arthur, you can afford it. We know who your father is."

She may have known who my father is, but I know who he is a lot better.

I haven't any idea how much money Father has in his coffers after seventy years in show business. All I know about the subject is what I read in the newspaper headlines every time he gets another divorce, and his ex-wife and her lawyers start tossing settlement figures around.

GROUCHO'S WIFE WANTS HALF
HIS FOUR MILLION

But whether it's four million or four thousand, I want to announce that no vast sums of Groucho's money have found their way into my checking account.

Not that he hasn't been an extremely generous father in every possible way.

Until I married and moved out of his house, Father kept me amply supplied with tennis balls, corned beef sandwiches, expensive orthodontia, new automobiles, and all the other necessities of life in the Beverly Hills ghetto.

And every birthday and Christmas—even today, and no matter where I happen to be in the world—he never forgets to send me a good-sized check. Over the years, these checks have ranged from $500 to $3,000 on occasion, the variable depending on four things: (1) whether he's steadily employed, (2) the current state of the stock market, (3) how much alimony he's paying his last wife, and (4) what his girlfriend of the moment is euchring him out of in exchange for posing as his secretary.

At the age of eighty, and with, I'm sure, more than enough resources in the bank to live like a millionaire for the rest of his life (even if he never works again), Father still worries about money.

And he economizes in foolish ways.

He lives in a six-thousand-square-foot contemporary home in the Trousdale section of Beverly Hills. It's fully equipped with a swimming pool, lava-rock fireplace, expensive paintings, and an electric bed. The whole package is easily worth $300,000 on today's market, and he owns it free and clear, never having believed in worrisome encumbrances like mortgages, or finding them necessary since he first came into big money.

Yet he tries to run the place with one elderly combination cook-housekeeper, who has her hands full just answering his phone. As a result, there's always enough dust in his house to give everyone who visits it an allergy for at least a week.

He had two broken-down couches in his barroom that weren't worth recovering. But when my wife, Lois, who's one of the best interior decorators in Hollywood, suggested that he donate them to the Salvation Army and start with new ones, which she'd get him wholesale, he couldn't see spending the money. So one of his girlfriends found some schlock upholsterer on Melrose Avenue to do the job for him, and now his barroom looks like Barker Brothers window.

On the same day he was deciding against the new couches, he bought $60,000 worth of stock, on a friend's recommendation.

While he was recovering from a recent operation, he blacked out on a sidewalk on the main drag of Beverly Hills, while taking his daily constitutional. His doctor suggested that as a precautionary measure, he stay out from behind the wheel of his Mercedes for a while, and let someone else do the driving.

Instead of hiring a chauffeur, which would have been the simple solution, he saddled his cook-housekeeper with the additional chore of driving him around town, leaving his house more unkempt than usual.

I've been to his house for dinner when he'd only have one small chicken for six people.

"For Christ's sake, why don't you buy two chickens?" I finally scolded him one night as he handed me a bony back and took a generous portion of white meat for himself.

"Don't be so quick to spend my money, Big Feet," he quickly retorted. "Just remember, white meat doesn't grow on trees."

At the same time, he will shop at the most outrageously overpriced market in town, and when someone tries to tell him he could get the identical quality for half the price at Safeway, he'll reply, "I don't believe in saving money on things I put into my stomach."

It was this kind of ambivalence in his spending habits that used to drive my mother right up the wall when she was married to him.

One moment he'd be buying her a six-thousand-dollar mink coat or a diamond ring, the next moment he'd be bawling her out for not turning off the lights when she left a room.

Or he'd take ten people out to dinner at the most expensive restaurant in town, but he'd park the car two blocks away so he wouldn't have to tip the car attendant. He'd also leave his hat in the car, so he wouldn't have to check it. This kind of thing humiliated Mother, but Father felt that the restaurant ought to absorb the cost of parking his car and hanging up his hat. "After all, they soak you enough for the meal," he'd say to justify it.

No matter how much it annoyed Mother, Father couldn't conquer his habit of saving money in insignificant ways.

Even in the palmiest days of the Marx Brothers' career, when their pictures were racking up record grosses all over the country, and their fame had catapulted the four of them onto the cover of *Time*, Father was diligently cutting corners. He knew it was foolish, that some people even considered those traits miserly, but he couldn't help it, because no matter how well he was doing careerwise, he always had an eye on the future. And a bleak future he imagined at that—one in which the Marx Brothers would be completely unemployable, even for honky-tonk night clubs, when he'd be dependent for his bread on the charity of his children or the county Welfare Program.

In good times or bad, Father was never without his insecurity syndrome for very long. Never an optimistic man by nature, Father was always at his gloomiest when he was shooting a film. He hated the hours, he loathed the script, and he considered most directors with whom he worked complete incompetents and a real threat to the Marx Brothers' theatrical career.

On top of that, I don't believe he ever made a film without coming home from the studio at least once during the shooting to tell us about a traumatic experience he'd had on the set that day. It would usually go something like this:

"I had a real shock this afternoon. I bumped into a fellow on the set who used to be a big movie star when we were in vaudeville. He made ten thousand dollars a week, had solid gold plumbing in his house, three swimming pools, five Rolls Royces, and a two-hundred-foot yacht. And now he's working as an extra for fifteen bucks a day on our picture, and he's glad to get that."

My mother, my sister, Miriam, and I were always glad to learn it wasn't something really important—like Harpo or Chico having heart attacks, or perhaps a delay in finishing the picture which would postpone *our* summer vacation trips. But Father could not take lightly these encounters with former movie stars who were now destitute. As soon as he could, he'd phone his insurance man and arrange to take out another fifty-thousand-dollar annuity as a bulwark against old age, infirmity, and the fickle movie public's disfavor.

If the stock market also happened to take a slight dip in the same week that Father encountered the destitute movie idol chances were pretty strong that we in the Marx household would be subjected to an economy wave—one that would destroy everything in its path, from charge accounts at Saks and Magnin's to dinners at Chasen's, and contemplated raises in our allowances.

Luckily for all of us, Father wasn't any more consistent in making the family stick to his austerity programs than he was about anything else in life. And before long all the charge accounts would be reopened, and our lives would return to normal until the next time Father had another scare on the set.

Of course, Father realizes that his spending habits are hard to keep up with. And he himself isn't sure why, even after all his successes, he can't make up his mind whether he is Aristotle Onassis or Scrooge. There seems little doubt that his frugal ways began as a direct outgrowth of an improvident childhood spent in a slum section of New

York City, where six dollars a month for rent was considered beyond his parents' modest means.

By now, the star who's close with a buck because of his early years has become almost a show business cliché. But clichés are born of the truth, and Father, like many another entertainer who's had to climb and claw his way to success through small-time vaudeville, has never been able to shake off, no matter how valiantly he tried, the disquieting memories of crooked theater managers who absconded with the actors' salaries, and nights stranded in tank towns without money for train fare home, or even for his next meal.

And it's left an indelible mark on him and a determination, even at his ripe old age, never to have to do without again. However, his concern about the future has occasionally spoiled his enjoyment of the present. He's never derived as much pleasure from his money as he should have, and his spending habits have caused friction in marriages that might otherwise have remained lasting and rewarding relationships.

CHAPTER 2

MY KINGDOM FOR A PORTER

FATHER didn't have a great deal to spend when he met Mother, although by that time, 1919, the Marx Brothers had, after many years of struggle, graduated from small-time vaudeville and scored somewhat of a triumph at the Palace, in an act called *Home Again.*

That they had reached that apogee of success was due in part to their comic genius, considerable luck (without which no entertainer makes it, Father is convinced), and a mother named Minnie, who didn't stop pushing until her boys had reached the top.

My grandmother, the legendary Minnie Marx, was a plump, vivacious blonde Jewess who had migrated to New York City from Dornum, Germany, in the last part of the nineteenth century, when she

13

was fifteen years old. To support herself, she worked as a seamstress in a straw hat factory on Manhattan's upper East Side.

Her future husband, Sam Marx, was an Alsatian Jew who had migrated to New York around the same time. According to Father, Sam's motivation for leaving Alsace-Lorraine was to escape induction into military service. However, it's more likely, since probably no army would have taken such a complete incompetent, that he came to America to escape the anti-Semitism which abounded in the old country and stood in his way of making a living.

Eventually, Minnie's and Sam's paths crossed—on a ferry boat to Staten Island one Sunday afternoon. Soon Sam was courting her steadily. They fell in love and eventually married, settling down in a brownstone flat on 92nd Street, across from Rupert's Brewery.

By profession, Sam—often known as "Frenchie"—was a tailor, and not a very good one. He was a much better lover, judging by his record. In the short span of thirteen years he begat six children. One died in infancy. The five who lived turned out to be the Marx Brothers.

Listed in the order of their appearance, they were:

Leonard Marx	(Chico)	1887
Arthur Marx	(Harpo)	1888
Julius Marx	(Groucho)	1890
Milton Marx	(Gummo)	1897
Herbert Marx	(Zeppo)	1901

"Pop knocked off quite a few others, too," claims Father, "but Mom never knew about those."

With a number of unemployed relatives and other assorted ne'er-do-wells also taking up residence in the Marx flat from time to time, there generally were more mouths to feed than food to fill them. Sam's take from the tailoring shop usually fell far short of what was needed to satisfy the grocer, the butcher and Greenbaum the landlord, whose six-dollar monthly rental charge did not exactly put him in a class with the robber barons of the day. Nevertheless, it was usually touch and go as to whether or not Sam and Minnie could come up with the rent and stave off eviction—at least for another month.

The result of such poverty was that Minnie, inspired by the success of her older brother, Al Shean (of Gallagher & Shean) in vaudeville, and driven by the understandable desire to eat regularly, decided to put her own boys in show business.

"After all, where else can people who don't know anything make such a good living?" averred Minnie with quite some perspicacity.

In the beginning, the Marx *frères* didn't have much to recommend them as performers. Chico had played the piano in a whorehouse; Harpo had worked as a bellhop in the Seville Hotel; Groucho had been a choir boy in a Catholic church; Gummo could sing, but only off key; and Zeppo had a good left hook and was nimble afoot from the training of trying to outrun the local truant officer.

But what the boys lacked in recognizable talent, the indomitable Minnie made up for with plenty of chutzpah when it came to buttonholing theater managers and booking agents, and talking them into giving her boys a chance. And what she couldn't do with chutzpah, she did by plying potential employers with bean soup concocted by Frenchie, whose wizardry as a chef is still fondly remembered by Father.

It took many years for the Marx Brothers to travel the short distance from 92nd Street to 47th and Broadway, where stands the much hallowed Palace. But as history shows, they finally did make it with *Home Again.*

History, however, has had very little to say about Father's conquest of Mother—an episode in the annals of romance that should take its place alongside such epic love stories as Abelard and Heloise, Romeo and Juliet, and perhaps Burton and Taylor.

The cupid in their flirtation turned out to be Zeppo, who had supplanted Gummo as the act's "straight man" when the latter, recognizing his lack of performing talent, sought refuge in the ladies'-dress business.

Zeppo's big specialty in *Home Again* was an adagio dance performed with the aid of a girl named Vickie Vixen. When Vickie quit the act in Cleveland, Ohio, because she could no longer stand her partner's amorous advances between performances, Zeppo recruited a local girl named Ruth Johnson.

Zeppo's new dance partner was young (eighteen), had a show-stopping face and figure, and she was also a Gentile—three qualities in women that always evoked extreme desire in the loins of Groucho Marx, but with the emphasis on the latter.

Lest there be any misunderstanding about this, Father is *not* anti-Semitic. He admires Golda Meir. He gives generously to all the Jewish charities. Most of his friends are Jewish, and he himself would rather dine on a corned beef sandwich or a piece of smoked whitefish than *canard à l'orange.*

He is what I would call an anti-Jewish chauvinist. Rather than look to the public like the typical show business "Professional Jew," who will be overly biased in favor of his people, he will go out of his way to appear not to be one at all. Incredible as it may seem, he never tasted a bagel until he was eighty-one years old, because the word "bagel" itself has a strongly ethnic connotation. He doesn't care for Barbra Streisand. And when we were contemplating the original Broadway production of *Minnie's Boys,* and the producer wanted to star Totie Fields as the mother of the Marx Brothers, Father turned him down flatly, stating emphatically, "I don't want that fat Jewish broad playing my mother."

"But wasn't your mother Jewish?" I kidded him.

"Yes, but nobody thinks the Marx Brothers are Jewish. Our fans think we're Italians."

According to Father, there's nothing strange or anti-anything about his attitude. "Jewish broads just don't appeal to me," he will tell you proudly.

The incident that fanned the flame of love between my parents occurred just inside the stage door of the theater they were playing, one night a few weeks after the new dancer had joined the cast. Father had just entered the theater, clutching his heavy Gibson guitar in its carrying case, when he noticed the blonde, blue-eyed beauty with the turned-up nose, standing by the mailbox, reading a letter.

Sidling up to her, Father wiggled his eyebrows at Zeppo's new partner and said, "What are you reading, Babe—a letter from your boy friend?"

When the demure Miss Johnson answered shyly that she had no boy friend, Father said, "Then how would you like to marry me? I need a wife to carry my guitar."

He playfully shoved the guitar into her hand. She looked at him with uncertainty for a moment, then smiled timorously and followed the brazen young star of the show up the stairs to his dressing room.

Recalling the incident at the time of their divorce nearly a quarter of a century later, Father commented that that was the most costly remark he's ever made.

"It would have been cheaper to hire a porter," he lamented miserably after the judge had just ordered him to turn over to Mother half of his $500,000 life's savings.

CHAPTER 3

LOVE
AND
MARRIAGE—
GROUCHO STYLE

PERHAPS because he came from a family of indigents himself, it was always one of Father's most fanciful desires to marry a rich
girl.

To his way of thinking, money is more important than love—a
state of mind he believes is evanescent at best, and therefore should not
be a serious consideration when choosing a wife. He always took good
care to emphasize this point whenever the subject of girls and related
subjects came up between us in my youth.

He hasn't, however, lived by his own belief—if that, indeed, is
what he truly believes. His three marriages—to women whose combined assets couldn't have kept one of them off welfare—are eloquent
testimony to the fact that his cynicism about love quickly vanishes the

moment he's in the company of a girl who's young, pretty and non-Jewish.

My mother's father, a Swedish immigrant named Oscar Johnson, was a journeyman carpenter. He was good at his trade, but always had to struggle to support his wife and two daughters.

No wife ever came to my father with less of a Dun and Bradstreet rating than Ruth Johnson. Which is probably why Father didn't get around to marrying her until 1920. He wanted to sock a little money away before taking on the responsibility of an additional mouth to feed. ("After all, white meat doesn't grow on trees.")

In the interim, they worked together in the same act, traveled the vaudeville circuits together, and dined together. But that's about all they did together, in spite of what Father might have had in mind the first time he enticed her to his dressing room.

Mother might have looked wanton and sexy while doing her adagio dance, but once off the stage, she was as proper and straight-laced as Pat Nixon.

Father, on the other hand, could boast of no great record as a conquistador of women in the towns along the Orpheum circuit prior to meeting Mother. Since he'd taken to the road he'd had a few fleeting sexual encounters with local hookers. And once he nearly succeeded in getting himself shot when he was caught in a hotel room with the wife of an actor on the bill with him.

But generally speaking, he never had the luck with women his brothers did. Chico, in particular, had the highest batting average of the four.

"He had a way with dames you just wouldn't believe," Father recalled to me one evening with more admiration in his voice than I've ever heard him conjure up for Chico's other talents. "He could walk into a strange theater where there were thirty chorus girls on the bill with us. And after four days, he'd have laid half of them. He had no fear. He'd walk up to a girl—a complete stranger—give her a little squeeze on the rear end, and the next thing you'd know, they'd be in the hay. Or else he'd charm them with the piano. He was the worst goddamn piano player I ever heard. Absolutely no ear. Half the time I'd have to walk out of the theater when he was doing his piano act. Yet he could sit down at a piano backstage and after one chorus of playing all the wrong harmonies, he'd have half a dozen great-looking broads drooling all over him. I guess today you'd call it sexual charisma."

Why there should have been anything lacking in Father's own sexual charisma in those days, I can't imagine. He was thirty years old, clean-shaven, with dark wavy hair, the features of a leading man, and a well-coordinated body.

In addition he was witty and entertaining, and rapidly blossoming into an intellectual. He'd been largely responsible for most of the writing in *Home Again*, to say nothing of their earlier acts, and a piece of his, published first in *Variety*, had been picked up by H. L. Mencken and reprinted in his *American Language*.

Perhaps it was the pungent aroma of those cheap cigars that were never out of his mouth or hand that kept him from being a second Valentino. Or maybe it was his strangely ungallant ways of treating the opposite sex as equals. In this respect he was way ahead of his time in giving the female animal the liberation they are so militantly demanding today.

Father himself isn't exactly sure when the seeds of his own version of Women's Lib first started sprouting in his consciousness, but if there's any truth to the following story, which he proudly relates, they must have begun to germinate at quite an early age.

It was the winter of 1903, Father had not yet been Bar Mitzvahed, and he was still living at home in the family brownstone, when he gathered up his nerve and invited out for a date the prettiest girl in the neighborhood—one Eleanor Karger.

Surprisingly, she accepted, and with seventy cents jangling in his pockets—two weeks of accumulated savings from running errands in the neighborhood—he took her to a matinee at Hammerstein's Victoria at 42nd and Broadway.

Father had figured the cost of the excursion to the penny: carfare downtown, ten cents; two tickets to the show, fifty cents; carfare back home, ten cents.

The one thing he hadn't anticipated was Miss Karger's sudden craving for one of the coconut candy bars that were being hawked by a candy butcher as they entered the lobby. Too embarrassed to deny the girl her coconut fix, the young sport plunked five cents down on the counter.

By the time the matinee was over, Father still hadn't figured out how the two of them were going to get all the way back to 92nd Street with only enough change left in his trouser pocket for one carfare. To make matters worse, it was starting to snow and it was bitter cold out on the street.

When Eleanor asked her escort why he was hesitating about jumping aboard the horse-drawn street car that was waiting outside the theater, he had no choice but to confess the truth.

As she mulled the problem over, he said, gallantly, "I'll tell you what I'll do—I'll toss you for it."

He tossed the nickel up in the air, and caught it on the back of his hand.

"Heads," exclaimed Eleanor joyously, thinking how fine it was to be squired by a boy with such a wonderful sense of humor.

Father uncovered the coin and peered at it closely. "Tails!" he exclaimed.

It was then that Eleanor got a sample of Women's Lib—Groucho style.

He tipped his cap to her, muttered an apologetic goodbye, and galloped after the already moving streetcar, leaving Eleanor Karger to walk alone from 42nd to 92nd Street, in a blinding snowstorm after dark.

Understandably, Father never saw Eleanor Karger again.

But Mother was not to be put off from capturing her man, either by Father's lack of gallantry or the smell of cigar smoke, which she was getting used to after their long engagement.

In February of 1920, while *Home Again* was playing a week's engagement at Chicago's McVicar's Theater, Mother and Father suddenly decided to get married.

Chicago seemed the appropriate spot for the ceremony. Sam and Minnie had been making the windy city their home base for the past five years, and in addition, the bride's mother and father also had moved there from Cleveland.

The moment they announced their intentions, several complications developed:

(1) They couldn't find a minister who would unite a Jewish boy with a Gentile girl—especially a couple who were in show business (which was not considered a respectable profession as late as 1920).
(2) The bride's mother, Josephine Delano, was not overjoyed at the prospect of having a Jewish son-in-law.

In addition to being slightly bigoted Josephine Delano was a religious kook—a jack of all denominations. At various moments in her spiritual life, she had practiced every religion in the book—Protestant, Christian Science, Mormon, Baptist, Seventh Day Adventist, and just about anything else you can think of. The one religion she had studiously avoided was Judaism.

And it mattered not to Mrs. Delano that Father wasn't a practicing Jew—that he hadn't been in a synagogue since his Bar Mitzvah, and that the only reason he had shown up then was to get a fountain pen.

After making some frantic last-minute phone calls, Joe Swerling, who was to be best man, finally solved the problem of who was to unite the lovers. He turned up a Justice of the Peace who not only was Jewish, but an ex-vaudevillian.

As for Grandma Delano, she never fully accepted the fact that her would-be son-in-law wasn't a member of one of her Christian religions, but after Mother showed her a clipping from the *Chicago Tribune*'s drama critic, Percy Hammond, predicting stardom for the Marx Brothers, she consented to let the ceremony proceed.

In gratitude for these turns of fortune, Father heckled the Justice of the Peace unmercifully all through the ceremony. (Harpo could have attested to this, because he was hiding behind a potted plant at the time and was moving the piece of greenery around the room, to make it appear that it was walking.)

When the Justice intoned, "We are gathered here to join this couple in holy matrimony," Father interrupted him with "It may be holy to you, Judge, but we have other ideas."

Coming down the home stretch—and pretty relieved that the ordeal was almost over—the Justice asked, "Do you, Julius, take this woman to be your lawful wedded wife?"

"We've gone this far," snapped Father. "We might as well go through with it."

There was no time for a honeymoon. In fact, there was barely time for a quick wedding dinner with the Brothers Marx and other *mishpocheh* before Mother and Father had to hurry back to the theater for that night's performance of *Home Again*.

CHAPTER 4

THE ACROBATS AND I

I CAN'T truthfully say how much of the next five years I actually remember and how much has been handed down to me by my parents. But piecing together fragments from both sources, I believe the following is a fairly accurate account of the Son of Groucho's years before five.

I was born at the Lenox Hill Hospital on Manhattan's upper East Side, in July of 1921.

I suspect, from scraps of dialogue that Mother and Father let slip during my formative years, that I was not exactly a product of planned parenthood. Mother was still a featured dancer in the act (with every intention of returning to show business as soon as her strength returned); and Father was not yet secure enough to take on intentionally the responsibility of still a third person.

But whether I was planned or not, I was treated most cordially from the very beginning. Mother even breast-fed me, which accounts, I'm sure, for my predilection for bosoms today. And Father changed and washed my diapers, in spite of the fact that by then he and his brothers were headliners on the Keith-Albee Circuit.

The Keith-Albee Circuit comprised such an enormous chain of vaudeville houses, in and around Manhattan, that a performer could play it for a solid year without once leaving greater New York City—a convenience that didn't go unappreciated by Father and the rest of his brothers, who had leased a house for the entire family in Richmond Hill, Long Island.

Groucho didn't take his duties as a proud father lightly. The night I was born *Home Again* was killing the audience at Keith's Flushing.

When Father heard the news from the stage manager, who relayed it to him from the wings, he stopped the show, stepped to the footlights and announced, "I have just been informed that my wife, Ruth, has made me the father of a six-pound bouncing baby. . . . When the baby stops bouncing, I'll let you know whether it's a boy or a girl."

For the rest of that week, whenever he could spare the time between shows, he'd rush straight to Mother's hospital room, which she shared with two other maternity patients because he didn't think he could afford a private room. There he'd sit on Mother's bed, reading *Variety*, cracking jokes with the other young mothers, and filling the room with pungent cigar smoke.

One evening, during the dinner-hour break between performances, Father lingered at the hospital so long that when he got back to the theater, the curtain was already going up on the Marx Brothers' act. Because he didn't have time to paste on the hirsute mustache he usually wore in his characterization of a school teacher, he grabbed a stick of black greasepaint off his dressing table and quickly smeared some of the blackener under his nose as he ran for the stage.

Father's jokes went over just as big that night with the greasepaint mustache, but when he returned to his dressing room after the show, he found the theater manager waiting for him, and he was livid.

"What's wrong?" asked Father, nervously.

"That mustache—it's just greasepaint."

"The audience didn't mind it. I may paint one on all the time. It's easier."

"Listen, Groucho," ranted the theater manager. "I'm paying for a hair mustache, and that's what I want."

Father refused to be intimidated, in spite of the manager's threats that he would report his insubordination to E. F. Albee, the then reigning czar of big-time vaudeville; and from that day until the Marx Brothers broke up as a team thirty years later, he painted on his black mustache.

So in an indirect way, I guess I'm responsible for a Groucho trademark that was to become as famous as Harpo's red wig and Chico's little green hat.

At the time, Father had no idea of the kind of fame that was in store for him and that mustache. All he really was aware of was that he could ad lib lines that could make an audience limp with laughter, and that he'd better hang onto the money he was making, as a hedge against the day when their contract with Keith-Albee would run out.

Actually, their futures were as secure as any vaudevillian's could be. They were tied to Keith-Albee for five years, and the act was getting $1500 a week. It wasn't all profit, of course. Out of the fifteen hundred they had to pay the other members of the cast, plus their own traveling and living expenses when they were on extended road trips away from New York City. Their individual salaries came closer to two hundred a week. But in those days there was very little income tax and two hundred a week was considered big money.

It wasn't, however, big enough to keep Father from worrying. He was living as frugally as possible.

On the road, Father insisted on staying with Mother in second-rate hotels and avoiding the more expensive restaurants. Once inside a bistro, he paid careful attention to the prices printed on the menu and ordered accordingly. Room service was also an extravagance to be avoided.

For several years after Mother had rejoined the cast following my birth, there wasn't even a nurse or a housekeeper to look after me. For a while there wasn't even a house. Just hotel rooms. It seemed to me we were always traveling—for what purpose I didn't know.

Mother, Father, and I usually shared one hotel room—frequently so tiny there wouldn't be a place in it for a crib. In that case, they'd do the next best thing—they'd put a blanket in a bureau drawer and tuck me in with the socks and underwear for the night.

With not even room for a crib, Father was forced to retreat to the bathroom to do his late-night reading—usually while perched on the toilet seat or the rim of the bathtub. Undeterred, he'd pore over every piece of reading material he could get his hands on—from Dickens to Benchley. And neither the hard seat nor the smell of diapers could stand in the way of his fierce determination to educate himself.

Mother used to say that it was a lucky thing for her that Father was such an avid reader. Otherwise, he probably would have taken a hotel room *without* a bath.

In addition to the inconvenience of three in a hotel room, there was the problem of what to do with me during the show, since Mother was still dancing in the act. Baby sitters were unheard of in those days, and they couldn't leave me at the theater during the performance because most vaudeville houses didn't have individual dressing rooms.

I was a very light sleeper when I was an infant, and a loud cryer. If they left me backstage during the performance, my shrieking could be heard out front in the audience above the sound of the orchestra.

Father finally had to prevail upon a troupe of acrobats on the same bill to stay with me in the hotel room while the Marx Brothers were on the stage. The acrobats opened the show, and after their performance just had time to rush back to the hotel before my mother and father left for the theater.

This arrangement worked out for a while, but finally Father had to let the acrobats go, because they couldn't refrain from rehearsing new stunts while waiting for my parents to return. Aside from what this was doing to the furniture, the guests in the room below were constantly complaining to the manager about the disturbance overhead. On one occasion, a hotel manager thought Father was beating up Mother and sent for the police. When the manager found acrobats occupying our room, he charged Father for five additional guests. That sort of thing *had* to stop.

While Father was scrimping to save a few bucks, Harpo, Chico and Zeppo, never ones to be frightened by the shadow of future failures, were living in comparative splendor.

They stopped at only the finest hotels along the vaudeville circuits, and ate at the most expensive restaurants. Frequently they'd occupy suites instead of single rooms, and Chico and his wife even hired a nurse to care for their daughter, Maxine, who was three years older than I.

Mother could never understand how the other brothers could afford such luxuries, while we, on the exact same income, were dining at Childs Cafeteria and otherwise living like schleppers.

"It'll catch up with them someday," Father would predict. "And then they'll regret they didn't put a little money away."

Zeppo finally solved our baby sitting problem—in a most unexpected way.

Ever since Mother had started dancing with him, they'd been feuding because she didn't like the way he kidded around during their number. Like his brothers, Zeppo could never be very serious on stage, and when he discovered that Mother didn't have much of a sense of humor, he used to take great delight in finding ways to torment her. For example, when Zeppo realized that my mother couldn't extricate herself from a back-bend position very gracefully under her own power, he'd let her struggle with the problem herself for what seemed like an interminable length of time before he'd condescendingly pull her to her feet. This was embarrassing to Mother, and at the conclusion of their act there would be an unpleasant scene in the wings.

But since my mother had her heart set on becoming a headline dancer, she put up with Zeppo's unchivalrous behavior until the Marx Brothers were playing the Biltmore Theater in Los Angeles one night. During the dance number Zeppo grew a little too playful and zestful. While swinging Mother around by her hands, he somehow let her slip through his grasp and she sailed out into the orchestra pit, and landed on the kettle drum.

Mother wasn't hurt physically, but she was humiliated, and after the show was over, she confronted Father and demanded that he say something to Zeppo about the way he was treating her.

"What are you bellyaching about?" cracked Father. "That's the first time you two ever had a decent finish to your act."

Mother was shocked to tears over such a response. She was young and innocent and hadn't been around Father long enough to realize something about his character that I was to discover myself a number of years later: No matter how much he loves you, he'll rarely stick up for you. He'll make some sort of a wisecrack instead to keep from getting involved. It's a form of cowardice that can be more frustrating than his monetary habits.

"You mean you're not going to do anything to Zep?" asked Mother after she had recovered her composure.

"What do you want me to do?—Fire Zep?" hollered Father. "He's one of the Four Marx Brothers."

"Then you'll have to get yourself another dancer. I refuse to work with him."

That ultimatum gave Father the perfect opening to suggest what he'd been wanting to get off his mind for a long time—that she quit dancing, and concentrate on being a mother and housewife. Her main talent lay in those directions, he felt.

It didn't assuage her disappointment any to learn that Chico's wife, Betty, was also quitting the act, at the mutual request of all the brothers, who had wisely decided that wives caused more friction around the theater than they were worth.

So a fall into the percussion section ended Mother's acting career. And while she took it like the proverbial "good trouper," and concentrated her energies on rearing a family from that day forward, it was a blow she never quite got over. The pain of it festered beneath the surface of their marriage, causing trouble between them right up to the very end.

CHAPTER 5

A STAR
IS BORN—
OR WOULD YOU
BELIEVE, FOUR?

THE hard times that Father had been predicting—almost welcoming, it seemed—finally befell the Marx Brothers when I was barely out of diapers.

It came on the heels of an apparent windfall.

While Father and his brothers were sitting around during their summer lay-off in 1922, Abe Lastfogel, their agent, came up with an offer to play their new act, *On the Mezzanine*, at the Coliseum Theater in London, England, for three weeks.

Naturally, they leaped at the opportunity. The pay was good, the job wouldn't interfere with any future bookings coming up on the Keith Circuit, and it would give them and their families a chance to see something of the world.

They left for England with high expectations. Now the whole world was going to be their stage—not just the United States.

But the trip seemed to have a jinx on it.

On the Mezzanine was an enormous flop in London. Jokes that had been killing the people in New York got boos and jeers from the English audience.

About halfway through the show came the crowning insult. The audience started lobbing pennies on the stage. In those days that was the Londoner's way of saying, "Yankee, go home!"

Father, feeling that all was lost anyway, stepped to the footlights, held up his hand for silence and announced in somber tones, "If you people are going to throw coins, I wish to hell you'd throw something a little more substantial—like shillings and guineas."

This brought down the house, and although it didn't prevent the management from canceling the act immediately after the performance, it changed what had promised to be a complete rout into a minor victory. Father's wisecrack on the brink of defeat not only won him the sympathy of the audience, but the line was quoted all over London, and it resulted in the act being booked by a rival theater chain.

For their second attempt at what my Father calls "Licking the Redcoats," the Marx Brothers discarded *On the Mezzanine* and resurrected *Home Again*. Its humor was dated, but apparently that's what the English music hall audiences wanted.

Home Again was a huge success in London, and afterwards it toured the provinces for months before the Marx Brothers returned to the United States.

They should have stayed in London.

When they returned to New York, they discovered that Albee was furious with them for accepting an engagement in London without his permission. Although they hadn't been aware of it, one of the small-print clauses in their contract stipulated that it was strictly up to Albee whether or not they could accept employment elsewhere, *even if he had no work for them on his own circuit.*

The Marxes claimed that they didn't know those were the rules. And besides, what difference did it make? Their trip to Europe hadn't interfered with any jobs Albee had for them, had it?

Albee glowered and said that wasn't the point. He then slapped them with a large fine.

The Marxes countered by calling Albee a dictator, setting fire to his wastebasket, and refusing to pay the fine.

Understanding, warm-hearted man with a great sense of humor that he was, Albee tore up their contract and swore he'd fix it so they'd never work in vaudeville again.

The Marx Brothers scoffed at Albee's blustering threat. They'd already been offered a contract by the Schubert chain, at more money, and now they were free to take it.

But the Schubert chain folded after a few months, taking the Marx Brothers' careers in big-time vaudeville down with it. There was nothing left but to start touring the sticks again. But they soon discovered they weren't getting many jobs in small-time vaudeville either. And after a while, none.

Albee, who was pulling strings in the background, was making his threat a reality.

The small theater owners were afraid to book the Marx Brothers for fear of reprisal action by the vaudeville czar. Unfortunately for the Marx Brothers, the smaller circuits were dependent on the overflow from Albee's circuit for their talent. If they crossed Albee in any way, he would see to it that their supply of talent was cut off, forcing their theaters to close.

So who needed the Marx Brothers?

The famine went on for several months, with things looking more and more desperate. Father had just about exhausted his savings buying bread for the three of us, and he was even considering going into another line of work (except no other line of work would have him), when Chico turned up with an offer to do a legitimate show.

It was one of the weirdest offers in the history of the legitimate theater. A thumbnail history of it goes something like this:

A shoe-string producer, Joseph M. Gaites, had produced a flop called *Love for Sale*, libretto by Will Johnstone, cartoonist of the *New York Evening World*, and music by his brother, Tom. Gaites walked away from the disaster with no money—just a warehouseful of expensive scenery and props.

Shortly afterwards, Gaites met a man named James P. Beury,

who was a successful coal dealer from Allentown, Pennsylvania. Beury not only had plenty of money, but he also owned the Walnut Street Theater in Philadelphia. The theater was dark, but with the summer tourist season approaching, Beury wanted desperately to put a show in it.

Gaites, smelling a sucker, promptly suggested that he build a musical show around his leftover scenery. The idea appealed to Beury, so Gaites quickly contacted Will Johnstone and asked him if he had any ideas.

Johnstone had none, until he bumped into Chico one afternoon standing forlornly in front of the Palace Theater.

"What are you doing?" asked Johnstone.

"Nothing," replied Chico, "and I don't even think I'm allowed to stand here."

Without any coaxing, Chico recounted the sad saga of the Marxes. Johnstone, who had seen them at the Palace, and been impressed, grabbed Chico by the arm and dragged him up to Gaites's office.

Gaites liked the idea of building a musical around the Four Marx Brothers and his leftover scenery but, not realizing their fortunes had sunk so low as they had, was fearful he couldn't offer them enough salary to make the venture worth their while.

Chico, on the other hand, was afraid to ask for too large a salary for fear of blowing the deal, so he said, "We don't want any salary. Just give us ten per cent of the gross."

Father was furious with Chico for offering to work without salary, but it turned out to be the smartest deal they ever made.

The show, hastily slapped together in three weeks' time, with my Father and Will Johnstone collaborating on the book, was a hodgepodge of some new material and many sure-fire gags and routines the Marx Brothers had been killing audiences with for years. It opened at the Walnut Street Theater in Philadelphia under the misleading misnomer of *I'll Say She Is*. Nobody to this day has been able to figure out the exact origin of the title, but it must have contained some kind of magic, for the show was an immediate success, both with the audience and the critics, and it played seventeen capacity weeks in Philadelphia before running out of customers.

At that point, they had to make a decision: Did they want to risk New York and a possible lambasting by the toughest critics of them all, which could mean folding? Or should they stay on the road and milk the less sophisticated towns, where their roughhouse type of comedy was more certain of being appreciated?

The producer decided on the latter course. Why should they kill a sure thing just because of a little vanity? So *I'll Say She Is* toured the United States for nearly a year. By then the show was as solid as the Chase Manhattan Bank. Every joke and comedy routine had been honed to perfection.

There was only one trouble. After a year, there weren't any other legitimate theater towns to play. It was either take *I'll Say She Is* to New York, or close the show.

Faced with being unemployed again, the Marxes had no choice but to risk going up against Alexander Woollcott and the rest of the New York critics, who no doubt were already sharpening their stilettos in anticipation.

I'll Say She Is opened at the Casino Theater in New York City on May 19, 1924. It came in so completely unheralded that *The New York Times* hadn't even planned on sending Woollcott to cover it. They assigned their second-string critic to attend the Marx Brothers' opening. But at the last minute, another show—the one Woollcott was supposed to cover—postponed its opening, so Woollcott changed his plans and deigned to see *I'll Say She Is* instead.

Father's always felt that that was the biggest break in the Marx Brothers' careers. Woollcott, at the time, occupied a pedestal of unparalleled importance in theatrical reviewing. "If he liked you, you were made."

He liked them.

Woollcott not only gave them a good review, he wrote a rave. The one he raved the most about was Harpo. He wrote:

"There should be dancing in the streets when a great clown comes to town, and this man is a great clown."

Singling Harpo out for such an encomium didn't exactly thrill Father. Harpo may have been his favorite brother, personally, but Father's always believed that the word—either spoken or written—deserves more praise than a few funny faces and some well-timed beeps on a rubber horn.

But if he was a wee bit envious of Harpo, he didn't let it spoil his enjoyment of seeing, the next morning, a line at the box office that wound clear around the block and up Broadway.

Minnie Marx's faith in her four sons had finally been vindicated.

Only one thing marred Minnie's complete enjoyment of her boys' triumphant return to Broadway's Great White Way.

On opening night, Minnie was getting dressed to go to the theater. While reaching for her hat, she fell off a stool and broke her leg.

But Minnie didn't let little things like a cast on her leg or the fact that she was in great pain keep her away from the Casino Theater that May night so long ago.

She insisted on being driven to the theater in an ambulance. There she was carried down the aisle and to her front-row seat by two white-coated attendants—just as the curtain was going up. And she remained in her seat, with her cast-encased leg propped up on the brass rail of the orchestra pit, *kvelling* triumphantly every time one of her boys socked over a joke, until the final cheer-laden curtain call.

Sam Marx, my grandfather, was as proud of his boys as Minnie— even though his grasp of the English language was pathetically small, and he didn't understand what half the jokes were about.

Remaining in his seat during intermission opening night, Sam overheard a couple in the row in front of him arguing about whether the Marx Brothers were real brothers.

The argument became pretty heated, with the wife stating that they were, and the husband insisting they were "fakes."

The argument naturally piqued Sam's interest, and finally he tapped the husband on the shoulder and said, "Oh, Mister, I think you are wrong. I know for sure the boys are brothers."

The man looked at Sam skeptically. "You know that for sure, do you?"

Sam nodded confidently.

"Want to make a little bet on it?" asked the stranger, taking out a handful of bills.

Sam considered the proposition a moment, then said, "Vot odds vill you giff me?"

As for me, I was too young to attend the opening at the Casino Theater and personally witness the Marx Brothers' transformation from just another roughhouse comedy act into internationally known stars who, from that evening forward, have never been out of the limelight.

I'm not even sure I knew what a star was, or exactly when it was that I first realized that Father was a celebrity, and not an ordinary nine-to-five wage-earning mortal like the fathers of other children on our block.

I remember hanging around backstage of a number of theaters while I was still in short pants, and having to duck out of the way of stagehands who were moving heavy pieces of scenery while the show was going on. I would gawk up in embarrassment at long-legged show girls in scanty costumes as they brushed by me to take their places on stage, and think how indecent it was to see their anatomy at such close range.

And I would visit Father in the dressing room he usually shared with Harpo and Chico. I remember watching him paint on his black mustache and heavy eyebrows. I remember watching Harpo practicing his harp and Chico fondling every show girl who came within pinching distance.

Through many actual performances, I stood in the wings watching Father and his brothers clowning on stage and sending the audience into convulsive laughter. Even though I didn't always know what the audience was laughing about or why they were applauding him, and I wasn't really aware of how famous the Marx Brothers were, I remember feeling terribly proud of that mustachioed gentleman up on the stage who was my father.

CHAPTER 6

THE
BEST THINGS
IN LIFE
AREN'T FREE

FATHER took advantage of his newly acquired fame and affluence by investing six thousand dollars in a seven-passenger Lincoln sedan, and signing a two-year lease for an apartment on 161st Street and Riverside Drive.

Although I have only fragmentary recollections of places we lived before then, the Riverside Drive apartment seems to be the first home I can remember with any clarity.

It was large and completely furnished, but not luxuriously so, or with any great élan. It was just good, durable Grand Rapids stuff, the kind you'd see in a department store window on Main Street, USA, or in Father's bedroom today.

But the rooms were large and comfortable.

37

I had a bedroom all to myself, with a crib, not a dresser drawer. And plenty of toys. I remember my first Christmas in that apartment. My bedroom, after Santa Claus's arrival, looked like a branch of F.A.O. Schwarz and Company. It was piled high with everything from a shiny red automobile that moved by pedal power to a set of matched golf clubs, cut down to fit my size. Just what a three-and-a-half-year-old needed! But who expected a gift from an uncle named Harpo to be practical?

Mother, who was developing into a first-class cook now that she was devoting her time to being a housewife, had a full-sized kitchen instead of just a hot plate.

And Father had a comfortable mohair reading chair and ottoman in the parlor. If there was one thing Father probably appreciated about his success more than any other convenience, it was the fact that he had been liberated at last from his lavatory-reading room. No longer was it necessary for him to get calluses on his seat while improving his brain.

The six-thousand-dollar Lincoln was delivered to Father at the stage door of the Casino Theater one Wednesday afternoon during the matinee. Though Father rarely waxes enthusiastic over anything, he was pretty excited when the stage manager called him out to the alley, to take delivery of his new automobile. The reason for his euphoria was understandable when you realize that at one time in his vaudeville career, Father and his brothers were forced to travel from town to town, in rain and snow, on motorcycles.

The Lincoln was his first luxury vehicle. And what luxury! It was as long as a hearse and painted black; it had white wall tires, and was decorated with all kinds of nickel-plated trimmings and gadgets. It even had a glassed-in chauffeur's compartment. No chauffeur, however. Father wasn't that affluent.

Chico was on the stage doing his piano solo at the exact moment the vehicle arrived, and the Napoleon sketch, featuring Groucho as the flamboyant Corsican, was to follow. Figuring Chico would be on for another ten minutes, Father hopped in the Lincoln, dressed as Napoleon, and went for a spin around the block.

The Lincoln performed up to his highest expectations, but Father had not counted on the heavy crosstown traffic, nor had he taken the one-way street into consideration. About the time the Napoleon sketch was to start, he was wedged in between two trucks three blocks from the theater, still trying to find a street where he could make a left turn.

"Chico had to play fourteen encores," remembers Father. "And this was pretty difficult since he only knew ten numbers."

In his desperation to get back to the theater, he made an illegal turn, and a policeman stopped him. One look at Father dressed as Napoleon convinced the gendarme that he was a refugee from Bellevue's psychiatric ward.

"But I tell you I'm one of the Marx Brothers," insisted Father, "and I'm due on the stage right this minute."

"If you're one of the Marx Brothers," said the skeptical cop, "let's hear you say something funny."

"If you're a policeman, let's see you arrest somebody," countered Father.

There was no reason why that line shouldn't have landed him in the nearest jail, but evidently the policeman felt that only a Marx Brother would have the nerve to say such a thing. He not only didn't arrest Father, but gave him a police escort back to the theater.

On most Sunday afternoons—a time when the average car owner would take his family for a drive in the country—Father would park our Lincoln somewhere in Central Park, and spend the rest of his day off polishing it. Mother and I would have to sit patiently on the grass, watching him.

Father could go down among the peasants without being pestered by autograph seekers because in those days a mustache was not part of his off-stage attire. And *sans* mustache, and in his rimless spectacles, he was unrecognizable. He could have been just another nice Jewish boy from the Bronx, with a degree in Business Administration from NYU.

Except that the average CPA couldn't afford such an elegant automobile.

One Sunday, when Mother and I were again watching the new Toast of Broadway polishing his Lincoln, a middle-aged burgher paused on the sidewalk to admire the flashy-looking car.

"That's a nice buggy, Mister," said the stranger, patting one of the Lincoln's fenders. "How much does a thing like that set you back?"

"Six thousand, five hundred and forty, F.O.B."

"Isn't that a lot of money for a young man like you to be spending on a motor car?" queried the man, looking at Father in his grease-stained undershirt.

"It's not actually mine," confessed Father. "I'm just the chauffeur. The family let me use it when they go to Europe. And that's the chauffeur's wife," he said, pointing to Mother. "And that's my son. At least my wife tells me he's my son!"

Father enjoyed his off-stage anonymity, for a couple of reasons. To begin with, he's never liked the adulation of fans *per se*—unless the fan was someone whose intellect he truly admired, like a George Kaufman or a Sid Perelman. Particularly anathema to him was the bothersome chore of signing autographs, which he was convinced the average fan tossed in the trash the moment the celebrity was out of sight.

And secondly, he always got a kick out of mingling with non-show business people, and trying to discover what they were currently thinking and saying.

Mother, on the other hand, was rarely amused by Father's reluctance to reveal his true identity—especially when it was responsible for causing inconvenience, like not being able to get into a popular restaurant or to get a good table.

After all those years of scrimping and living in third-rate hotels along the small-time vaudeville circuits, Mother felt Father was entitled, now that he had achieved stardom, to use his name to gain entrée to places denied the average citizen. Not only was it his right, but he owed it to her, his wife.

But Father—either because of an inherently perverse nature, or else because he really believed in living up to the true meaning of democracy—would tell Mother that he did not feel a celebrity had any right to use his name to curry favor with headwaiters or room clerks in order to get a better table or room, thereby taking advantage of people less famous.

This would always be an issue between them when Father took the family out to dinner—especially if the restaurant was crowded and Father had forgotten to make a reservation.

I can see the scene now. I've lived through it dozens of times.

As the maître de approached our party Mother would nudge Father in the ribs and whisper, "Now be sure to tell him who you are, Grouch."

"Sure," he'd say, turning to the maître de.

"The name's Jackson," Father would announce proudly. "Sam Jackson." And then, indicating Mother and me: "And this is Mrs. Jackson, and Master Jackson."

"There'll be a thirty-minute wait, Mr. Jackson."

For some reason, Father was crazy about the name Jackson, and Mother would always do a slow burn whenever he used it at a time like this.

"Groucho!" Mother would implore him heatedly. *"Tell him who you are."*

"If I can't get in under the name of a real American like Jackson, then I don't want to eat here," he'd reply. "I don't like restaurants where you have to be a celebrity to be seated."

"Then you should have made a reservation," she'd scold him. "You just can't walk into a restaurant on a Thursday night without a reservation and expect to get a table."

At this point, we'd either leave for another bistro, or else Father would appear to acquiesce and he'd tackle the maître de a second time. "Garçon, I don't like to throw my weight around, but my real name is Julius H. Marx. And this is Mrs. Marx and this is Master Marx."

To no one's surprise, Julius Marx got us no closer to a table than Sam Jackson did.

"You know that's not what I meant," Mother would berate Father as we headed for another restaurant.

"Julius Marx is my name, isn't it?"

"It's not the one people know you by."

She never cured him of giving the name of Jackson at a restaurant, but her role as the "chauffeur's wife" came to an end soon after the opening of *The Coconuts*.

The Coconuts, a satire on the Florida land boom, written by George S. Kaufman, Morris Ryskind and Irving Berlin, followed *I'll Say She Is* onto Broadway the next season and was an even bigger hit than its predecessor. With a weekly salary now larger than President

Coolidge's, and a rapidly swelling bank account, Father suddenly felt secure enough to change his life-style for the better.

He no longer bought ready-made clothing. He had all of his suits and shirts custom tailored by Earl Benham, who catered especially to the Broadway celebrity trade—Jolson, Cantor, George M. Cohan, to name but a few of his customers. Benham charged two hundred dollars for his cheapest suit—quite a fancy price for those days.

Father also acquiesced to Mother's suggestion that they hire live-in help—in this case a German couple named Otto and Frieda, who had just a fragmentary command of the English language. Frieda cooked and looked after me while Otto butlered, kept the Lincoln's nickel plating in high glow, chauffeured Father back and forth to the theater, and confused us all with his "station house" dialect.

Since Father spoke German, having been taught the language by his mother, he was the only one who could communicate with the Teutonic couple. It therefore fell on his shoulders to plan the menus, and to tell them how he wanted the household run—a role he fell into so easily he never relinquished it even after we had help Mother could communicate with.

There was another drawback to having Otto and Frieda living with us. We only had two bedrooms in our small un-chic apartment.

Father responded to this challenge by driving Mother and me out to Long Island one Sunday, and buying a house in Great Neck—an hour's ride away from Manhattan.

It was a two-story, ten-room stucco house with a slate roof, and it stood on a knoll on a wooded acre of ground. The whole layout cost twenty-seven thousand dollars, and Father paid all cash for it, exclaiming gleefully as he wrote out the check.

"Now, no landlord's ever going to tell me I have to move because I don't have the money for the rent."

No ex-wife has ever been able to eject him from his home, either. Through three straight divorces, Father's always managed to hang onto his security blanket—his house.

CHAPTER 7

AN
OFF-BROADWAY
CHILDHOOD

FATHER couldn't have found a better place to raise a growing boy than Great Neck, Long Island, during the mid-twenties.

Though some of the Broadway and literary crowd (Eddie Cantor, Al Jolson, Ring Lardner, Zelda and F. Scott Fitzgerald) had already discovered Great Neck and moved there before we did, the area was still sparsely populated, and virtually untouched by the big real estate developers.

Our house, for example, overlooked hundreds of acres of deep forest rich with birch and oak trees, unpolluted ponds and streams, and all sorts of wild flora—lush ferns, Jack-in-the-Pulpit, violets and wild raspberries and blackberries. There was also an abundance of rabbits, squirrels, frogs, owls, garter snakes and everything else necessary to make life interesting for a boy bent on becoming another Huck Finn.

A few miles away was the Long Island Sound, with its boating, swimming and fishing facilities, and a number of impressive-looking waterfront estates, where the super-rich owned their own yachts which were tied to their own piers in front of their homes.

Great Neck Village was right out of Sinclair Lewis—one Main Street featuring a bank, a toy and stationery store, a haberdashery, Bretman's Confectionery, and the Great Neck Playhouse, a small movie theater, where I'd sometimes go on Saturday afternoons to watch Tom Mix shooting it out with Indians and other bad guys.

Add to such physical wonders a father named Groucho (and throw in a couple of uncles named Harpo and Chico, who also lived on Long Island), and a boy couldn't ask for a better set-up for having fun.

No son ever had a more doting father than I had. Or a more conscientious one. Or a more entertaining one. Or a father who was more of a buddy.

But then again, not many fathers have the opportunity to hang around the house during the day as much as mine did. Except for Wednesday and Saturday afternoons, when he'd drive into Manhattan for matinee performances, his daylight hours were free to devote to me.

That was perhaps the nicest dividend of having a father who was starring on Broadway.

About once a month, when he was appearing in his third straight Broadway hit, *Animal Crackers*, Father would let me ride into the city with him on Saturday matinee days. He'd take me to lunch at his favorite eating spot—Dinty Moore's, where all the show people ate because it was handy to the theaters—and then he'd let me stand backstage and watch the performance from the wings.

Animal Crackers was probably more sophisticated than their other two shows, but if an eight-year-old couldn't understand every joke and nuance, at least I could appreciate the slapstick. Harpo, for example, making his first entrance at a formal dinner party in a long, flowing cape. When the butler removed the cape, Harpo was revealed wearing nothing but swimming trunks. (Once he forgot the trunks, and a Broadway audience was treated to a Harpo Marx version of *Oh, Calcutta!*)

Or Harpo chasing a blonde across the stage. Why he was so eager to catch her I didn't know for quite a few years.

Or Chico clowning at the piano.

In *Animal Crackers* Father portrayed Captain Spalding, a big-game hunter returning to civilization after months in the African jungle. His first entrance was made in a sedan chair carried on stage by four husky black men.

After alighting, Captain Spalding, dressed in boots, riding pants and a pith helmet, would reach for his wallet and ask the head sedan bearer how much the fare was.

The black man would mumble something unintelligible in his native tongue, to which Captain Spalding would exclaim indignantly, "Eight dollars from Africa to 45th Street? That's an outrage. I told you not to go through the park."

One day, I happened to be standing near Father when he was preparing to climb into the sedan chair and he invited me to ride on stage with him. I did, and after overcoming my initial fright at seeing all those faces staring at me, I enjoyed the experience—especially when Father turned to one of the slaves, as they were getting ready to carry me off again and said, "Driver, take this boy to the nearest drug store and get him an ice cream cone."

The audience must have been as puzzled as I was delighted.

Out of boredom, Father and his brothers were always ad libbing new lines or pieces of business that weren't in the script. They used to drive their authors crazy. George Kaufman, in particular, looked on Father's attempts to change his dialogue with a jaundiced eye. Alexander Woollcott loved to tell the story of the day Kaufman invited him to drop into the theater to watch a few minutes of *Animal Crackers* from the SRO section. At one moment in the show Kaufman turned to Woollcott, and said bitterly, "Be quiet a minute, Alex—I think I just heard one of the original lines."

Following my first exposure to an audience, I was always pestering Father to let me ride on stage with him again, in the sedan chair. Usually he'd cooperate, but if he thought I was overdoing it, he'd shake his head "No!"

One day after he turned me down for the third Saturday in a row, I whiningly asked him, "Why?"

"You're getting to be a ham, that's why. I don't like it."

"But you're a ham."

"Yes, but I don't want my son to be one. Being an actor's a lousy life. Be a doctor or a lawyer, but don't try to be an actor just because I'm one."

Perhaps to distract me from a theatrical career, Father decided to get me interested in the great outdoors. He introduced me to horseback riding.

Father had had considerable experience with horses in his youth. Before embarking on a career in show business, he'd worked for a short period in a livery stable. And later, when he was touring in small-time vaudeville, he'd been stranded out West, where hunger had forced him to take a job driving a horse-drawn delivery wagon between Denver and Cripple Creek, Colorado.

Because of his inexperience as a horse handler, he let the team of horses run away from him one day while he was traversing a narrow mountain trail. The wagon cracked up just short of going over a cliff, and Father and the horses escaped with their lives, but the wagonload of supplies was destroyed and Father had to flee the state on foot to keep from being tarred and feathered by the owner of the lost cargo.

The memory of that distant disaster did not dampen Father's enthusiasm for passing along to me all the savvy he had picked up during his own illustrious career as an equestrian, and one afternoon found the two of us down at the Great Neck Riding Academy renting a couple of two-dollar-an-hour thoroughbreds.

The riding trail snaked its way through very dense forest, and once mounted, Father didn't seem as sure of his seat on the English saddle as I did. And I'd never been on a horse before in my life, except to ride the ponies in Central Park.

Perhaps Father's horse was more spirited than mine. At any rate, his mount shied at every little thing along the trail, and kept bobbing his head up and down in a manner that was so distracting to Father that he finally asked me if I'd mind trading horses with him.

Being an obedient son, I obligingly hopped to the ground, handed

Father the reins to my horse and jumped up in the saddle he had just vacated.

The ride proceeded another two hundred yards, when we came to a large tree that had fallen across the trail. My former horse, leading the way with Father astride him, stepped carefully across the log to safety. But my new mount, believing he was in the Grand National steeplechase, took a sudden and unexpected leap into the wild blue yonder, and I went sailing over his head and into the bramble bushes, where I landed on my back, unhurt but pretty shaken up and frightened.

After dismounting and making sure I was all right, Father started to laugh.

"What's funny?" I asked, still trembling from the experience.

"That horse I gave you is a jumper."

"Why'd you give him to me?" I persisted as tears started rolling down my cheeks. "I could have gotten hurt!"

Continuing to grin, he said, "That'll teach you—never trust your father!"

I trusted Father even less after our outing to Coney Island. It was a hot summer day, the traffic between Great Neck and the amusement park had been bumper to bumper, and Father would have much preferred to be curled up in the hammock in our back yard reading *The New Yorker* than to be engulfed in the huge crowd at Coney.

But Father had promised to take me there, and Father never reneged on promises—especially to children. Besides, ever since his own childhood, when he couldn't afford to go on the rides, he had considered Coney Island the ultimate in juvenile entertainment and was determined not to let his own son miss out on all that fun.

I was equally positive I would enjoy myself. But once we arrived at the amusement park, I was afraid to try anything more daring than the Merry-Go-Round and the frozen custard stand.

Father was pretty disgusted with me when I refused to go on even the junior roller coaster.

"I drove forty miles in a heat wave to find out our son's a coward," Father complained to Mother as he bought tickets to enter the Fun House, whose main attraction was a hundred-foot slide.

"Our son's no more of a coward than you," said Mother protectively. "I don't see *you* going on any of the rides, Groucho."

"I'm not a coward," replied Father. "I merely get sick to my stomach at any kind of motion."

"Well, I'm not a coward, either," I said.

"Then let's see you go down that big slide," said Father, pointing to it with his cigar. "I'll buy you another frozen custard if you do."

With the courage of an astronaut, I swiftly clambered up the hundred steps to the top of the slide and perched myself on the glossy point-of-departure. But as I gazed down at the bottom of the slide, which seemed farther away than the floor of the Grand Canyon, I lost my nerve.

I sat frozen at the top of the slide for nearly an hour while all around me other kids were running up the steps and fearlessly going over the brink, some even head first. Meanwhile, down below Father was exhorting me onward with frantic hand motions and occasional expletives, like, "Schlemiel, don't be a schlemiel! Jump like the *poor* kids."

I was relieved when I finally lost sight of him and Mother in the crowd of proud parents at the bottom of the slide. I figured they'd probably got fed up with my cowardice, and gone for a walk. If I played my cards right, I could sneak back to the ground floor by way of the stairs, and when I found them I'd lie and tell them I'd come down the slide.

I was about to put this stratagem into action when I felt a sudden push from behind, and the next thing I knew, I was hurtling down the precipice. As I made my descent, I caught a glimpse of Father standing at the top of the slide, grinning victoriously.

Shortly after our Coney Island contretemps, Father decided that we ought to join a beach club. After investigating a number of them, he drove us over to the Sands Point Bath and Sun Club one August afternoon and filled out an application. On Mother's advice, he wisely put down "Groucho" where the blank asked for his first name. But it didn't help. He was told by the stuffy head of the membership committee that he couldn't be a member because he was Jewish.

For the first time in his life, Father was speechless. But he recovered quickly.

"My son's only half Jewish," he shot back. "Would it be all right if he went in the water up to his knees?"

However, Father *was* allowed to join Lakeville Country Club—at the time, perhaps the finest golfing layout on Long Island's North Shore. The initiation fee was five thousand dollars, which was a lot of money for the way Father played golf, but Eddie Cantor, Al Jolson and Ruby Keeler (who was married to Jolson at the time) were all members, and Father enjoyed their company, so he splurged. Besides, there was no reason for Father to believe he couldn't become a scratch shooter if he applied himself. He already had a hole-in-one to his credit—made at the Brae Burn Country Club in Boston a couple of years earlier. It had been quite an exciting experience for him, too.

Because he was a world-famous comedian, news of his feat made the front page of *The Boston Globe*'s sports section the morning after it happened, along with a picture of Father in a little box. The box was flanked on one side by a picture of Bobby Jones and on the other by Walter Hagen. The caption read simply: "Groucho joins the immortals."

That afternoon, when Father showed up at Brae Burn to take his daily exercise, he found he was being trailed by a phalanx of newspaper reporters and photographers.

Under that kind of pressure, Father took a twenty-two on the same hole where he'd previously scored the ace, and about a hundred and twenty-two for the entire round.

The next morning the sports page ran the same illustration, with one change. There was a blank space in the box where Father's picture had been. And underneath it, the caption read "Groucho leaves the immortals."

Father was plagued with that kind of luck during most of his golfing career. For twelve years, he and Mother would play eighteen holes of golf every day that it wasn't snowing, raining, or that he didn't have to work. Every day he'd step out on the tee in golfing knickers and argyle socks, his mind spinning with all the tips he read in the latest "How to Play" book the night before, and every day he'd be absolutely convinced he was going to shoot par. But when he finally hung up his clubs for good (threw them away, as a matter of fact, over a cliff at Pebble Beach), he still had never broken ninety.

Nobody could ever figure out this phenomenon. Father had one of the finest practice swings in the world. No golf professional could ever find a flaw in it. But as soon as you put a ball down in front of him, his game fell apart.

Unlike a lot of golfers, he didn't have any one shot that gave him trouble. His short game was as bad as his woods, and his putting was especially atrocious. He could never be sure of sinking any putt over a foot long. Once at Lakeville, with but a single hole to play, and needing just a bogey for an 89, Father again got the shakes, and five-putted from less than three feet. He was so furious with himself that he hurled his putter to the green, embedding it about a foot deep in the velvety green turf that had been brought over to Lakeville from Scotland.

The greens committee was shocked, and initiated a movement to have this usually mild-mannered actor tossed out of the club. But they did give him a chance to defend himself at the expulsion proceedings. And defend himself he did, with a brilliance even Clarence Darrow would have envied.

"If you throw me out, you'll be sorry," he argued. "If I'm not a member, I won't have to play golf. And if I don't have to play golf, it'll be a pleasure—not punishment. You want to make me happy for doing what I did?"

In view of the defendant's logic and honesty, the committee reconsidered and allowed Father to remain a member. To show his gratitude, while playing Lakeville's famed water hole the next day, Father killed one of the club's prized swans with a wild two-iron shot. This unnerved him so that when he was making his final approach to the eighteenth green, he topped the ball and sent it flying through the windshield of the club president's Rolls Royce.

Father has never been able to understand his lack of aptitude for the ancient and honorable Scottish game.

It's certainly nothing that runs in the family. Chico and Harpo were always able to shoot in the low eighties and high seventies, and Zeppo, even today, and approaching the age of seventy, still makes a pretty good living hustling golf at Tamerisk Country Club in Palm Springs.

Father has consistently refused to let his golfing inability get him down. "After all, everyone has some kind of an albatross," he points out philosophically. "Sam Snead's never won the U.S. Open. Wilt the Stilt's lousy from the free-throw line. And Nixon never made Governor of California."

Oddly enough, when he was young, Father had all the attributes of a fine athlete: good coordination, stamina, and an ability to think quickly in a tight situation—as evidenced by the way he tricked me into trading horses with him the day he introduced me to saddle riding.

He swam well—that is to say, he never drowned; he could beat Mother at tennis; and he was quite expert with a ball, bat and glove. In his vaudeville touring days, as a matter of fact, he played catcher for a semi-pro team composed of other performers on the same bill with him, and they played the local hot shots in all the towns along the Orpheum Circuit.

When I was old enough to swing a bat, Father organized baseball games for me and the other kids in the neighborhood, and he usually would compete himself. If we were shorthanded, he'd frequently ring in one of his visiting celebrity friends—Eddie Cantor or Ed Wynn, and, once, Will Rogers.

Will Rogers, who was starring in the Ziegfeld Follies on Broadway, and was about forty at the time, was a better horseman than a baseball player, but that didn't stop him from getting in the spirit of our contests.

I remember one incident in particular involving Rogers. He was playing second base for the opposing team and quite a way off the bag. I was the runner on first; when the batter drilled a line drive deep to short, I streaked for second. Simultaneously, the shortstop scooped up the ball and rifled it to Rogers, for the force-out. But Rogers was still about twenty feet off second, and made no attempt to tag me as I ran by and reached the bag standing up.

I was safe by a country mile, as the saying goes, but Rogers took one look at me standing smugly on second base, and yelled, "You're out!"

"I can't be!" I shouted back. "You were nowhere near second base."

Rogers furrowed up his brow and scratched his head as he considered my accusation—then said, completely unruffled: "Listen, kid—when you get to be my age, anyplace you stand is second base!"

At the time, I was a little too young and agile to appreciate that remark. But in retrospect, I can say it's one of the great lines about growing old.

CHAPTER 8

EVERYTHING
I DIDN'T REALLY
WANT TO KNOW
ABOUT SEX—AND
A FEW THINGS MORE

IF I've given you the impression that life with Groucho was all *Animal Crackers* and *Monkey Business*, I'd like to correct that notion at once.

There comes a time in every boy's life—even Son of Groucho's life—when he must face up to some of the more serious aspects of living—like sex, and religion.

My sexual education began when I noticed a large swelling in Mother's abdomen one day when she was stepping out of the shower. The swelling later turned out to be my sister, Miriam, but at the time I merely thought that Mother had eaten too much lunch, and I mentioned it to her.

Mother's face flushed a deep red, and as she hurriedly covered her nakedness with a towel, she informed me that there was a baby in her stomach.

I was shocked that she'd eaten an entire baby for lunch, and said so.

"I didn't eat it," she replied.

"Then how did it get there?"

Mother smiled shyly, and said it was about time that Father and I had a little talk.

The talk occurred several days later when Father and I were riding together in the rumble seat of his new convertible Packard, which was rolling along a country road beside a pasture where cattle were grazing.

One of the bulls wasn't grazing; he was coupled to the rear of a rather attractive female Jersey.

"You know what those two animals are doing?" asked Father, pointing them out to me.

"Wrestling?" I ventured.

"They're making baby cows," he informed me.

As I looked at him in complete bewilderment, he continued, but a little uneasily:

"You see, the bull puts his penis in the female's counterpart, some seeds shoot out, and pretty soon a baby cow starts to grow inside the mother's stomach. And two years later he'll be paying her child support!"

From that he segued into the fact that humans procreate in a similar fashion, and then he made the prediction that pretty soon I was going to have a little sister or brother.

I didn't believe him. How could you trust anything this man said? I thought he was merely being funny.

Four months later, when I had to share my bathroom with an infant girl, a bathinette and a tyrannical trained nurse named Mrs. Kirky, I didn't think he was so funny.

The new infant in the house, plus Mother's flat stomach were fairly convincing evidence, even to a young skeptic like me, that storks don't bring babies. However, I still couldn't understand how the baby made it from such a confining area as a mother's stomach to the outside world.

From my questions, Father deduced there was still something lacking in my sex education. However, I guess he was too embarrassed to delve into the subject in any greater depth himself. He waited a couple of years, and one day when he went into the city to see Doctor Hoffman, a psychiatrist who was presumably helping him conquer his insomnia, he brought me along. After Father's session with Doctor Hoffman was over, I was called out of the waiting room and into the Doctor's inner sanctum. There I saw Father whisper something into the Doctor's ear, following which Father ducked out into the outer office, and I was told to take a seat.

Hoffman thereupon delivered a lecture, couched in highly technical medical terms, on the reproductive process. He illustrated his talk by drawing, on a blackboard, pictures of male and female sex organs, the ovum and how it's fertilized by the male, the fetus in the womb, the baby's final journey down the vaginal passage and out into the world, and everything else you ought to know about sex if you're going to be a gynecologist. Pure textbook stuff—cold and clinical, but nothing practical like how did you get a girl to let you fertilize her egg in the first place.

When the talk was over, Father asked Hoffman, "Did you tell him how to protect himself in the clinches?"

"Protect himself?" repeated Hoffman, dully.

"Yes. I don't want Arthur coming down with some social disease or knocking up a girl."

"The young man's only eight years old," pointed out Hoffman. "Aren't you being a little premature?"

"He's a Marx," said Father. "I can't take any chances!"

Doctor Hoffman quickly filled me in on the uses of a male contraceptive, and we left.

On the way home in the car, Father asked me how I liked the talk, and I told him I thought it was pretty boring.

"Someday you'll thank me," said Father. "Mom and Pop were too ignorant to tell me anything about sex when I was a kid. I wound up catching the clap from some whore I met on the road when I was fourteen. I hope I've saved you from that bit."

He did. But he never did cure his insomnia.

My religious education also began around the time Miriam was born, when Grandma Jo (Mother's mother) came to visit us from Chicago.

Grandma Jo was not only a jack of all religions, but she was forever proselytizing whatever faith she happened to be caught up in at the moment. And at the moment of her visit to us, Grandma Jo was on a Christian Science kick, having just recovered from an attack of asthma that she was convinced would have been the death of her if it hadn't been for a practitioner she'd been seeing.

At the dinner table one night, Grandma Jo tried to convert Father to Mary Baker Eddy's faith-healing ways—by pointing out to him how a fortune could be saved in doctors' bills and medicine.

Father pooh-poohed the whole faith-healing bit, and in the ensuing conversation about religion in general, wound up pleading guilty to not only being an agnostic, but a *Jewish* agnostic—obviously the worst kind.

Grandma Jo was shocked, but not as shocked as she was to learn that Mother and Father weren't encouraging me to worship God under any label, and that in fact, I'd never even been inside a Sunday School—Jewish or any other kind.

"That's heathenism—depriving that youngster of spiritual learning!" snorted Grandma Jo indignantly.

"I haven't deprived him of anything," shot back Father. "If he wants to go to Sunday School it's all right with me. But I'll bet he doesn't want to, do you, Art?"

"I'd rather play baseball with the kids," I answered.

"How's he going to know what he wants if he's never been?" asked Grandma Jo.

"She's right, Grouch—" joined in my mother, who had never attended church since she'd left home. "At least let him try it."

"He goes to school all week," pointed out Father. "Why does he have to go on Sunday, too?"

"The discipline will do him good," persisted Mother.

The upshot of the conversation was that Father gave Grandma Jo permission to enroll me in the Sunday School class at the Church of Christ, Scientist in Great Neck Village the following Sunday.

For openers, my Sunday School teacher told the class the story of the Nativity, the Crucifixion and the Resurrection.

I thought it was about as interesting as Doctor Hoffman's lecture on sex, and I could hardly wait for the class to be over so I could get back to the house and start playing baseball with Father.

"Well, what did you learn at Sunday school today?" asked Father as he, Mother, Grandma Jo and I sat down to have lunch on our screened-in porch.

I gave him a *Reader's Digest* version of what the Sunday School teacher had told the class.

"You believe that story—that Jesus Christ was killed and then came back to life?" asked Father.

"That's what they told us," I replied.

"That sounds like a fairy tale written by Hans Christian Andersen," said Father skeptically. "I don't believe people come back to life —not even Jesus Christ! What else did you learn?"

I told him about Mary Baker Eddy's *Science and Mind*, and how marvelous medical cures had been effected without doctors or medicine.

"I don't believe that, either," snorted Father.

"A Christian Science practitioner cured my asthma," said Grandma Jo defensively.

"It probably would have gone away by itself," said Father logically.

"She tried all kinds of doctors," said Mother.

"What about a guy with a bad appendix?" persisted Father. "How does Mary Baker Eddy handle a thing like that—let it burst and the patient dies of blood poisoning?"

"Now, Grouch—you don't have to be so literal," Mother rebuked him.

"I think the kid's wasting his time going to Sunday School, when he could be out in the fresh air playing," said Father.

"Well, I don't," replied Mother, sticking up for Grandma Jo out of sheer filial loyalty. "It won't hurt Arthur to have to do something he doesn't want—for once in his life."

"Do as you please," said Father. "But if you ask me, he could learn more by staying home and reading *The Life of Frank Harris*."

At Mother's insistence I remained an unwilling disciple of Mary Baker Eddy's for about six months—or up until the time Grandma Jo nearly died of double pneumonia and had to spend four weeks in an oxygen tent. Following her recovery, at the hands of a very expensive Park Avenue doctor paid for by Father, Grandma Jo became a Quaker and I was allowed to return to baseball on Sunday mornings.

CHAPTER 9

TRY
A LITTLE
TENDERNESS

ON the surface, Mother's and Father's marriage seemed to have a lot going for it in those halcyon days before the 1929 market crash.

Father was a big star, making important money, in good health and not quite forty years old.

Mother, after eight years of marriage and two little dividends, was extremely youthful-looking, and still more beautiful than half the show girls on Broadway.

But temperamentally, they were unsuited.

Father was strong and forceful. Mother was timid—almost pathologically so—with a great desire for some tenderness and understanding, and a strong need to be loved.

I believe Father loved Mother—as much as he can love any

59

woman. That is to say, he considered her a sex object, pure and simple. She was also a pretty package to have on his arm when he strolled into a restaurant or otherwise ventured forth into polite society, a good mother, and a reliable person to leave at home with the kids when he was at the theater or away on the road (as he sometimes had to be) without her.

But for straight companionship, he's always preferred the company of other men, feeling he could never have anything really in common with a woman but sex. He's never, for example, been able to say of any of his wives, "She's also my best friend."

As for the tenderness Mother craved, that's an emotion that Father always rationed out pretty frugally. He may feel it, but he is ashamed to display it in public, or see it displayed by others. Sometimes it actually outrages him to see lovers being affectionate in public.

At a family gathering at his house one night, Father severely reprimanded Melinda, his second wife's daughter, for daring to kiss her new husband on the lips while they were sitting on the couch together before dinner.

"That sort of thing should be done behind locked doors!" Father rebuked her, sounding more like Queen Victoria than Groucho Marx.

Melinda's fiery response was that she'd kiss her husband anyplace and any damn time she felt like it. Whereupon she picked up her purse and stormed out of the house, hand in hand with her husband.

Melinda and Father didn't speak for nearly a year after that.

Father is aware of his shortcomings in this department. Just recently he confessed to me, "You know, today at Hillcrest I heard Jack Benny talking to Mary on the phone. You know what he kept calling her?—'Dollface'! I guess if I'd have spoken that way to *my* wives, maybe I wouldn't have been divorced three times."

Paradoxically, another source of real friction between my parents was Father's sense of humor. Mother never quite understood it. In that regard she wasn't too unlike many of her sex. A poll taken at the height of the Marx Brothers' popularity revealed that their fans were predominately male. Sixty-five percent of the women polled didn't care for the Marx Brothers' type of humor at all.

Mother also didn't understand his compulsion to be funny at serious moments. She had a fairly good sense of humor, but it was limited to laughing at the things that normally evoke laughter—a witty line, or a funny situation, and at the proper time, like on stage. But she had very little sense of humor about herself. And around Father that can be a serious handicap.

Go to Father with a serious problem, and nine times out of ten he'll make a joke about it. The only time you can be sure he'll take a problem seriously is when it's his own.

It isn't that, deep down inside, he may not have *any* empathy for your problems. It's simply that he's so impelled to live up to his image as a great wit that his urge to say something funny is virtually uncontrollable. Besides, if he showed tenderness or real understanding it might be construed as a sign of weakness. So he throws up a smoke screen of wisecracks to hide behind.

God forbid anyone should think Groucho Marx is weak—even when he's checking into a hospital for major surgery.

In September of 1970, I drove Father to the hospital at UCLA, where he was to undergo serious abdominal surgery. He was so weak from an infected bladder that he had to be wheeled from the car to the Admitting Office.

In the Admitting Office, which was spilling over into the corridor with would-be patients, a dowager-type nurse, who was obviously much harassed by the mob, signed Father in. Simultaneously she informed him that he couldn't keep more than five dollars in cash on him during his stay in the hospital, and turned his wallet, containing two hundred dollars, over to me.

"But suppose I want a girl to come to my room and take off all her clothes and lie down with me?" asked Father. "What kind of a girl can I get for five dollars?"

Mother didn't enjoy that kind of humor, any more than the admitting nurse did. If she'd have been there, she'd have said, "Grouch—can't you see the girl's busy? Stop annoying her!"

And he would accuse her of not having a sense of humor, and the fight would be on.

In addition to his sense of humor (which could be vexing to anyone under the wrong conditions) Father was a more self-sufficient person than Mother. He could read or play the guitar by the hour, or putter in the garden, trimming hedges or sniffing apple blossoms, and never need any outside entertainment.

But Mother had to be constantly on the go—to a speakeasy or a movie, or off for a ride on Long Island Sound on somebody's yacht. Like the song of the same name, Mother was one of those people who needed people. But not necessarily the kind of people Father was traveling with in those days. Following their initial success Father and his brothers were being lionized by the Broadway crowd. All the famous wits of that era—Dorothy Parker, Bob Benchley, George Kaufman, Heywood Broun, F. P. Adams, Harold Ross, George Jean Nathan, and Alexander Woollcott—took the Marx Brothers to their bosoms and were fighting for their company. They were being quoted in all the columns, and wined and dined by the Long Island and Manhattan smart sets.

The Marx Brothers were great assets at any social affair. In addition to their comic talents, Harpo, Chico and Zeppo were expert bridge and croquet players. Harpo and Chico could entertain musically. And Father could sing a tongue-twisting song and insult all the guests.

Although it pleased Father to be the center of so much idolatry, he didn't enjoy the social life as much as his brothers, nor was he as suited to it. Strange as it may seem, Groucho's always been a bit of an introvert. He didn't care to participate in games like cards or croquet, and his piano playing, though adequate to accompany himself badly, was nothing he cared to display in public. So he had to rely on conversation to make himself noticed. And in the fast intellectual company he was keeping—Kaufman, Benchley, Woollcott, and Parker—he sometimes felt at a loss because of his lack of a formal education.

Occasionally, he didn't even know what they were referring to when they mentioned some esoteric literary figure like a Ronald Firbank or a Virginia Woolf. But, feeling obligated to say something if he didn't want to look like a schnook, he took to interrupting their conversations by twisting their pontifical statements around into jokes, or turning their big words into outrageous puns. Two of my favorites from Father's pun-making period:

"You want some ice water? I'll give you an onion. That'll make your eyes water,"

and

"The Mexican weather report: chili today and hot tamale."

It's hard to believe that puns such as those could enhance anyone's reputation as a great wit and ad lib artist. But as Father discovered soon after he became a successful comedian, people laughed at almost anything he said—if Groucho said it, it had to be funny. And they thought Father was an intellectual, even though he knew he was just covering up his educational shortcomings.

Being pretty but not witty, Mother had no such subterfuge on which to fall back to cover her own feelings of inferiority when she was forced to mingle with Father's fast-talking set.

Mother had quit high school after her third year to go into show business, and not mistakenly, considered most of Father's friends her intellectual superiors. To make up for her lack of formal education, she did her utmost to read all the books on *The Times* best-seller list, studied French in the evenings when Father was at the theater (as he was six nights a week), and even took bridge lessons so she wouldn't make a fool of herself when she was invited to play bridge with the other wives in their set.

Mother was young and bright, and therefore able to learn quickly. Still she was terrified that she might make a *faux pas* and be laughed at. Or that she would lose at bridge, and wouldn't be able to pay her debts. The women played for high stakes (a half a cent a point), and Father didn't give Mother spending money to throw away on games of chance.

One of our neighbors was Bobby North, a Broadway producer. He and his wife, Stella, lived in a much more luxurious house than ours, and once a week she would throw a bridge party, and would always invite Mother.

Stella was a warm and gracious hostess, but Mother never felt comfortable around the other women in Stella North's group. She felt way out of her element—intellectually and financially.

Across the street from us lived an elderly couple named Parks. Mrs. Parks was a hopeless alcoholic. Her husband was always hiding bottles from her, or smashing them in the sink, or seeking other ways to keep her sober for a few days. When Mrs. Parks would grow unbearably desperate, she'd sometimes drop in on Mother and mooch a shot from Father's stock of bootlegged bourbon, and Mother would be too timid to turn her down.

One day Mrs. Parks dropped in on Mother just before she was leaving for her weekly ordeal at the Norths' bridge party. Noticing that Mother seemed nervous, Mrs. Parks suggested that she try a drink before going to her game.

"I don't drink," said Mother.

"A little will give you confidence," insisted Mrs. Parks.

Feeling maybe it was worth a try, Mother took a small shot before leaving the house.

That one drink was a turning point in Mother's life.

When she discovered that alcohol helped her lose her inhibitions around the other wives, the imbibing of it before social occasions soon became a regular and unbreakable habit.

Next she discovered that sneaking a drink or two before the guests arrived at her own house gave her the courage to feel more at ease when she and Father were entertaining important friends.

Mother wanted desperately to do things properly, and she had learned considerable about the fine points of being a hostess from observing how the other wives, like Stella North, handled the social graces at their bridge and dinner parties.

But Father was a "meat and potatoes" man. He didn't care for what he called "trick vegetables"—eggplant, artichoke, cauliflower au gratin. And he also couldn't stand any kind of pomp. He hated flowers or candlelight on the dining table, claiming that they made him feel as if he were eating in a funeral parlor.

What he disliked most of all was formal service—by a maid or butler. "They bring the meat," he would complain, "and twenty minutes later when the meat's ice cold, they bring in the potatoes and vegetables. Why can't we just put it all on the table like Mom used to do when we were kids?"

When Mother would explain to him that wasn't how things were done in polite society, he'd reply, "What about the people who can't afford a maid or a butler to pass the food? I'll bet *they* get their meat and potatoes all at the same time."

Another habit of Father's that used to annoy Mother was his insistence on having dinner at the time *he* wanted to eat.

If a guest was a few minutes late, and Father was hungry, he'd shout, "Svensk—put the food on the table!"

"But the Norths aren't here yet," Mother would protest.

"That's their hard luck. I asked them for seven. It's now twenty after. If they want to eat, they can be on time—just like we are when we go to their house."

Mother would want to slide under the table with embarrassment when the guests would arrive to find her and Father half way through dinner.

Father liked to eat early for two reasons: (1) He wasn't much of a drinker—one old fashioned before dinner, perhaps a glass of wine or beer with dinner. (2) He enjoyed having us kids with him at the dinner table but, of course, we couldn't stay up late. On company nights Mother felt we should eat in the kitchen. "The kids don't eat with the grown-ups at anybody else's house," Mother would complain whenever the issue was raised.

"I don't care. I don't see them all day. When can I see them if I don't eat with them?" Father would argue.

"But you *do* see them all day," Mother would point out.

"Well, not enough," Father would retort.

In these arguments, I'd of course be rooting for Father to be victorious, because it was infinitely more fun to be at the table and listen to him trading cracks with George Kaufman or Sid Perelman than to hear Otto and Frieda bickering in a language I couldn't understand, in the kitchen.

Being the more stubborn of the two, Father would usually get his way.

The arguments over protocol were endless, for Father was as determined to eat on time and to have his meat with the vegetables as Mother was anxious to set a pretty table and show the other wives that Mrs. Groucho Marx hadn't been "brought up in a stable," as she put it.

To find the courage to confront Father on these issues, Mother

would, with more and more frequency, go to the bottle first for a forti-
fying nip or two.

Father might acquiesce about the flowers and candles until the
company had arrived and everyone was seated around the dinner table.
At that point, he'd usually announce, "Folks, now that you've all seen
the candles and flowers, we'll dispense with them." And then he—with
Otto's help—would whip the decorations off the table and onto the
sideboard or into the kitchen.

The other guests, of course, would think Father's behavior terribly amusing ("Isn't Groucho a scream?"), and Mother would go along
with it on the surface. But inside it hurt, and she'd barely be able to
fight back the tears as she sat there helplessly and watched her pretty
table destroyed.

Chances were, she still wouldn't have recovered from her defeat
by bedtime. In that case, she'd sneak another quick drink in order to
calm her nerves so she could get to sleep.

Father, who always considered himself a model husband, would
have been shocked to know that Mother was turning to the bottle to
make her life with him more bearable.

Father always recognized the fact that he was more of an eccentric than most husbands. At the same time, he'll go to his death bed believing that any woman who didn't consider him a good catch just
didn't know the right things to look for in a man.

"After all," I've heard him state at least once during every marriage, "I'm not a gambler. I don't get drunk and come home and beat
up my wife. I entertain my kids. And I make enough money to keep
my family in Cadillacs, mink coats and tennis rackets. What else does a
wife want?"

When he was younger, he also liked to do the marketing and tell
the cook what to have for dinner (and sometimes how to prepare
it).

Like most wives, Mother wasn't crazy about her husband's inter-
fering with the running of the house, but there were certain advantages
to his doing the marketing. He'd usually go to the most expensive food
specialty shop in town—the one he had warned her not to patronize—
and he'd come home loaded down with all kinds of imported delicacies
and out-of-season fruits and vegetables.

"A dollar five for this little piece of cheese?" Mother would exclaim. "If I brought this home you'd bawl me out for being extravagant."

"It's worth it, Svensk. I can't stand to eat that goyisher cheese you buy. Those packaged brands taste like ear wax."

"But you told me not to go to Jorgensen's."

"It's okay for cheese, meat and vegetables. Just don't buy your canned goods there."

But when the monthly food expenditures rose precipitously, Father would get after Mother.

"What's the matter with the A&P?" he'd want to know. "But Grouch," Mother would protest. "*You* told me to go to Jorgensen's."

"That was last month when we were in a bull market. Today General Motors dropped five points. If you'd read the financial page you'd know where to shop."

Their arguments over money were endless, and frequently hilarious, looking back on them from this vantage point, anyway.

When I first took up horseback riding, Father sent Mother and me to New York City to buy a pair of riding pants.

We found an outfit that appealed to me at Macy's. It was a good buy—only nine dollars—and we sent it home C.O.D. since Mother didn't have the cash to pay for it. But later in the week, when the delivery man arrived at the door of our Great Neck home with the pants and announced that it would take nine dollars to complete the transaction, Father looked at Mother as if she'd gone bananas to be so extravagant and refused to come up with the money.

"After this, let *me* buy Arthur's clothes," announced Father.

The next day he took me to Abercrombie and Fitch and bought me a riding outfit for forty dollars. On the way home he gave me a lecture on how women don't know the value of money.

When I pointed out to him that he had spent more than Mother had, he replied, "You only get what you pay for. In the long run, you save money by buying the best."

My mother was a very timid person in those days, and with no Women's Lib movement to give her the courage to stand up for her rights, she was no match for Father when it came to arguing about monetary matters—which was usually at the dinner table.

Father didn't mind buying things, but he didn't like to be surprised by her. The moment she bought something—whether it be a dress for herself, or a piece of furniture badly needed for the house—and he hadn't been apprised of the purchase ahead of time, he'd roar out that he couldn't afford it, and demand that she return the item to the store.

If she refused, or burst into tears, which was her usual reaction, he'd send her away from the table to eat dinner by herself in the kitchen.

I was only six when I witnessed the first of these scenes—I think she had bought a red cloche hat he wouldn't let her keep—but I was surprised to see a mother and grown woman treated that way. I thought only naughty kids got sent away from the dinner table, I remember saying to Father.

"I can't be upset when I have to be funny in front of an audience in an hour," he explained, glancing nervously at his watch.

Anyway, it was the first hint I had that a wife could never be treated like an equal in my father's house.

Eventually Mother found a method of fighting back.

In order to get her hands on a little extra spending money, and without having to go through the demeaning experience of asking Father for funds, Mother took to the habit of stealing change that he had forgotten to empty out of the pockets of his suits hanging in his closet.

Father had an extensive wardrobe of custom-tailored clothes, and as careful as he was about money in other ways, he was too lazy to empty loose change from his pockets. Frequently, he'd leave as much as two or three dollars in quarters and dimes in each suit, and perhaps a couple of stray one-dollar bills as well.

On a good day, Mother could pick herself up ten or twelve dollars just by disappearing into his closet with a whisk broom and pretending to be brushing the lint off Father's suits.

As I grew older, but my allowance remained the same, I caught on to why Mother was always so diligent about cleaning Father's closet. To supplement my own meager allowance, I soon started making forays into his closet myself.

Since I got up earlier than Mother, who slept until noon alongside Father, I usually could beat her to Father's pockets by quite a few hours, especially since the entrance to his closet was in the hall outside his bedroom.

Father never caught on, but after showing up at his closet a few times and discovering his pockets were completely bare, Mother must have thought he had.

It was a lousy trick to play on Mother, and to this day I regret not offering to split my ill-gotten gains with her.

In a strange way, I actually did Mother a service. The sudden drying up of her source of revenue gave her the courage—that plus a couple of shots of bootlegged whiskey—to ask Father for a regular allowance to spend as she pleased.

He gave in, eventually. He always does. He's basically extremely generous and a softy. But he never stopped worrying that he was spending too much money, and not putting enough away for the proverbial rainy day.

Which was why none of us who ever lived in the same house with him was ever able to keep ahead of his spending habits.

As frustrating as Father's monetary inconsistencies could be, his behavior in regard to maintaining law and order among the small fry in our family was downright puzzling.

Father could never make up his mind whether to be a disciplinarian or a soft touch. I think he felt that, for our own good, a little discipline was necessary. But usually when he was at the point of meting out punishment, his sense of humor would get the best of him.

He didn't believe in spankings, and if Mother dared lay a hand on us, no matter how justified she was, he'd become furious.

"But, Grouch—I caught Arthur and Junior Hanft smoking cigarettes in the wood shed."

"Well, hitting him won't help."

"Just what do you suggest?"

"Use psychology. Take away something he really likes."

"All right. What?"

"His cigarette lighter."

If my sister or I did something exceptionally naughty—like lying or breaking an expensive antique—he'd put us to bed and threaten to make us go without dinner.

But he'd rarely keep his threat. He'd let us worry about it right up until the meal hour, at which point he'd knock on our door and say, "Okay, if you think you can behave yourself, you can come out now. There's no reason why I should have to eat Frieda's cooking and not you."

He didn't have the heart to make anyone go without food, having gone hungry so many times himself in his youth on 92nd Street. Besides, he preferred having his children around him at the dinner table to most of the grown-ups he knew—and that included his wives.

One thing that really infuriated Father was to be awakened when he was trying to sleep in the morning. He'd rarely not follow through on a punishment meted out for waking him early.

On show nights he rarely got to bed before one in the morning. He liked to sleep until around noon the following day. But with noisy children in the house, it was a rare morning that he'd be granted that luxury. It wasn't that we were so noisy or inconsiderate, but Father was an extremely light sleeper. He could hear the cook whispering to the milkman at the back door a hundred feet away. And he was almost certain to hear Miriam or me tip-toe up or down the staircase which was just outside his and Mother's bedroom door. No matter how mouselike we tried to be, the stairs would creak under the weight of our bodies. One of the crosses Father had to bear in life was that he never owned a house that was well built enough to have stairs that didn't creak.

The moment he'd hear me running up the stairs to my bedroom to fetch my baseball mitt or fishing pole, Father would be out on the landing in his sleeping coat, shouting at me to be quiet.

If I awakened him more than once in a morning, he'd order me to take off my clothes and spend the rest of the day in bed.

Once I remember telling him, "It's not my fault."

"Who did those big feet I heard belong to?"

"If you'd get a better house, the stairs wouldn't be so noisy."

"I tell you what, Big Feet. When you make enough money to buy that kind of a house, I'll move in with you. Now GO — TO — YOUR — ROOM!"

After I'd been unfairly incarcerated for three days in a row one summer vacation, I decided I couldn't take it any longer. I'd run away from home.

So I escaped from my bedroom by a rope from the window to the garage roof, loaded my wagon with supplies—like my baseball mitt and a peanut butter sandwich—and started down Shorewood Drive towards Great Neck Village.

It was an extremely hot day, and I was awfully tired and thirsty by the time I pulled my wagon all the way into the village—almost five miles away.

I had no money on me (Mother having beaten me to Father's coat pockets that morning) and no idea where I was going. But by late afternoon I found myself standing on the sidewalk in front of Bretman's Confectionery Store, with my nose pressed against the plate glass window, watching the people at the fountain inside guzzling sodas.

I'd only been there a few minutes, when I heard Mother's voice behind me exclaim in relief: "There he is, Groucho!"

I turned, and saw Mother and Father double parked in the Packard.

"What are you doing here?" asked Father, jumping out onto the sidewalk.

"Running away," I answered.

"Do you have any money on you?" he asked.

I shook my head negatively.

"Here's a dollar," said Father, handing me a bill. "You can't run away without money."

He started to get back into the car. I suddenly felt alone.

"Wait a minute—can I go back with you?" I asked, running over to him.

"I thought you didn't like it at home."

"I changed my mind."

"Okay, hop in," he said, giving me a hug and opening the car door. "But next time let us know when you're going to run away from home, so we can rent your room out."

He didn't even ask for his dollar back.

It was a better deal being a son than a wife.

CHAPTER 10

CHICO
HAS THE
LAST LAUGH

AS the summer of 1929 slid by, Father was finding less and less time for meddling in household affairs.

Earlier in the year the Marx Brothers had signed a three-picture deal with Paramount Studios. Their first two films would be *Coconuts* and *Animal Crackers*, from the stage shows of the same name.

Because *Animal Crackers* was still playing to SRO on Broadway, and its producer (Sam Harris) had no intention of closing it, the Marx Brothers couldn't go to Hollywood to start their picture careers. *Coconuts* had to be filmed at Paramount's Astoria, Long Island, studios, during the day, while the Marx Brothers were appearing on Broadway at night.

Though Father was young enough to take on the twin assignments, it didn't exactly please him to have to get up at six in the morning, in order to be on a drafty sound stage in Astoria, and in full costume, by eight.

In addition to the fact that he considered having to be funny before noon a Herculean assignment, he felt it was also an intrusion on his privacy. Morning was the time of day when he enjoyed sitting around the house in his bathrobe and slippers, reading the New York newspapers (both *The Times* and *The Tribune*), and complaining about the cook's coffee ("Why can't I ever get a cup of coffee that doesn't taste like dish water?"). Moreover he never slept well when he knew he had to rise early in the morning. Any eight A.M. call by the Assistant Director was sure to give him instant insomnia and necessitate a sleeping pill, which usually wouldn't work on him until just before it was time to get up. This would make him crankier than ever if he happened to hear Miriam or me sneaking up or down the stairs on our way to and from the kitchen.

The mechanics of picture making (with its dozens of retakes) made Father nervous. And directors annoyed him. I don't recall Father ever being satisfied with any movie director he's worked with, and he's worked with some of the finest, from Leo McCarey to Mervyn LeRoy. "Why do they have to tell *me* how to be funny?" he would rant at the dinner table after a particularly vexing day of shooting. "I've been playing this material on Broadway for two years. I ought to know how it goes by this time. If I don't, I ought to quit and go into the dress business with Gummo."

I remember my first excursion to Paramount Astoria to watch him shoot a scene from *Coconuts*—the famous "blueprint" scene, in which he and Chico were talking about building a house.

Movie studios forty years ago looked about the same as they do today. The cameras might have been bulkier and more primitive in appearance, and the sound equipment more temperamental and likely to break down, but basically there's been hardly a change in the physical setup.

At that time—only a couple of years after Warner Brothers had made the first talking picture, *The Jazz Singer*, starring Al Jolson—

sound recording equipment was clumsy and extremely sensitive to all the wrong things, like the rumble of a truck passing by on the street in front of the studio, or a toilet flushing in the men's room.

The simple action of folding a piece of paper like a blueprint for the house-planning scene caused such a crackling on the sound track that it drowned out the accompanying dialogue between Father and Chico.

After the twenty-seventh retake, the director finally thought of soaking the blueprints in water until they were too limp to crackle. That worked, but they dripped enough water on Father's pants during the ensuing retakes to cause him to come down with a cold later in the week. Predictably, by the time the director had thought up his brilliant scheme, Chico's mind had wandered to the seventh race at Pimlico, and they had to shoot the scene thirteen times more because he kept blowing his lines.

Father was an extremely quick study when he was young. Although his dialogue was usually the trickiest to remember—because there was more of it and he had to speak it fast—he could usually reel off his lines letter-perfect in the first couple of takes.

So if an actor he was playing with didn't know his part, or if the director would insist on more takes than was absolutely necessary just to play safe, Father would blow his stack, and start talking about going into another line of work—preferably writing.

"What kind of directing talent does that take?" Father would often complain to me when we'd be driving back to Great Neck after I'd spent a long day with him at Astoria. "If a director shoots enough footage, something's bound to be good—if only by accident."

By the time I was nine years old I had grown pretty blasé about watching movies being shot, or hanging around studios and mingling with film stars. I was too active a boy to be able to take the long waits between camera setups or to put up with the monotony of hearing the same dialogue being mouthed over and over while I had to maintain absolute silence.

Things finally reached a point where I'd even rather go to school than have to spend another day at the studio. At least school was out at three o'clock; the studio day frequently lasted until seven or seven-thirty in the evening.

Kids my own age who were dying to see the inside of a studio or to ogle movie stars couldn't understand how I could eschew what they imagined was a pretty groovy way of spending a day.

But Father understood. "I don't blame you," he'd say after I'd turned down an invitation to accompany him to the studio for perhaps the dozenth time. "I'd rather stay home and play baseball, too."

Father's mind was rarely on baseball in those boom days before the 1929 stock market crash.

If he had a day off he'd usually spend it at his broker's—the Great Neck branch of Newman Brothers & Worms—studying the ticker tape and otherwise keeping tabs on his rapidly growing portfolio of stocks. Often he'd drag me along, promising that we'd only stay a few minutes—minutes that frequently turned into hours.

Like everyone else with money to burn in those days, Father was investing all his savings in the stock market. And not too wisely—also like everyone else. He would take a tip from just about anyone—from the bellhop at the Ritz in Boston (who persuaded him to load up on Union Carbide) to his good friend and neighbor in Great Neck, Eddie Cantor.

Cantor was headlining at the Palace when Father dropped into his dressing room one afternoon after catching his act at the matinee.

At the time Cantor was just getting off the phone with Herbert Bayard Swope, who had given him a tip to buy Goldman Sachs, at 135 dollars a share, because the insiders were certain it would go to 150 by the end of the week. After hanging up on Swope, Cantor passed the tip along to Father. Never one to ignore financial advice from an expert such as Cantor, Father immediately phoned his stock broker at Newman Brothers & Worms and ordered him to buy two hundred shares of Goldman Sachs. He paid twenty-seven thousand dollars for the stock, and when the crash came two weeks later Goldman Sachs was worth nothing. "Imagine that!" recalls Father lugubriously. "I paid twenty-seven thousand dollars plus the price of a ticket to hear Eddie sing 'If You Knew Susie' and talk about Ida and the five kids. Eddie's act was good, but not that good."

Max Gordon, producer of many Broadway hits, including *The Women* and *Born Yesterday*, was a frequent visitor to our house in Great Neck during the days when playing the market was everyone's favorite sport except for sex and drinking poisonous liquor. Gordon was such an afficionado of the market that he rarely talked about anything else. I dubbed him "Stock Market Gordon," and for some reason he got such a kick out of it that he told me that if I ever wrote a play I should send it to him first. Thirty years later I did, he produced it, it flopped, and he's never spoken to me since.

Gordon couldn't get over the profits he and Father were making in the stock market—paper profits, that is.

"Marx," Gordon gloated one day after Auburn Motors had gone up over a hundred points in the short time it had taken him and Father to play eighteen holes of golf. "We're foolish ever to work. How long has this racket been going on?"

A few days later the market began its historic collapse.

Father had to do something he'd never done before in his life, and vowed he'd never have to do. He borrowed money, to cover the stocks he had bought on margin.

But with stocks dropping as much as a hundred points in a day (Goldman Sachs, included) he soon was wiped out of his life's savings —over $250,000, and was in debt up to his mustache besides.

Returning home from the brokerage after scribbling out his last check, and seeing it go down the drain along with the rest of his money, Father walked through the front door just as the phone was ringing. Wearily he picked up the receiver. It was Max Gordon on the other end.

"Marx," exclaimed Gordon, "the jig is up!"

I wasn't at the theater that night, but Marx lore has it that Father was so distraught that he didn't want to appear on the stage. As curtain time drew nearer, he sat brooding in his dressing room, making not the slightest move to get into costume. How could he be funny when widows had been wiped out of their life's savings, bankers were jumping out of windows, and he himself—the one member of the Marx family who was not a spendthrift or a gambler—was hopelessly in debt?

No doubt he was thinking of the many times he had berated Chico for throwing away his money in card and crap games, and writing checks that were always bouncing and getting Chico (and the rest of the brothers) in trouble with the mob.

Where was the justice of it all? Father had lost everything—even his sense of humor. And who could blame him?

As the orchestra struck up the opening notes of the overture, Chico strolled into Father's dressing room, patted him comfortingly on the back and said, "Well, Grouch—that'll teach you to save your money. Now you're a pauper, just like your brother Chico."

"Stop trying to make me feel good," growled Father.

"Don't let it get you down, Grouch. I've been in debt all my life. You'd be surprised at how easy it is to live without money—once you get used to it. I don't even have insomnia. I sleep like a babe."

"I noticed that—especially on the set when you should be listening to the director."

Chico laughed good-naturedly. You couldn't insult my Uncle Chico. "Look at it this way, Grouch. You lose your money in the market. I toss mine away on dames and gambling. Who has the most fun?"

As Chico's philosophy sank in, Father smiled appreciatively, and started to put on his make-up.

CHAPTER 11

A
SPY
IN THE
GRAVEYARD

WITH the approach of the great depression, our days in Great Neck were numbered. But not because we couldn't afford to live there any longer.

Times were grim, but not for Father.

While millions were out of work and standing in breadlines, and former business tycoons were posted on street corners, peddling apples for five cents apiece, Father was still earning two thousand dollars a week from his share of *Animal Crackers*, plus additional income from the Marx Brothers' first picture efforts. *Coconuts* was already in release, and a hit, and the Marx Brothers were on a percentage of the profits. All except Zeppo, that is; he was never considered an equal member of the team. He was just an employee, earning a weekly salary. ("Why do you think I turned to gambling?" quips Zeppo today.)

I'm not saying that we in the Marx family didn't feel the pinch in some ways. Father was a little more conscious of expenses, and somewhat more insistent that we not waste electricity and water by leaving the lights on or the tap running when we left a room. He also dismissed the German couple who were working for us, and supplanted them with a cleaning maid. Mother always claimed he didn't *have* to get rid of the couple—that the Depression was just a good excuse *not* to have formal service in the dining room, so he could once more have his meat and vegetables all at the same time. Actually, he liked Mother's cooking better than Frieda's. Mother may have been a Swede, but her matzoh ball soup and pot roast and potato pancakes were beyond compare.

"She's better than Lindy's," Max Gordon would extoll, turning to Father at our dinner table. "Marx—you've got it made!"

When *Animal Crackers* closed in the spring of 1930, after a two-year run, Father and his brothers decided that they'd had their fill of Broadway. Working six nights a week was a grind they could do without. It was fatiguing and boring to have to mouth the same dialogue night after night, week after week; and the rigid schedule cut into their social lives. They couldn't live like normal people—having to gulp down their dinner early so they could make the curtain, then finishing their chores around midnight, when everyone else was preparing to go to bed.

Of course, they couldn't have afforded to abandon Broadway if Hollywood hadn't been beckoning. But by then, and despite the Depression, every major movie studio was anxious to put them under contract.

As soon as they made known their intentions, Paramount, having the inside track, immediately signed them for three more pictures—to be made in Southern California, where the physical setup was better and the living easier.

The move to a warmer clime would also please my grandparents, for Minnie and Sam were approaching seventy, and the winters in the East were becoming too severe for them. This was very much in the Marx Brothers' minds when they finally decided to pull up stakes and move West.

But before Hollywood, a trip to Europe first had to be squeezed in.

The Marx Brothers were wanted for a six-week vaudeville engagement at the Columbus Theater in London. Harpo, Chico and Zeppo, born bons vivants, besides sensing a chance to pick up some extra money at cards during the crossing, were in favor of taking the job.

But Father, a born homebody, said, "Oh, no. We're movie stars now. We're not going back to vaudeville."

The other brothers were still working on Father to change his mind, when Zeppo had a family get-together one evening at his plush apartment in Manhattan, just for the brothers, their wives, and Minnie and Sam.

Children were excluded, but from the report I got afterwards, there was plenty of good heavy kosher cooking, and they all ate themselves into a stupor. Afterwards, Chico, as was his custom, departed for a card game across town, and those remaining retired to the terrace, where they played ping pong, a new game that was currently all the rage.

Minnie, being young at heart, if not in body, played three hard sets of ping pong herself—and with a little too much enthusiasm, considering her sixty-five years, the heat of the Indian summer night, and the fact that she was about forty pounds overweight.

Fade out. Fade in. Father and Mother came home from Zeppo's around midnight. Father tucked in my bed covers and gave me a good-night kiss, as was his nightly custom, and then the two of them retired to their bedroom.

About an hour later, I heard the phone ring, and the sounds of Mother and Father getting back into their clothes and their bedroom door opening again.

Clad in pajamas, I intercepted them on the stair landing, and asked them where they were going.

"To your Uncle Zep's," said Father.

"Your grandmother's taken sick," explained Mother. "Go back to bed."

And then they left.

They didn't return until the maid was feeding me breakfast the next morning. They both looked beat as they came in the door. Father's pallor was particularly gray.

"How's Grandma?" I asked.

Tears welled up in Father's eyes, and he couldn't reply. He shook his head, gave me a quick kiss, and exited for the bedroom.

"Grandma Marx had a stroke," explained Mother. "Last night, just as she was leaving your Uncle Zep's. She never recovered consciousness."

Believing it unnecessary to subject children to medieval ordeals, Father wouldn't allow me to attend the funeral, which took place in the Jewish sector of one of those huge cemeteries in Queens that you see on your way into Manhattan from Kennedy Airport. But Father gave me a full report, at the dinner table that evening.

It was raining—why must it always rain on funeral days?—but the turnout was gratifying. My grandmother had had many friends, for all of her sons' friends were admirers of Minnie as well.

Alexander Woollcott, perhaps her most ardent admirer, stood between Father and Harpo, buttressing them against his bulky figure, as the casket was lowered into the grave.

The rabbi intoned his final words, which in turn were punctuated by the dull thud of the first shovelful of earth being thrown onto the casket top. As Harpo and Father turned to go, Woollcott, with a pixyish smile, called their attention to a neighboring headstone on which the name "BRIAN KELLY" was prominently engraved.

"Groucho," whispered Woollcott as he indicated Kelly's headstone, "methinks there's a spy in this graveyard."

At the dinner table that night, Father told us how grateful he'd always be to Woollcott for lightening up that dreadful moment when he was saying a final good-bye to his mother.

At the same time he recalled how, on his way to and from Manhattan by car, he'd often passed right in front of Minnie's and Sam's house in Little Neck, without stopping in to say "Hello" to them. "It wouldn't have hurt me to drop in for five minutes and visit with Mom. She'd have gotten a big kick out of seeing me. But, no, I was too busy getting to my dressing room at the theater. Now, it's too late. She was a great dame."

Father was having the usual attack of guilt that strikes whenever there's a death in the family.

But I've often wondered if Father noticed the loss of his mother quite so much as the other brothers did. I know, because he intimated as much to me, that he was slightly resentful of the fact that Chico was Minnie's favorite. Which wasn't surprising. Chico was her first-born. In Minnie's eyes, he could do no wrong. Chico got the piano lessons when there was only money for one of the brothers to learn. And Chico was the one member of the family who could make her smile when she was feeling blue—just by clowning at the piano.

It was a relationship Father couldn't help resenting.

And I know one other thing. Father has never quite believed the myth that the Marx Brothers couldn't have made it without Minnie's help.

"That's a lot of horseshit," Father once confessed to me. "Sure, Mom gave us a little push. But *we* did all the work. *We* were the ones with the talent."

But coupled with the loss of his savings, Minnie's death was a traumatic enough experience to make him decide that he could well use that trip to Europe, and a change of scenery.

CHAPTER 12

THE EDUCATION OF A BORN TRUANT

WHENEVER any journey longer than a drive into Manhattan was contemplated, there was sure to be a discussion in our house between Mother and Father that went something like this:

GROUCHO: I think we should take the kids. Don't you, Svensk?

MOTHER: Certainly not. Arthur's in the middle of a school semester. And Miriam's only three years old.

GROUCHO: We took Arthur to London when he was only a year.

MOTHER: Sure, and I was stuck in a hotel room taking care of him while you and your brothers were running around London.

GROUCHO: That's simply solved. We'll bring Miriam's nurse.

MOTHER: What about Arthur's school?

GROUCHO: Listen, Svensk, he'll learn more seeing Europe than he will from some two-hundred-dollar-a-month school teacher.

Naturally, I'd be rooting for Father in any of these discussions. I hated the confinement and routine of the classroom, and I was bored by most of my contemporaries and teachers. Somehow they just didn't measure up—intellectually or on just a plain "fun" basis—to the people I was always meeting through Father—Kaufman, Benchley, Perelman, Ring Lardner, Woollcott, F. Scott Fitzgerald, Jolson, Will Rogers, Babe Ruth, Jimmy Walker, Jack Dempsey, Eddie Cantor, to name but a few of the people Mother and Father entertained at our house.

However, I was too diffident—a residual effect, I suspect, of having a man like Groucho for a father—to be very vocal about my contempt for the educational establishment, and the people with whom I had to associate therein. I just suffered quietly, like most introverts.

Part of my hatred—or was it simply fear?—of the formal classroom stemmed from our family's extensive traveling during my grammar school years, and the fact that I was always having to change schools and make new friends. Before I was ten years old I'd been across the country twelve times, and to Europe twice, and those were the days when a trip to the Coast wasn't just a four-hour hop by jet. It took four days on the best trains to go to Los Angeles, and a week, or more, to sail across the Atlantic on a good liner.

Because Father and his brothers road-toured *Coconuts* and *Animal Crackers* extensively during my grammar school years, and Father didn't like to leave his family at home while he played extended engagements in the major cities, I could find myself in and out of as many as four different learning establishments in the course of a school year.

Getting adjusted to the widely varied educational systems of New York, Chicago, Cleveland or Los Angeles would have been traumatic enough if I'd started each new school at the beginning of a semester. But most of the time I'd be yanked out of a school in the middle of a term, and be expected to take up the work in the new school wherever it was, and whenever I was dropped into it.

A dedicated scholar, which I can assure you I was not, would have found that a difficult assignment—especially without the services of a professional tutor to help him. But the only tutors I ever had were Mother and Father, neither of whom had finished school themselves.

As a result, I usually fell behind my contemporaries—in whatever part of the country I happened to be matriculating—and suffered the normal humiliation of feeling I wasn't as smart as my friends.

I never flunked, but I never did as well as I might have, either.

Although it improved my knowledge of geography, being constantly on the move also made it difficult for me to make friends, and once made, to keep them.

By the time I weathered the usual period of hostility reserved for a new student in a classroom, the Marx Brothers' engagement in town would come to its normal conclusion, and we'd be packing to leave for another section of the country.

If I'd been mature enough to take the long-range view, I might have seen that the more I was out of school—a form of running away from responsibility—the more uncomfortable I'd feel in it when I had to rejoin a formal class. Therefore, I'd be better off if Mother won the battle and I had to stay behind.

But, paradoxically, the insecurity I felt in school was so compounded by my constantly having to leave it that it only made me more eager than ever to latch onto any excuse not to have to attend.

I quickly acquired the short-sighted (but typically juvenile) philosophy of "live today and worry about catching up with the rest of the class tomorrow." The fact that I never did quite catch up never stopped me from rationalizing, along with Father, that I'd learn more by seeing Europe than I would by staying home and attending Kensington Grammar School.

If Father had been honest, he'd have admitted that he wanted me along for the company—so he'd have someone to have a catch with when he needed a little exercise.

At any rate, it wasn't necessary for me to root very hard for Father's side. In my memory, our side only lost once—when he and Mother took a trip to Hawaii by ship when I was in my sophomore year at Beverly High.

Somehow Mother persuaded Father to leave me home. I was so angry that I ditched school and went to the beach for the entire four weeks they were away. I wound up getting a "D" in geometry, a grade which later kept me from being accepted by Columbia University. Boy, did I show *them*.

In 1930, Mother and Father reached a compromise. They would take me to Europe, but I was not to be idle. Mother would obtain my school assignments from my teacher, and during the trip Father would tutor me.

You can imagine how much I learned with Father doing the tutoring. My first lesson on board the liner *Paris* during our Atlantic crossing will give you a slight idea.

"Here's a good one, Big Feet. Now listen very carefully: A farmer has one hundred acres of peach trees . . . there are fifty peach trees to an acre . . . and each tree at harvesting time bears fifty peaches. After picking them, what will the farmer have?"

I figured it out in my arithmetic notebook, and gave him the answer: "Twenty-five thousand peaches."

"Wrong," snapped Father. "He'd have a sore back."

"Be serious, Grouch—" Mother scolded him. "That kind of tutoring will do him no good at all."

"The hell it won't," retorted Father. "Suppose vaudeville comes back, and he wants to get up an act? A joke like that could come in very handy."

A short time later, Mother wound up taking over the tutoring chores, which was probably what Father wanted in the first place. It left all his time free for being seasick.

CHAPTER 13

OCCUPATION: SMUGGLER

SHIPBOARD life, with its attendant social activities—drinking, dancing, and organized games—always brought out the worst in Mother's and Father's relationship. It magnified, as nothing else could, the things that they *didn't* have in common.

Mother, with her Norse blood, was a good sailor. In the stormiest of weather, she could always have what she referred to as a "gay time." All she needed were a couple of old fashioneds, a small dance combo, and some people equally intent on being gay.

Father, on the other hand, probably had more Doctor Brown's Celery Tonic than blood coursing through his veins. He couldn't step on a dock without getting a queasy feeling in his stomach. And the word "gay" was absolutely anathema to him. Even today it sends a shudder up his spine. To him, it can have only one meaning—drinking and dancing.

We sailed aboard the *Paris* on December 23, 1930, and in the kind of style no family who had recently been pauperized by the stock market had a right to expect. Our family of four, plus Sadie, the nurse, occupied the Royal Suite—three full-size bedrooms, a kitchen, dining room, butler's pantry, and a living room containing among other furnishings, a grand piano.

It was typical of Father to splurge when others were tightening their purse strings. Even royalty couldn't afford the Royal Suite in those depressed times. Which is probably what induced the French Line to give Father a special rate—five hundred dollars for the whole package, meals included.

I'm sure the French Line made money on Father's meals that week.

Father's face was already starting to turn green the moment he set foot in the foyer of the Royal Suite. By the time we were sailing past the Statue of Liberty he was already lying down. And by the first dinner call he had already thrown up twice, and had taken to his bed with a copy of *The New Yorker*.

The seas and weather on the North Atlantic that December were particularly tempestuous. I traveled the South Pacific for an entire year during World War II, and never once saw skies so gray or waves quite so mountainous.

When the ship rolled to one side, she lay wallowing in the trough for a frighteningly long time—as if she might never right herself again.

Our steward, a kind of road company Maurice Chevalier named Henri, kept insisting, every time he brought something to our suite, that the weather was *"magnifique"* and that the ocean was *"Très* Smooooooooooooooooooooooooooothe."

"Then why am I throwing up?" Father would ask him.

Despite Henri's assurance, dishes fell off the tables in the dining salon every night, even though they were clamped down, and ropes had to be strung along the passageways, so that the passengers had something to hold onto. In the dining salon, one evening after a particularly violent lurch of the ship, my Aunt Betty (Chico's wife), dressed to the teeth in a beaded Chanel creation, fell over backwards in her chair and slid clear across the dance floor on her back.

Considering the violence of the crossing it was understandable how Father could be seasick—to everyone but Mother, who, like most people who've never suffered from that oceanic malady, find it difficult to have empathy for the victim.

Mother was absolutely convinced that Father was malingering so that he'd be able to avoid mixing with the other passengers and have a legitimate excuse for being a recluse for the entire voyage.

She may have been partially right in her diagnosis. After the second day out, Father was well enough to start taking brisk turns around the deck with me or to play shuffleboard; and once he participated in a deck tennis exhibition with Karel Koslo, the then reigning professional tennis champ.

He even felt sprightly enough to heckle the First Mate during a lifeboat drill the fourth morning at sea.

"Any questions?" asked the First Mate, after he'd carefully outlined the abandon-ship procedure, and shown us how to tie on our life jackets.

"Yes," piped up Father, raising his hand. "Is it true that on French ships, it's women and children last?"

It only took a few of those jokes to convince Mother that Father couldn't have been as seasick as he pretended.

Father, on the other hand, argued that it was the fresh air on deck that kept him mobile during the daylight hours, and that it was those "damn shipboard smells" *inside* our suite and in the dining salon that incapacitated him for indoor sports.

One indoor sport he hated with a passion was dinner dancing—one of the mainstays on any ship's calendar of social events. "What kind of a way is that for two grown people to spend an evening?" Father used to complain, when he wished to justify his reluctance to take to the dance floor with his wife or any other female at his table who was eyeing him hopefully. "Dancing's only good if you're on the make for some broad and you need an excuse to keep your arm around her waist all evening. But once she's hooked you, and you've already seen her with her clothes off, what fun is there in just holding her waist? I'd rather talk to George Kaufman."

Conversely, Mother, with her background as a professional dancer, could think of no more enjoyable way to spend an evening— whether it be on land or sea. She was so fond of dancing that she could even enjoy it *with* Father as her partner.

Father was no Fred Astaire, another good reason why he eschewed the dance floor. One quick, dutiful spin around the floor with Mother was about the extent of his terpsichore. After that, she'd be on her own.

Since Mother was as attractive as she was a good dancer, she found no shortage of males willing to substitute for Father on the dance floor. This was doubly true on board a ship, where, it seemed, there was always a plethora of single men on the prowl for receptive, beautiful females with money.

Many of these were the conventional gigolo types, complete with waxed mustaches, charming French and Italian accents, and suave hand-kissing manners.

"You can spot a gigolo because he always stands up when a broad enters the room," says Father, who wouldn't stand up if the First Lady entered the room.

One male passenger who always stood up—and even bowed— when Mother entered the cocktail lounge was a handsome Prussian, who was an unsuccessful exporter of ladies' beaded handbags. He became so enamored of Mother that he followed her all the way to Southern California. When she made it clear that she had only been interested in him as a dance partner, he quickly switched alliances and turned his attentions to a sixty-five-year-old heiress. He swindled the old lady out of her life savings, was caught and wound up doing time in San Quentin. However, he somehow hung onto his ill-gotten money, and after his release from prison, invested it wisely. The last I heard of this charmer, he owned most of the real estate around Malibu, including a very successful roadhouse, and was running for Mayor of that posh beach community, which proves that crime *does* pay.

Mother recognized her pursuers for what they were, but didn't seem to mind as long as they were good dancers. Father didn't mind either—as long as *he* didn't have to talk to them. He had every confidence in Mother's moral standards, and felt free to retire early and let her dance the night away.

There were a few times, however, when, as Mrs. Groucho Marx, Mother liked to have her husband around—if only to show him off.

Like the night of the Captain's ball.

Mother was delighted that she and Father had been invited to sit at the Captain's table, and appalled when Father turned the invitation down flat. "Go back and tell the Captain that this is a very bumpy trip and I don't want to eat with such a lousy driver," Father informed the Captain's emissary, who delivered the invitation.

"Groucho—it's an honor," pleaded Mother when the messenger turned to go.

"Some honor—sitting with some schmuck who's got gold stripes on his sleeve and who probably can't even do a hornpipe. Besides, he'll expect me to sit there and be funny all evening."

"Well, you won't dance—you might as well be funny," Mother pointed out with considerable logic.

But the Captain, like most victims of Father's sharp tongue, didn't realize he was being insulted. Within fifteen minutes the messenger was back with a note from the Captain saying he hoped Father would be just as funny at the party that night.

Faced with such flattering intransigence, Father had no choice but to accept, and, in fact, seemed fairly resigned to his fate, until the evening of the party, when he and Mother were in their cabin, starting to get dressed for the affair. Then he discovered for the first time (or at least pretended to discover) that he had to wear a tuxedo.

I was in the adjoining cabin, wishing I didn't have to be stuck eating dinner with just my three-year-old sister and the nurse, when the argument broke out. Since the door connecting our two cabins was open, I could see and hear the whole scene very clearly.

"But I don't want to wear a tux," complained Father, who was just stepping into the pants of a very dapper pin-striped business suit.

"You have to, Grouch," insisted Mother, who didn't have a stitch of clothing on except her silk panties. "This is the biggest event of the crossing."

"I don't care about that. I'm on this scow for a vacation. And wearing a stiff collar isn't my idea of a vacation."

"But they won't let you in the dining room without one."

"If this two-hundred-dollar custom-tailored suit isn't good enough for those phonies, then I'll eat in the children's dining room. I'd rather eat with the kids, anyway. Kids like you for yourself—not because of what you wear." (In that sense, he was the world's first hippie.)

"Grouch—don't do this to me," said Mother. "I've got a new gown."

"Nobody's stopping *you* from going," said Father, starting to put on his jacket.

Father always preferred informal attire if he could get away with it, but he seemed unusually stubborn about not yielding to conformity on that occasion. Probably he didn't feel good after so many rough days at sea, and that made him irritable.

At any rate, the argument quickly blossomed into the worst kind of acrimony, with each calling the other every uncomplimentary name they could think of. And it culminated with Father slamming out the door, and Mother reduced to tears, which cascaded down her cheeks and off onto her bare breasts. It was a scene I've never forgotten—probably because it augured things to come.

As I sat eating dinner with Father, Miriam and the nurse in the children's dining room, I wondered if this was the end of the Marx family as a unit. Although I'd seen Mother in tears before, I'd never heard the two quarrel quite so bitterly.

Father may have been thinking the same thing, for he was awfully quiet, for him, as he sat toying with his food during dinner.

It was the first time I wasn't really happy to have Father for a dinner companion.

But I didn't have him for long.

About eight o'clock, he started glancing at his watch, and by eight-fifteen—as the strains of the orchestra began drifting down from the main salon—Father stood up suddenly, gave Miriam and me each a quick kiss, and instructed the nurse to see that we didn't stay up too late. Then he ducked through the door to the main dining salon.

According to Mother, who was sitting at the Captain's right, she was as pleased as she was shocked to see Father slip quietly into his place beside her. She didn't even mind the fact that he hadn't changed into a tuxedo.

"What are you going to tell the Captain?" she asked Father in a whisper. "I told him you were seasick."

"Don't worry," Father reassured her. "I'll take care of him."

And he turned to the Captain.

"You made a quick recover—*ee,*" said the white-haired old Captain with great dignity.

"I wasn't sick," explained Father. "I just didn't want to wear a tuxedo." He then put his hand on the Captain's gold-braided sleeve, and said, "Tell me, Cap, old boy—how come you're not wearing a tuxedo?"

If she'd had a gun, Mother probably would have shot Father. But when the Captain threw back his head and laughed heartily, the tension was broken.

Mother started to laugh, too, and she and Father kissed and made up.

"Shall we dance?" said Father, bowing in imitation of the handbag exporter, and pulling Mother out onto the polished floor.

The rest of the voyage was "smooooooooooooooooooooooooooth" sailing.

So was our stay abroad.

Seeing London for the first time, with Father as my tour guide, was almost as educational as being tutored in mathematics by him.

We stayed at the Savoy—at the time the most expensive hotel in London. But we almost didn't when Father was told the price of our rooms as he was about to sign the register.

"That's an outrage," said Father, turning to go. "Come on, Svensk, let's look for another hotel."

This was a scene I'd witnessed many times in the past—whether we were checking into a hotel in a major city, or into a ski lodge at a mountain resort where there was no other place to stay. Father would always balk at the price of the first hotel we were checking into, depart in a fit of righteous indignation to look for more reasonable lodgings, and then, after finding nothing equally luxurious for less money, would sheepishly return to the hotel where he had the original reservations.

But it was two in the morning when we arrived at the Savoy, the city was enveloped in one of its famous pea-soup fogs, and we were all exhausted after a long train ride to London from Dover.

With two tired cranky kids on her hands—to say nothing of Father's guitar—Mother quickly made it known that *she* had no intention of setting foot outside the lobby door to go traipsing around a strange city in the fog in a vain search for a reasonably priced hotel.

Besides, Harpo, Chico and Zeppo had already registered and were on their way to their rooms. What kind of a nut would Father look like if he didn't follow their example, and be a sport? So he consented.

"Why not? You only live once," said Mother, who was a great coiner of phrases.

"Okay, but there's not going to be room service," threatened Father. "I'm not made of money. We'll go out for breakfast."

What he meant was, Arthur, Miriam and Sadie would go out for breakfast. He and Mother slept late, and enjoyed room service for the entire six weeks we were there. Following the example of his brothers, Father was at last learning to relax a bit about his spending.

And why not? There may have been a Depression back in the States, but the vaudeville show they were doing in London was a hit, and they had a fat picture contract in Hollywood to return to as soon as their stint abroad was over.

While Mother and the other wives spent their days shopping, Father took me on the standard tour of London's sights—London Bridge, Westminster Abbey, Changing of the Guard at Buckingham Palace, the Tower of London, and the House of Parliament. In the House of Parliament, in the middle of a heated debate between Ramsay MacDonald and the leader of the opposition, Father stood up in the visitors' gallery, and at the top of his voice started singing, "When Irish Eyes Are Smiling." We were thrown out, and requested never to return.

It's a good thing Mother wasn't along; she'd never have gotten over the humiliation. But by the age of ten, I'd become fairly inured to his pranks and could usually laugh them off.

After we'd exhausted the sight-seeing spots, Father bought a soccer ball at Harrod's and we kicked the pigskin around every day in Hyde Park—until a Bobby informed us that we weren't allowed to use the "Queen's grazing ground" for "athletic endeavour."

"The Queen's grazing ground!" exclaimed Father. "What's the matter with the food at Buckingham Palace that she has to come out here and eat grass?"

"Her *sheep* graze here," explained the Bobby, a little nonplussed at such disrespect.

After that we had to settle for the alley in back of the Savoy for our soccer playing grounds.

Every afternoon I went to the theater with Father, and from a seat in the first row watched the Marx Brothers go through their antics on stage. Their act was mostly a potpourri of famous bits they had done in the past, but English audiences hadn't seen any of it, so it was fresh to them, if not to me. What *I* enjoyed most—outside of the fact that you could order tea and sandwiches from your seat—was watching the English vaudeville acts who were on the same bill—jugglers, dancers, acrobats, magicians.

One of the acts featured a trick unicycle rider. Near the climax of his routine, he'd suddenly look as if he'd lost control of his bike, go zooming up to the apron of the stage, and hang there tottering—as if he were about to fall into the lap of a dignified dowager in the seat beside me. She, in turn, would scream with fright and jump out of her chair, and the audience would go into spasms of laughter.

This happened every day for four weeks, to the same woman. And every time it happened I wondered why they didn't hire a better bicycle rider.

"Schlemiel!" said Father when I asked him about it. "All your years with me in vaudeville, and you still don't know a 'plant' when you see one?"

When the same thing happened the following matinee, I screamed and jumped out of my seat before the dowager could. The audience didn't laugh at all. It was a good lesson in comedy writing. Upsetting dignity begets laughs—frightening little boys doesn't.

On the nights he had off, Father was a social lion. Because of their reputations for being such witty comedians, the Marxes and their wives were invited everywhere. Among others, Father got to meet some of his favorite authors—J. B. Priestly, Noel Coward, Aldous Huxley, A. P. Herbert and T. S. Eliot. He and the latter became close friends, and kept up a spirited correspondence until Eliot's death.

It was Eliot who arranged for Father to have lunch with Somerset Maugham, at the author's private club. Father was excited at the prospect. Maugham, the teller of all those South Sea adventure stories, was his favorite author—and the one person he truly admired, and would rather have been, if there were such a thing as two human beings trading places.

But when Father came back from lunch with Maugham, he was extremely upset. When Mother asked him what was wrong, he replied unhappily, "Somerset Maugham's a *faygeleh!* How do you like that?"

Though the Marx Brothers were popular in London's show business and literary circles, they weren't getting much play from the Royal Family.

Father had promised to introduce me to Edward, the Prince of Wales, who had once dropped into his dressing room after seeing a performance of *Animal Crackers* on Broadway and had invited the Marx Brothers to look him up if they were ever in London.

Father looked him up, but was informed that the Royal Family was in mourning for some distant relative who had recently passed away. The only person of royal lineage who wasn't in mourning was the Duke of Manchester, who was kind of an old roué playboy.

He invited the Marx Brothers and their families to visit him at his estate in Manchester one Sunday. His fifty-room manor house was set back from the road in a beautiful pastoral setting, where sheep and thoroughbred horses were grazing. It looked like a perfect spot to spend a Sunday. I could envision myself going horseback riding, and maybe even on a fox hunt.

But January in Great Britain is not an ideal time for outdoor sports. There was an icy drizzle that kept us all inside, in front of the fireplace, in which, strangely enough, no fire was burning.

Father hadn't brought a sweater, and felt he was courting pneumonia, sitting in a damp cavernous room whose quaint stone floor was uncarpeted.

Finally he couldn't take the cold any longer.

"Hey, Duke," said Father. "How about turning on a little heat before I freeze my ass off?"

The Duke smiled ruefully and confessed to Father that there was no central heating system, and that he had no money to buy logs for the fireplace.

"Don't they pay you fellahs?" asked Father.

The Duke confessed that he received a yearly allowance from the government, but that he had already gone through it at the gaming tables in Monte Carlo.

On the way home, in the rented limousine, Father turned to Chico, who was beside him in the back seat, and said, "See, Chick—the same thing will happen to you if you don't stop gambling!"

"Wanna bet?" smiled Chico.

"I mean it, Ravelli. Save your money. Someday you may not be making any."

"In that case, I'll live off you. You save enough for both of us."

Father was never able to frighten Chico.

But he did throw quite a scare into all of us—when we were going through Customs on our way back into the United States, after debarking from the liner *Europa*.

Like most Americans who traveled to Europe in those high-tariff days, Mother and Father had made quite a few purchases that they weren't planning to declare on their way back into the country. Mother was scared to death of being caught and told Father he ought to slip the customs inspector "a little something" in return for not being too thorough when he inspected our luggage on the pier. "Everyone does it," added Mother nervously.

"I don't believe in bribery," replied Father. "If we're going to smuggle, at least let's be honest about it."

His perverse sense of humor again over-powered his better judgment when he filled out his Declaration of Purchases form.

NAME:	Julius H. Marx
ADDRESS:	21 Lincoln Road, Great Neck, Long Island
BORN:	Yes.
HAIR:	Very little.
OCCUPATION:	Smuggler.
PURCHASES:	Wouldn't you like to know?

As was the accepted custom of the day, Harpo, Chico and Zeppo had slipped their customs men a few bills and went through their inspections without delay. While they departed in taxi cabs for their respective homes, we were detained on the dock, with our customs man going through every piece of luggage with the care he normally must have reserved for the head of a jewel or opium smuggling ring.

Mother was furious at the way her carefully packed dresses were being mussed, and highly critical of Father for being so stubborn about giving our customs inspector a gratuity.

"Never mind that," said Father, annoyed. Then, in a very loud stage whisper, he asked: "What did you do with the opium? Do you still have it in your girdle?"

We were promptly taken to the Customs Office on the pier, segregated by sex, and made to undress. Father hadn't counted on his practical joke getting so far out of hand.

CHAPTER 14

A
SKUNK
IN THE
GARDEN
OF ALLAH

N 1931, when the Marx Brothers settled out West for good, Southern California was an ecologist's dream. No smog, no freeways. No tall buildings. And hardly any factories.

To Easterners, used to frigid wintry weather and hot muggy summers when you couldn't sleep, Southern California, with its warm dry days and cool nights, was about as close to paradise as you could get.

The phrase "No matter how hot it gets here during the day, you can always use a blanket at night" quickly became a cliché because it was employed so often by enthusiastic transplants trying to sell Southern California to friends and relatives still living in more severe climes.

After the long trek across the desert by *Super Chief*, the fragrance of orange blossoms overwhelmed the new settler as he stepped off the train in Pasadena, where most of the "in" people of that era debarked because it saved them from having to see the shabby side of downtown Los Angeles on their way to and from their palatial homes in Hollywood, Beverly Hills and Malibu.

A horseback-riding path divided Sunset Boulevard down its center. A good deal of Beverly Hills was a bean field. The area between Beverly Hills and Santa Monica (today known as Westwood, Bel Air and Brentwood) was largely unpopulated, with its only sign of civilization being the UCLA campus. Only it wasn't the great seat of higher learning it is today. UCLA was just an adjunct of the mother university at Berkeley—a couple of brick buildings, virtually unlandscaped, and an athletic field. It was such an unimpressive layout—and so little known—that most passers-by had to stop and ask, "What's that over there?"

Los Angeles's peripheral towns were little more than harvesting centers for citrus fruit growers. San Fernando Valley was completely rural, consisting mostly of small ranches and fruit orchards and the old Mack Sennett Studio. A few miles to the north was the kind of rugged Western terrain you'd previously only seen in Tom Mix movies. And there were more Indians in Palm Springs than Jews.

The only first-class restaurant in Hollywood was the Brown Derby. Grauman's Chinese was about the only theater. And you couldn't get a corned beef on rye anywhere—you had to have it flown out from the East. But transcontinental flying was in its infancy, planes weren't very safe, or dependable, and your corned beef sandwich was just as liable to wind up on a jagged mountain peak in the Rockies as in your stomach.

About the only things in abundance were movie studios and citrus trees, causing George Kaufman to comment, on one of his infrequent visits to the Coast, "Southern California is a great place to live if you're an orange."

Or a movie star.

Will Rogers' ranch took up most of the Santa Monica mountains. Pickfair, a Valhalla of sorts, where Douglas Fairbanks chased Mary Pickford through marble halls, was perched on a hilltop overlooking

Beverly Hills, for all the peasants to see. Marion Davies, Harold Lloyd and Charlie Chaplin could boast of bathrooms with solid gold bath tubs.

Even "B" picture stars lived in homes with swimming pools and tennis courts, and drove splashy convertibles, and threw wild parties—the kind where movie actors got drunk and knocked their wives' lovers into the pools, and starlets went down on studio executives under the tables, between courses.

Chico, not to be outdone by Douglas Fairbanks, rented a thirty-room Spanish hacienda on Sunset Boulevard, complete with tennis court, swimming pool, five acres of fruit and palm trees, and a live-in gardener, who had his own house on the premises. Harpo, still a bachelor, was shacked up in a smaller place, but it, too, had a swimming pool. And Zeppo leased a fabulous duplex in a building that had its own swimming pool and tennis court.

But sticking true to form, Father never went Hollywood in his mode of living. Until he was sixty years old, in fact, he never owned a house with a swimming pool, though he did rent one for a brief time one summer. But the pool didn't have a filtering system and was usually filled with so much green slime only frogs would swim in it.

While the Marx Brothers were making their first three pictures for Paramount—*Monkey Business, Horsefeathers* and *Duck Soup*—we lived in a series of rented houses that were about as spectacular-looking as the gardener's place on Chico's estate.

Like many newcomers to the West, we started off in a hillside home, in a place called Hollywoodland. It was a Spanish house that clung to the side of a steep cliff. You had to go downstairs to reach the bedrooms. It not only didn't have a swimming pool or tennis court, it didn't even have a yard. One false step and you were smashed to smithereens on the concrete pavement of a bus stop a half mile below. But it did have a spectacular view of the city—only there wasn't much city to look at in those days.

Our neighbors were a few homo sapiens, but mostly yucca plants, rattlesnakes, rabbits, coyotes, hawks, skunks and once in a while a mountain lion who'd wander down from the higher hills to gobble up someone's poodle or fox terrier.

If you drove an automobile, our Eagle's Nest wasn't too difficult to reach—provided you didn't get car sick on the twisty, narrow, mountain roads, or weren't drunk.

But for a schoolboy, who was still a couple of years away from sneaking out the family car, it was not the handiest place to live. Unless I wanted to take the long way around by road, it was necessary to negotiate a flight of five hundred steps down the mountainside to the bus stop, where I embarked for Cheromoya Grammar School. It wasn't so bad going down, but you were courting a heart attack every time you climbed up the five hundred steps in the tropical California sunshine.

Nevertheless, sometimes I'd be so anxious to put mileage between me and Cheromoya School that I'd run up the steps, two at a time. It was good leg training for a future tennis player, but that wasn't why I did it. I hated Cheromoya.

My schoolmates there were just like most of the others I'd run into during our many moves around the country—unfriendly. However, these were Westerners—tall, Gentile, and more taciturn than Eastern schoolboys, and they wore long pants and a few even sported high-heel cowboy boots. Because my parents insisted, I still went to school garbed in rather sissyish short pants, and plain Oxfords, which made me a bit of a freak. I was also half-Jewish and only the Jewish half showed.

My first day at Cheromoya, the other boys looked at me silently and suspiciously—the way the heavies in a Western appraise the hero when he first rides into Durango. Since I wasn't the hero type (my Father still wouldn't let me have a B.B. gun), I was ready to jump back on the *Chief*, with or without my parents, and head east.

Fortunately, Arthur Sheekman, one of Father's script writers, and a good friend of the family's, sensed my discomfiture. He showed up at the house one day with a pair of long corduroys for me, and advised me to wear them no matter how my parents felt about it. I did, and from that moment on, I was accepted at Cheromoya—especially after Father invited the whole class to Paramount one day to watch him shoot a scene from *Monkey Business*.

Paramount Studio in Hollywood was a lot handier to our new home than Paramount-Astoria was to Great Neck—just a five-minute drive through palm-lined streets—but the convenience of this had no noticeable salutary effects on Father's usual disposition when filming or preparing a picture.

If anything, Father was unhappier working in Hollywood than he'd ever been in the East—mainly because he felt he was surrounded, now more than before, by people who didn't know what they were doing. And most of them didn't—from the heads of the studios on down.

In the early thirties the talking picture was a relatively new art form, and almost anything projected on a motion picture screen made money.

Most people working in Hollywood's creative vineyards had migrated west from other forms of show business—mainly the New York theater—either because they had been unsuccessful in their former pursuits as playwrights, novelists or actors, or because the lure of the big money studios were paying was too tempting to ignore.

But there were more "no talents" working at the studios in Hollywood in those days than anything else.

Many studio heads themselves were new to film making. Sam Goldwyn, for example, had been in the glove manufacturing business before entering into partnership with Louis B. Mayer and forming Metro-Goldwyn-Mayer. And Harry Cohn had been a song plugger, and before that an unsuccessful singer in vaudeville.

But Father's main gripe was with the writing talent Paramount assigned to Marx Brothers pictures in the beginning.

Monkey Business was Father's first experience in making a picture that wasn't based on an already proven Broadway property. Having to start from scratch with the typical Hollywood hacks who infested the studios only magnified the problem and increased Father's anxiety.

In all fairness to those who tried and failed, fashioning a Marx Brothers vehicle wasn't the easiest assignment a writer—even the very gifted—could have.

Every person who had ever seen a Marx Brothers show or movie, and who owned a typewriter, *thought* he could write for them. But few came through when the chips were down. A writer might be glib as hell and keep everyone in stitches, in a story conference, but when you put a piece of paper in front of him, he'd come up with ersatz Marx Brothers material—pallid imitations of their style, but lacking true wit and comic inventiveness.

In *Monkey Business*, *Duck Soup* and *Horsefeathers*, for example, the scripts were overloaded with lines such as Zeppo saying to Groucho (who played his father), "Anything further, Father?" and Groucho replying, "Or anything farther, further. Or anything farther, further, Father?"

The rhythm of the Grouchoism was there, but not the side-splitting humor. It was simply zany, and that wasn't enough to please Father—or most audiences—for the length of an entire picture.

Another problem: a writer's forte might be writing witty lines for Groucho, but he wouldn't be able to invent pantomime for Harpo, or be facile with Italian dialect humor for Chico. Or he might be good on their characterizations, but might not know how to devise a story that would accommodate three zany creatures, whose appearances alone were enough to make you wonder if they had been spawned somewhere off in outer space and question whether they were actually humans.

At a recent party, the hostess introduced me to a lady, and, of course, couldn't wait to add that I was Groucho's son.

The lady shook her head in wonderment at her hostess' revelation.

"You don't believe Groucho's my father?" I said.

"Well, I don't think you'd lie," she replied. "It's just that, well, when I see Groucho on the screen in that painted mustache and frock coat, it seems so out of the question that he does things other human beings do—like fathering children. I mean, how could he? I just don't believe that man would ever take off his clothes or put down his cigar long enough to make love."

It was a description of Father I'd never heard before, but after thinking it over, I could easily see how a movie fan, especially a female, might get the idea that he would never do anything so serious as removing his clothes and copulating.

Subconsciously, that image of Groucho must have presented a problem to many an author setting out to write a script for him and the rest of his brothers. What was this madman if he wasn't a human being? Some kind of a mechanical doll that you wound up and jokes came tumbling out of? What was his motivation in the world? Where had he come from? Where was he going?

These same questions applied to Harpo and Chico as well—both of whom were more caricature than real people. What kind of situation could they be involved in? Certainly they couldn't fall in love like other earthlings. Or have a business problem. So what was there to root for, or to empathize with?

The late producing genius Irving Thalberg, who was responsible for making two of their better films—*A Night at the Opera* and *A Day at the Races*—recognized this problem and found a solution. "We have to involve you fellows with ordinary people, who have ordinary problems, and you try to help them," he explained to Father when they were preparing *A Night at the Opera.*

But when the Marx Brothers first started out in Hollywood, nobody knew the formula. Everyone connected with their projects was floundering—from writer to director, to the Marx Brothers themselves. They were doing formula anything-for-a-laugh lines and scenes, but nothing substantial in the way of a story or identifiable situations.

S. J. Perelman, a past master at writing a witty line, a double entendre, or twisting a large word into a guffaw-evoking pun, seemed like a natural to write for the Marx Brothers, and Groucho in particular. And, indeed, he was better than many, but he fell into the same trap. He mistook tongue-twisting repartee and high-flown hyperbole for genuine humor, and zany scenes for identifiable situations. Besides, it was apparent that he wasn't a dramatist. His humor is better read than heard. After slaving over a hot typewriter on several of their early pictures, and getting credit along with a host of other writers, Perelman gladly quit the movie business to return to *The New Yorker* and the kind of writing for which he was best suited.

Another problem of getting capable writing help stemmed from the fact that many successful playwrights and novelists of that era who might have become good screenwriters looked down their noses at studio scripting jobs. Part of this resulted from snobbishness, but mostly it was because they distrusted a medium where authors had virtually no control of their own material. As a result top writers resisted studios' efforts to lure them into picture-making mills.

A few succumbed—especially when important money was dangled in front of them; and a few others would deign to write for films only when they needed to refurbish their bank accounts.

But many held onto their integrity until it was no longer possible to make a good living in the theater.

George S. Kaufman, who had co-authored both *Coconuts* and *Animal Crackers*, was one of the stubbornest hold-outs.

He didn't need the money, but the Marx Brothers needed him desperately, Father felt. One day Father called him long distance and filled him full of glowing tales about the fantastic salaries Hollywood movie writers were pulling down every week.

"No—no," said Kaufman. "I don't care how much they pay me. I hate it out there!"

"But, George," pleaded Father, hoping to persuade him with his fine choice of cliché, "the streets out here are paved with gold."

There was a moment's pause, and then Kaufman said, "You mean, you have to bend over and pick it up?"

It wasn't until years later, when the Marx Brothers signed to make two pictures for Irving Thalberg, that Father was able to seduce George Kaufman into writing for them again.

Working for Irving Thalberg turned out to be one of the truly rewarding and happy experiences of Father's motion picture career. Although the word "genius" was thrown around loosely in Hollywood in those days, most people who ever had anything to do with Thalberg were pretty much in agreement that in his case the encomium wasn't an exaggeration.

Thalberg was an admirer of the Marx Brothers' talents, but not of their last three pictures for Paramount. *Duck Soup*, their final film for Paramount, had been an enormous bust at the box office, and while it is extremely popular in revivals today because of its anti-war sentiments, its failure then was the main reason why Paramount didn't pick up their option.

Thalberg recognized that there were some enormously funny things in *Duck Soup*, but felt it was lacking the same ingredients to make it a successs that had been in their last three pictures—sympathetic characters and a sound story.

To get these ingredients, Thalberg stated that he was willing to go to any lengths, and any expense.

"Too bad we can't get Kaufman and Ryskind to write it," suggested Father, glumly.

"Why can't we?" asked Thalberg.

"Because Kaufman said he won't go anyplace where he can't be in Times Square in twenty minutes," replied Father.

"Let me try," said Thalberg, and within an hour he was on the long-distance phone with George S. Kaufman and had persuaded him to tackle the new Marx Brothers picture with his old partner, Morrie Ryskind.

It was a happy day for the Marx Brothers and their fans alike when Thalberg threw Kaufman and Ryskind together again. For the fruit of their collaborative efforts turned out to be *A Night at the Opera* —one of the all-time comedy film classics.

With due respect to Kaufman and Ryskind, *A Night at the Opera* might not have been the classic it is if Father and Thalberg hadn't hit upon a revolutionary way of making comedies.

It came about one afternoon during a story conference in Thalberg's bungalow, when the Marx Brothers, the two authors and the producer were sitting around doing the final editing of the script.

Father appeared more apprehensive than usual, which caused Thalberg to ask him if he had some reservations about the script. "I think the writing's fine," answered Father, "but somehow I just don't have much confidence in comedy that hasn't been tried out on the stage. That's why *Animal Crackers* and *Coconuts* were so good. The comedy was sure-fire. But once you commit comedy to film, it's too late to change a line if it doesn't work. That's been part of our trouble."

Thalberg thought the problem over, and then came up with the idea of putting together a tab vaudeville show from the five main comedy scenes that had been written for the picture. "You'll try them out in four or five towns, make your changes, and *then* we'll shoot the picture," said the clear-thinking Thalberg. "What could be simpler than that?" It wasn't simple. Trying out the comedy scenes on the road was almost as gargantuan a job as breaking in a new musical for Broadway.

But it paid off, and *A Night at the Opera* became a hit, as did *A Day at the Races*, which was also made by the try-out system.

Father might have been disappointed in the quality of some of their early films, but *Monkey Business* and *Horsefeathers* were good enough to land the Marx Brothers on the cover of *Time* one week and insure their reputations as the country's leading comics.

Since it was apparent that the Marx Brothers' futures were in Hollywood, Father decided to sell the Great Neck house and, with the cash realized, buy one on the West Coast. But the Depression was deepening: there were no buyers.

At the end of our lease, Father and Mother decided to move anyway, for they were tiring of our hilltop perch. In addition to the fact that our house slid down the hill a little bit farther with each torrential rain, there was no flat area within five miles where children could play. Among the children, I include Father and all his script writers, who, after they'd finish a story conference in our patio, would join me and my boyfriends on the street for a game of baseball. Arthur Sheekman, Nat Perrin, Sid Perelman, Herman Manckiewicz, Will Johnstone, Harry Ruby, Bert Kalmer, Morrie Ryskind and anyone else who happened to be working for Father at the time were likely to be among our players.

You haven't seen baseball really played until you've watched Sid Perelman hotfooting it for home in a double-breasted business suit, or Harry Ruby going back for a high fly and disappearing over the side of a steep cliff.

We never actually lost any writers that way, but dozens of baseballs sailed over the mountainside, never to be seen again. Which was another reason Father decided to move. ("Baseballs don't grow on trees.")

There was another drawback to living in Hollywoodland. On one of the few occasions when Father got loaded at a party, he nearly drove the Cadillac over the cliff on the way home. Fortunately, he was able to stop the car on the rim of the cliff, with only its radiator and front wheels hanging out over the precipice. Mother and Father were able to escape, and the auto club managed to save the car. But as far as my parents were concerned, they'd had their fill of mountain living.

From then on, Father decided, it was the flatlands of Beverly Hills for the Groucho Marx family.

While he was waiting to find a good buy in Beverly Hills, Father moved us into the Garden of Allah, on Sunset Boulevard.

The Garden of Allah has long since been torn down to make room for another bank, but in those days it was the place into which most Hollywood novitiates moved upon coming to the West Coast, because it epitomized life in the movie capital as it was reputed to be led according to the fan magazines and columnists.

The Garden of Allah featured an immense swimming pool surrounded by lush tropical planting and a number of posh Spanish bungalows whose tenants were either drunk or in bed with somebody else's wife (or husband) or sitting at typewriters in their patios agonizing over movie scripts.

When we moved in, some of the Garden of Allah's most celebrated guests—or should I say "celebrating"?—were Bob Benchley, Charles Butterworth, Dorothy Parker, Alan Campbell, John O'Hara, F. Scott Fitzgerald, and Maureen O'Sullivan and Johnny Farrow.

At almost any time of the day or night you were likely to see Bob Benchley lolling beside the pool with a martini shaker in his hand, or hear Johnny Farrow beating up his wife in their bungalow.

It looked like a "fun" place when Father showed us around the grounds the day he and Mother were making up their minds which bungalow to lease. At last we were going to get a taste of what it was really like to live like a movie star's family. No more cave dwelling in the mountains. We were going to be *très chic*.

The day before the chic Marxes were to come down out of the hills, Fritz, our chic dachshund, chased a skunk down its hole. Because of the peculiar way our house was designed—with the bedrooms down below—the skunk's abode adjoined Mother's bedroom closet. There was just a thin layer of plaster separating the two.

In the ensuing fight to the finish between Fritz and the skunk, some of the plaster was knocked open in Mother's closet, enabling the skunk to perfume a good deal of her wardrobe.

We never knew what became of the skunk—perhaps Walt Disney signed him for a picture—but when Fritz emerged victorious from the hole, he smelled as bad as any living creature could possibly smell, including the skunk himself.

Obviously, he'd been doused with skunk juice at close range.

Now, in case anyone isn't familiar with what happens when you get the full treatment from a skunk, let me explain—you can't get rid of such a powerful odor simply by washing. It has to wear off gradually. This usually takes a month. But we had to move into the Garden of Allah the next day, and no boarding kennel had a vacancy.

Mother solved her dress problem by burning the clothing that had been hit by the skunk. But you can't cremate a dachshund just because he smells bad. The SPCA won't allow it. Besides, Fritz was a much-loved member of the family.

So we kept Fritz in the car when we were checking into the Garden of Allah, and sneaked him into our bungalow after we were settled.

However, out-of-sight, out-of-mind doesn't apply to skunk odor. The skunk smell not only permeated our car and bungalow, making it impossible to sleep (or even inhale deeply), but it was noticeable from as far away as the pool area. Not only that, by now the odor had impregnated the rest of our clothing. Mother, Father, Miriam and I all were beginning to smell like skunks—just by associating with Fritz.

All the celebrities at the pool who had seemed so friendly the day we were looking the place over were now casting distasteful glances in our direction when we walked about the premises. And if we attempted to strike up a conversation, they'd get up and walk away. They were too polite to say anything, but from the way they avoided us, it was obvious they felt that the entire Groucho Marx family could use a "Man's" deodorant.

Coincidentally, Bob Benchley was on a drinking bender that was putting the other alcoholics at the hotel to shame. He'd already had one attack of DT's, and he'd been advised by his doctor that he better go on the wagon if he wanted to avoid a second, more serious bout with the hallucinatory disease.

Benchley didn't believe he was drinking that heavily until, in a half-inebriated condition, he wandered into our bungalow by mistake one day and found himself face to face with Fritz, whose body odor had not improved one whit since we had moved in, despite daily scrubbings in the laundry tub.

Usually we kept Fritz in a closet or in the car when we were expecting visitors, but Benchley was our first drop-in trade. As he sniffed the air distastefully, it was obvious he wished he'd dropped into someone else's bungalow.

"Is there a skunk in here?" Benchley asked Father, who was sitting in a chair reading the newspaper.

"What kind of a remark is that?" retorted Father. "Do I go into *your* bungalow and ask *you* if *you're* living with a skunk? I don't care who you're living with, as long as it isn't your wife."

"But, Groucho, I could swear I smell a skunk," insisted the puzzled Benchley.

"You're imagining things," said Father. "You're probably drinking too much."

"It's that four-footed hot dog who's the culprit," said Benchley, pointing to Fritz accusingly.

Father smiled guiltily. "Well, I didn't want to tell you," confessed Father, "but that really is a skunk."

"Why does he look like a dachshund?"

"I'm going into a new business, Bob," said Father. "I'm raising skunks that look like dachshunds."

"I think *you've* been drinking," said Benchley.

"It makes a lot of sense," said Father. "You see, Bob, if I can get all the skunks in the world to look like dachshunds, and all the dachshunds to look like skunks, then there'll be striped dachshunds, and I'll make a fortune selling them to furriers."

No one knows for sure if that incident is the reason Benchley went on the wagon, but at any rate, he stopped drinking for a month.

Between sharing a hotel bungalow with a dog that smelled like a skunk and having to rise at 6 A.M. every morning to get to the set, the case of insomnia Father developed as a result of losing all his money in the crash reached pathological proportions by the time we were living at the Garden of Allah.

He tried everything. Pills. Ear plugs. Sleeping masks. Hot Ovaltine. Yoga exercises. Deep-breathing exercises. Hot baths. Cold baths. Lukewarm baths. Massages. Seeing a psychiatrist. Beer before bedtime.

Hard mattresses. Soft mattresses. The floor. A chair. Music—jazz and classical. He even tried reading Thomas Mann.

Nothing worked on him except a Chester Morris movie. But that was before TV, and most movie houses closed at one o'clock, when the head usher would roust him out of his seat so that he could close up the theater. By the time he was tucked in his bed at home, Father would be wide awake for the rest of the night.

He finally became so desperate that he even sought advice from Benchley, a fellow insomniac.

Being an expert on insomnia cures, Benchley suggested to Father that he try taking a hot bath scented with a pine needle solution every night before turning in.

Willing to grasp at any straw, Father bought a bottle of the pine-needle solution the next day, and that night before going to bed he doctored his tub water with it and immersed himself. The pine-needle soak appeared to be the answer—until Father fell asleep in the tub, and nearly drowned.

Mother, who found him gurgling beneath the water, had to pull him out and give him mouth to mouth resuscitation, which was probably the first time they'd kissed on the lips in years.

CHAPTER 15

THE
SPORTING
LIFE

BY the time Fritz smelled like a dachshund again, the vagabond Marxes had moved to another rented house—this one in Beverly Hills, and in the Hawthorne School District where we eventually settled down for good.

Although at first I missed the ice skating and sleigh riding of the Eastern winters, I quickly grew to love Southern California for all the other things it offered. You could play outdoors all year around. You didn't have to wear heavy clothing. You could ride your bike to school without getting soaked in a sudden thundershower. And you could swim whenever anybody invited you to his or her house (and you didn't have to go in the water only up to your knees).

If I was really desperate for something to do, I'd accompany Father to the studio and watch the Marx Brothers shoot their latest picture. But I had to be pretty desperate—desperation born of having my best friend away all summer, or the weather being too inclement for outdoor sports. How many times could I get a thrill out of watching Bing Crosby or Shirley Temple eating lunch in the commissary? Besides, I knew everything in *Horsefeathers* and *Duck Soup* by heart by the time they reached the shooting stage, for Father used to make me earn my allowance by cueing him in his lines when he was learning his part.

What I enjoyed more than anything when we first came to California was the horseback riding. When he wasn't shooting, Father would take the whole family riding three or four times a week.

Horseback riding was very much in vogue in Hollywood's infancy—probably because there was so much wide-open space. You could ride a horse all the way to the beach, without fear of getting gunned down by a Lincoln Continental or an Easy Rider.

Father loved to put on his jodhpurs and beret and spend the afternoon on the back of a horse. I think riding appealed to him because it was the one sport where he could keep talking while he was getting his exercise. In golf he was expected to keep quiet. Because that was virtually an impossibility for him, his company was anathema to the serious golfer. Even the great Ben Hogan couldn't concentrate with Father in the same foursome. While Father cracked jokes in the background, Hogan topped his drive off the fourth tee at Hillcrest one day, and the ball rolled exactly four feet. No one had ever seen Hogan do *that* before.

But while Father was on the back of a strong steed, he could be as garrulous as he pleased, and he pleased quite a lot.

If he wasn't complaining about the incompetence at the studios while we rode, Father would regale us with stories of his early vaudeville days. Or keep us abreast of current events ("Really, Arthur, you ought to start reading Walter Lippmann. If you're going to be a writer, you have to know everything. You can't just read the sports page."). Or else he'd be a philosopher: "There's nothing quite so good for the inside of a man as the outside of a horse."

Generally, we'd ride out of Dubrocks Riding Academy in San Fernando Valley. Dubrocks is now Studio City. In those days it was the largest livery stable in Southern California. And the most popular, too, for the rentals were only two dollars an hour, and the stable was accessible to the most interesting riding trails—many of them winding through fruit orchards, where, if you so desired, you could reach up and filch an apricot or an orange from an overhanging branch when the owner wasn't looking.

Father and Miriam (who was only six) and I soon became quite expert at handling horses. But after a couple of spills, Mother never was very comfortable aboard a horse, and thereafter only went along to show off her latest riding habits.

One week-end, when we were staying at a dude ranch in Palm Springs, the four of us decided to take a ride to the falls in Tacquitz Canyon. Mother, as usual, was dressed for Central Park—jodhpurs, a velvet coat and a brown derby. Certainly not the outfit for cow punching.

Halfway up to the falls, our horses came to a deep stream which had to be forded. Because it was an unusually hot day even for Palm Springs, and Mother didn't know how to handle her steed, he decided to roll over and cool off in the water, with Mother still clinging to him. Mother wasn't hurt, but as she waded out of the stream, soaking wet right up to her brown derby, she announced she would never get on a horse again.

"What should I do—call a taxi?" asked Father.

For several years, the three of us kept up the horseback-riding tradition.

One day Father tied his horse in front of a small frame bungalow in San Fernando Valley, bade us do the same, and strode up to the front door.

"I want to see a friend," he explained, ringing the bell.

A red, bulbous nose, its owner in bathrobe and slippers, soon appeared in the doorway. It was W. C. Fields. He greeted Father warmly, and pretended to be happy to meet his children.

Afterwards, he showed us around the house. Towards the end of the tour, he opened a door and pointed inside to a large room that was filled from floor to ceiling with cases of bourbon. It looked like a warehouse for a wholesale liquor distributor.

"Why so much?" asked Father.

"I'll tell you why, Groucho," said Fields in his inimitable drawl. "That's in case prohibition ever comes back. Can't afford to be caught short a second time."

Father loved the equestrian life so much that for a time he even considered buying a ranch in the valley, and making that his permanent home. But Mother talked him out of it. In addition to being afraid of horses, she was also afraid she'd never get Father out of the house at night if he lived so far from town.

One morning—we were living in the shack with the slime-green pool at the time—Father was at the Bank of America in Beverly Hills, when he heard of a brand new house on Hillcrest Drive that the mortgage department was repossessing.

It was a two story Monterey-Colonial, with fourteen rooms—including six complete baths, a billiard room, servants' quarters for three and an upstairs pantry. Everyone in the family could have a separate bedroom, including Mother and Father.

Its builder had gone broke in the depression, and Father could have it for only $23,000, if he moved fast.

He moved fast. We were in escrow by late that afternoon. With my usual luck, the house didn't have a swimming pool or a tennis court. But it had "room for a pool," as the real estate salesman handling the deal pointed out.

Father still hadn't made up his mind whether or not to put in a pool by the time I got married and moved away.

It wasn't much of a hardship, however, for Chico's baronial estate was now only a block from our new home. And after Chico gave it up to move his family to Malibu, Harpo took over the lease and stayed there for years.

It didn't matter to me which one of those two uncles owned it, for they both were as fond of me as I was of them, and I was given carte blanche to use the swimming pool and tennis court any time I desired.

It was during this period that Father decided—perhaps because of the proximity of Harpo's court and the fact that he enjoyed Harpo's company so much—that tennis ought to be our family sport.

Mother hated golf and horseback riding. Father just hated golf, but he was starting to tire of the long automobile drive through the hills to Dubrocks in the Valley.

But tennis was something we could all do together.

Besides, it was rapidly becoming the favorite sport of the picture colony, now that there was a Depression on and nobody could afford polo. You couldn't pick up a fan magazine or newspaper without seeing a picture of Gilbert Roland or Errol Flynn or Ben Lyons, dressed in white gabardine trousers and cable-stitch sweater, leaping around a tennis court or else just posing by the net with some glamorous female.

Harpo had forsaken croquet for tennis, and was now taking lessons on his court. And so were Zeppo and his wife, Marion, and also Chico and my cousin, Maxine. So why shouldn't the Groucho Marxes get in the same swing of things?

Father wasn't a complete tyro at the sport. When we lived in the East, he and Mother had potched balls back and forth on the courts in Central Park and at Rip's on 63rd Street. In addition, Father had always been an enthusiastic follower of big-time tennis. In the fall, he'd often gone to Forest Hills during the National Championships to see Bill Tilden, Susan Lenglen, Helen Wills, Rene LaCoste and the rest of the important names of that era play.

Mother and Father had given up tennis for golf, and golf for horseback riding. But now that their interest had been re-kindled by Harpo and Zeppo's enthusiasm for tennis, they were anxious for me to start swinging a racket, too.

Having heard from most of my friends that tennis was a sissy sport, I wasn't too sure I wanted to be part of the whole thing. But when Father and Mother dragged me to the Pacific Southwest Tennis Championships at the Los Angeles Tennis Club, and I saw Ellsworth Vines, Fred Perry and Frank Shields socking the ball around, I quickly changed my mind.

Tennis appealed to me even more after Harpo invited a group of the touring tennis players, including Fred Perry and Van Ryn and Allison (the National Doubles champions) up to his court one Sunday afternoon to play with his friends.

After the grown-ups had had their fun, Perry showed me how to hold a racket, gave me a few pointers on how to stroke the ball, and then let me hit a few with him. When I seemed to show some aptitude for the game, Perry told Father that he thought I had the makings of a great player if I'd take a few lessons from a good pro and work hard.

And then he made me a present of his brand new Slazenger tennis racket.

That was all the push I needed.

We all took lessons from Harpo's pro for a while, but he was a nicer guy than he was a good teacher and player. In six months I was able to beat him, so Father decided it was time to move on to someone better. After trying a few other pros around Hollywood, I finally wound up under the auspices of Eleanor Tennant.

Tennant, a former ranking player herself, was a masculine-looking, leathery-skinned woman of forty, who had the use of Marian Davies and William Randolph Hearst's court, on their estate in Beverly Hills.

Her assistant was a blonde, buxom nineteen-year-old named Alice Marble, whose job it was to bat balls across the net to the pupils as Tennant drilled them in their strokes. Afterwards, Marble would go around the court and pick up the balls and put them back in the teaching basket.

Two years later Alice Marble won the singles titles at Wimbledon and Forest Hills, and was being compared with the greatest of them all—Helen Wills Moody.

One day, Mother—who did most of the child-schlepping in our family when Father was working—brought me to the Hearst court for my lesson a few minutes early. Tennant was still on the court with her last pupil—a freckle-faced, tousle-haired boy who didn't seem much taller than the professional-sized racket he was swinging.

But he played pretty well, and when we were introduced to him at the end of his lesson, he seemed to have all the assurance of an emcee at the Trocadero.

After the boy had gone—doing kind of a "Shuffle Off to Buffalo" exit—Tennant explained to us that he was an actor; that he was currently appearing as "Puck" in a production of *Midsummer Night's Dream* at the Hollywood Bowl; and that his father was a baggy-pants comedian at the Burbank Burlesque Theater on Skid Row in Los Angeles.

"He's a remarkable kid," said Tennant, "but I'm really worried about him. He has no home life. I don't think he ever eats or sleeps regularly. And he's already smoking a pack a day. I don't know what's going to become of him."

The kid's name was Mickey Rooney.

Because of our mutual interest in the game, Mickey and I saw quite a bit of each other for a few months. If we weren't playing singles together, we'd team up and take on whatever grown-ups were around.

Because he seemed like such a waif, Mother and Father invited him over to our house to dinner regularly—to fatten him up.

Then, almost before we knew it, Mickey was a big star, making more money per week than Father, and we never saw each other—except to wave "hello" in passing—until thirty-five years later, when my collaborator and I wrote and produced his television series.

After I'd been taking lessons and playing tennis for about a year, I could beat most of the grown-ups who hung around Harpo's court. Admittedly, this wasn't much of an accomplishment, when you considered who frequented the place: Ben Hecht and Charlie MacArthur; H. N. Swanson, the literary agent; George and Ira Gershwin; Bill Perlberg, who was then a ten-percenter with William Morris; Harpo's numerous girlfriends; and Oscar Levant.

Levant didn't come to play tennis. He just sat in the sunshine in his rumpled dark blue suit and insulted the other guests—mainly Father. You could really feel the friction when those two got together—I guess because Father had once tossed Levant out of our New York apartment when the latter showed up at a party uninvited and asked Father how he could have such dull friends.

But Harpo didn't care what Father thought about Levant. He loved his company—probably because of his piano playing—and he always had him around. Sometimes Levant lived on the premises when he didn't have a job and couldn't support himself.

However, it wasn't my fault that the people at Harpo's weren't Wimbledon caliber. I did my job. I took on all grown-ups and usually beat them, making me most unpopular with everyone but Father. He was extremely pleased that the money he'd spent on lessons had brought such quick results, and he'd even taken to going around town and boasting about my game to his friends, foes and relatives.

One night at our dinner table, Father made the mistake of spout-

ing off about my game in front of my Uncle Zeppo and Aunt Marion.
Zeppo and Marion, in addition to being naturally great competitors,
were taking their own tennis quite seriously in those days. So seriously,
in fact, they had given up playing at Harpo's (because the competition
wasn't "good enough") and had joined the Beverly Hills Tennis Club,
where the really fine players of the movie colony hung out—Gilbert
Roland, Solly Biano, Norman Krasna, Errol Flynn and Ben Lyons, to
name just a few. Among the "A" women players there, Marion was
considered in the top two, so when Father boasted to my aunt and
uncle that he thought I was the best tennis player in the Marx family,
Zeppo and Marion started to snicker.

Zeppo allowed that "Art might be pretty good for a boy," but
then quickly added, "but he's certainly not in Marion's class."

"She can't beat Arthur," said Father confidently.

"How much would you like to bet?" shot back Zeppo, always
eager to risk his money. "A hundred dollars?"

Not a betting man himself, Father's complexion turned the color
of our white tablecloth.

"Put up or shut up!" said Marion as Father hesitated.

Father turned to me. "Do you think you can beat your Aunt Marion, Big Feet?"

"I think so," I answered, but deep inside I wasn't too certain of
how I'd play with all that money riding on me.

"Okay, you've got a bet," said Father, reaching for his wallet.

The match was arranged for the following Sunday at noon, on
Zeppo and Marion's home grounds—the Beverly Hills Tennis Club.

The Beverly Hills Tennis Club was—and still is—located in the
manufacturing district of Beverly Hills, between Beverly Boulevard
and Third Street, and within smelling distance of the Wonder Bread
Factory. It was a small club, with just six courts, a rambling, ranchy-
looking clubhouse, and no more than a hundred members—most of
them in the film industry. The club was little known, in fact, outside
movie circles.

The real bastion of tennis in Southern California in those days
was the Los Angeles Tennis Club, down on Melrose and Vine. The
Los Angeles Club had twenty courts, a large clubhouse and a tennis

stadium. Most of the world's top-ranking players went there to practice when they came to town.

But the Los Angeles Tennis Club did not take in Jewish members. They may have had—as they have today—one or two "token" Jews, but I have a feeling the management made a mistake about them, and somehow was convinced that they were Gentile.

At any rate, there was a definite need for a second club in town. This void was filled by a man named Milton Holmes, a Jew, and one of the finest tennis coaches in the United States, when he formed the Beverly Hills Tennis Club with Fred B. Alexander, a Davis Cup star of a by-gone era. Because of its handy location, the new club soon attracted most of the film industry's top names—whether they be Jew, Gentile or Chicano. There were no racial restrictions. You just had to be connected with the picture business in some way.

A list of a few of the important names who were members then— Fredric March, Nelson Eddy, Paul Lukas, Constance Bennett, Carole Lombard, Gary Cooper, Cary Grant, Peter Lorre, Ben Lyons, Bebe Daniels, Ginger Rogers, Gilbert Roland, Ann Sothern, Basil Rathbone, John Garfield, Robert Montgomery, Errol Flynn, David Selznick, Frank Capra, Bob Riskin, Norman Krasna, Willie Wyler, Charlie Chaplin, Paulette Goddard, Irwin Shaw, Billy Wilder, Gene Raymond and Clark Gable—reads like a *Who's Who* of the Late-Late Show.

Because of the glamour that came to be associated with the place, many of the top tennis stars of the world also started to hang out there —Bill Tilden, Ellsworth Vines, Frank Shields, Fred Perry, and a couple of then unknown kids, Don Budge and Gene Mako.

All those people, of course, weren't sitting on the veranda that faced the Number One Court that Sunday when Mother and Father walked into the Beverly Hills Tennis Club with me. But there were enough strange faces to make me nervous.

I think Zeppo and Marion had deliberately talked up the match beforehand, so that there would be a big crowd, and lots of excitement, and I, being young and used to the quiet around Harpo's court, would get the shakes.

Well, I *was* nervous. For the first couple of games I could hardly keep the ball in play. As I looked over at the veranda, I could see Zeppo smirking, and Father, paler than usual, and extremely silent, probably thinking about what he could have done with a hundred dollars if he hadn't thrown it away on me.

But then I discovered something about Marion's game—she had great form (not only her strokes but her figure), but, like most women, she ran as if both feet were glued to the concrete. Moreover, she couldn't play net at all. I started drop-shotting and pulling her in close to the net, and then I'd lob over her head. Most girls don't like to be lobbed to, anyway. It throws off their timing, and ruffles their dignity.

After the first two games it was no contest. If I recall correctly, I won 6-2, 6-1.

I felt sorry for my aunt as we walked off the court together. She— at least a half a foot taller than I—seemed on the verge of tears, and was hardly able to speak. But I was pleased that I'd come through for Father.

As I stood toweling off on the veranda, accepting congratulations from Father and Mother and some of the club members, Zeppo suddenly turned away from Marion, whom he'd been consoling, and said in a loud voice, "Listen, Groucho. The kid may be able to beat my wife, but I'll bet you he can't beat me!"

Zeppo was just a "B" player on the men's ladder, but, being a man and naturally more athletic than the average woman, he figured he could make up in brawn for what he lacked in skill and orthodox strokes.

"Okay, double or nothing," replied Father, who, in his euphoria over my victory, was turning into a regular Nick the Greek.

Zeppo didn't even bother to put on tennis clothes. He just stripped off the jacket of his Eddie Schmidt suit, loosened his tie, and slipped into a pair of tennis sneakers.

He was tougher than Marion. I couldn't bring *him* to the net and lob, because he had a strong overhead and volley from playing doubles with the "A" players. However, I did manage to outsteady him from the back court, and outlast him, too. His chain-smoking was finally catching up with him. By the time I won the first set, 6-4, and was leading 3-0 in the second, Zeppo had to default from sheer exhaustion.

I got a big kick out of watching Zeppo pull a huge roll of bills from his pocket, count out two hundred dollars and hand them over to Father. In a small way, I was finally getting to repay Father for all those chocolate sodas and tennis lessons he had bought me in the past.

I felt even better about it when Father gave me twenty-five dollars as my share of the victory spoils. It was the first money I'd ever earned. As I stood on the veranda, counting my money and making sure Father hadn't short-changed me, Milton Holmes approached us and invited Father to join the club.

"What for?" asked Father, upon learning a family membership cost five hundred dollars. "We can always play at Harpo's."

"If you want the kid to be a champ, he'll have to practice against tougher competition than he can get at Harpo's," said Holmes. "And he should enter all the junior tournaments, too. I'll be glad to coach him."

It didn't take much prodding from me to get Father to write out a check for five hundred dollars.

It was the first step in the making of a tennis bum out of me, and an alcoholic out of Mother.

CHAPTER 16

WHO WANTS
TO LIVE OVER
A FISH STORE
IN BOSTON?

HAVING a place like the Beverly Hills Tennis Club in which to hang out was an education—even to a boy who'd been raised around as many show business personalities as I had.

Our club, in the mid-thirties, was more than just a place for ham actors to flex their tennis muscles, and pretty starlets to model the latest court fashions. It was a "home away from home" for some of the finest creative talent in the film industry—Frank Capra, Bob Riskin, Norman Krasna, Irwin Shaw, Dore Schary, Elliott Nugent, Willie Wyler, Joe Cohn, Mervyn LeRoy, Billy Wilder, Moss Hart, and all at the height of their creative powers.

A mutual interest in tennis had, of course, attracted most of these gentlemen to the club in the first place. But tennis wasn't the only thing that drew them there. They enjoyed the company of other people in show business, but even more than that, they liked the food at the club, for it wasn't typical restaurant fare. It was home cooking, prepared by Milton Holmes's wife, Jay. At least, everyone presumed Jay was his wife, for they slept together in the same little room in the back of the club house.

The serving was done by Jay, too—boardinghouse style, at one long wooden table on the club's veranda. In the winter months, when the weather was bad, meals were served in the club's combination parlor-trophy room—a rustic-looking retreat with pegged wooden floors, comfortable leather furniture and a huge stone fireplace.

Jay's lunches were home cooking at its finest. "Most homes *wish* they had food like that," was the way Father put it.

Plebeian dishes but with a gourmet's touch. Pot roast and potato pancakes. Corned beef and cabbage. Cheese blintzes. Pigs in a blanket. Stewed chicken and dumplings. And for dessert, maybe a little strudel or deep dish apple pie smothered in home-made whipped cream. Just the sort of meal you needed before taking to the tennis court to do battle under a blazing Southern California sun—if you needed to have a heart attack, that is.

But who cared about heart attacks? Where else in Southern California could you eat so well and enjoy good talk with so many of your compatriots?

Jay's culinary artistry was such an attraction that most of the club's bachelors—and a few of its married members, too—showed up regularly to have breakfast on the veranda. While munching on toasted bagels, smoked salmon, cream cheese and jelly, French pancakes and other delicacies whipped up by Jay on demand, they'd read the trade papers, discuss the various picture deals that they or their agents were making, and exchange advice on how to solve their mutual problems—script, money and girl.

The men who had specific studio assignments would usually leave for their studio lots after breakfast, and return again later in the afternoon to squeeze in a couple of sets of tennis before going home.

If they were "between pictures," a euphemism for being unemployed, they'd often spend the entire day there, playing tennis, basking in the sun, and watching the exhibition matches on Court Number

One between Milton Holmes and whatever visiting tennis stars he was entertaining that day.

It was a private joke among the members that you didn't have to read the "trades" to find out whether or not a particular actor, writer or director was unemployed. You could tell by the quality of his tennis game.

Thus, if Gilbert Roland (one of the top three at the club for many years) was serving a lot of aces, was striking his topspin forehand with more ferocity and accuracy than usual, and wasn't missing backhands, it was a safe bet he wasn't spending much time before the cameras.

By the same token, if Norman Krasna (also one of the big three) started dumping easy volleys into the net, or began running out of gas by the second set, it was probably because he was stuck at some studio on a long-term writing assignment that didn't permit him to sneak away from his office even late in the afternoons.

Luckily, I had no employment problems to interfere with my tennis practicing. Just Beverly Hills High School stood between me and my main goal in life at the time—to become the best player at the tennis club. And I was determined that no school was going to thwart my efforts.

In my freshman year, Beverly High was probably as pleasant a place as you could find to get an education, if an education was what you were after. It had a small student body (only about 800 pupils compared with today's 3500); light and airy classrooms, gayly colored umbrella tables on the terrace outside the cafeteria; and, in general, a country-clubbish atmosphere. As a matter of fact, the west side of Beverly High's campus bordered an eighteen-hole golf course, whose beautiful manicured fairways and greens occupied the space where Century City and what remains of Twentieth Century–Fox stand today.

But country-clubbish or not, I could hardly wait for the bell to ring at the end of the school day, so that I could hop on my bike and pedal over to the club, where I was almost certain to find a good match. On weekends and vacations, I'd often be there looking for a game as early as eight in the morning.

If the place was deserted, or if one of the "A" players didn't consider me stiff enough competition to bother with, I'd take a playing lesson from Milton Holmes, or hit some balls against the backboard, until the grown-ups on the neighboring court complained about the noise and made me quit.

After we'd been members for a few months, I could beat everyone at the club, except Gilbert Roland, Ben Lyons and Norman Krasna. They were the top three on the men's "A" ladder, and were all pretty evenly matched. They took turns knocking each other off the top rung, the outcome of their spirited encounters often hanging on such a slender thread as who made the biggest pig of himself at lunch, or who *didn't* get laid the previous night.

Unless Roland, Lyons or Krasna happened to be suffering from huge hangovers or chronic employment, I stood little chance of winning more than two or three games a set from any of them—my first year as a member.

This gave them the excuse they needed to avoid playing me, if they so wished. And as my game continued to improve with practice, they "so wished" more and more frequently. They had nothing to gain by beating me. So the feeling was, who wants to risk his reputation against a high school freshman who was barely five feet tall in street shoes? If one *had* to get knocked off his top-of-the-ladder perch, it was far less humiliating to fall at the hands of a contemporary—a grown man, at least. So the word was out—avoid Marx *fils* if you can!

If I couldn't pressure one of the big three into playing me, or if Milton Holmes was busy giving a lesson to Robert Taylor or Carole Lombard, I might have to lower myself and play in the same foursome with Mother and Father.

For a while, Mother took her tennis very seriously. She had a steady, if unorthodox, backcourt game, and a great deal of determination. She also had youth on her side—she was only thirty-five—and she was naturally athletic and light on her feet. So after we'd been members for a few months she could beat most of the women at our club, and a good many of the men.

Father, on the other hand, was never able to take a sport very seriously. Tennis was no exception. He played a brand of tennis that the "A" players at the club referred to as "schlepper" or "alta cocker" doubles.

Father wasn't totally inept on the tennis court, nor was he actually an alta cocker yet. But he was slowing down, and his interest in running after a tennis ball was diminishing. He was forty-five, and quite conscious of the fact that in five years he would be fifty.

Nevertheless, when he set his mind to it, and stopped cracking jokes on the tennis court, he could hold his own in a foursome of alta cockers. He had a dependable forehand, which he kiddingly referred to as "Iron Mike," and a lob high enough to seed a cloud. But the killer instinct necessary to be a winning athlete was absent when he competed in tennis, or any sport, for that matter.

His neatest trick with a racket was to sit on its head between points, and rest—while he waited for someone else in his foursome to pick up the balls and return them to the server.

The only person who could stir up Father's competitive instinct on the court was Mother. He took great delight in soundly whipping her, mainly because she hated so to lose to him. For some reason he could always beat Mother, even after she was considered to be the better player of the two.

But it took more than Iron Mike to send Mother to the showers. Father kept up a running fire of funny patter all through their matches —until Mother could no longer concentrate on the game.

If jokes and Iron Mike failed him, he'd then have to rely on disconcerting her with a parody he'd composed, to the tune of "Break the News to Mother."

> Just hit the ball to Mother,
> And you won't have to hit another.
> And if you bring her to the net,
> You'll find the Swede's even more inept.

This ditty, when sung in a baritone loud enough to be heard by the people dining on the veranda, would infuriate Mother. Her face would turn purple with anger, and her normally steady game would fall apart instantly.

One of the high points in Father's tennis career was when he and I won a men's doubles tournament at the club. But by then I was a ranking player, and the best around. I just ordered him to keep sitting on his racket, while I virtually played singles against our opponents.

But perhaps an even higher point was an exhibition doubles match that pitted Father and Ellsworth Vines (the world's professional champ) against Charlie Chaplin and Fred Perry (who had just won his third Wimbledon title), to commemorate the grand opening of our remodeled clubhouse.

It was a well-publicized Hollywood affair, complete with kleig lights, newsreel cameramen, and lots of people.

Chaplin played about the same brand of tennis as Father, but he took his game more seriously—a fatal mistake.

Father walked out on the court carrying twelve rackets and a large suitcase. To Chaplin's annoyance, Father refused to divulge the suitcase's contents.

"Never mind what's in there," he told Chaplin. "Do I go around asking you what's in your suitcase?"

"I don't have a suitcase," replied Chaplin, failing to see the humor.

"Why in hell haven't you?" asked Father in a voice loud enough to make the gallery start laughing. "What kind of a tennis player are you, going around without a suitcase?"

Father played the first two games of the match sitting on his racket, with disastrous results. Chaplin and Perry won both games. When Perry served, Father finally got off his racket and somehow managed to hit a weak return to Chaplin at the net.

But just as Chaplin was about to put the ball away for the point, Father yelled, "Watch out, Charlie!"

Chaplin looked away from the ball, and missed it completely. "Did you have to speak when I was striking the ball?" asked the annoyed Chaplin.

"I just wanted to warn you that I'm going to give you Iron Mike," yelled Father. "So you'd better get down behind the net. I don't want to be responsible for hurting you."

Chaplin (who, paradoxically, seemed to have little sense of humor when he wasn't performing) became so nettled by the laughs Father was getting that his game fell completely apart, and, incidentally, so did the match.

Finally, Father had everyone in such hysterics that even Vines and Perry couldn't hit a ball over the net. At that point Father brought his suitcase to mid-court, opened it and started spreading a picnic lunch, from Nate & Al's, out on a blanket.

"Let's play tennis," demanded Chaplin. "I didn't come here to be your straight man."

"Well, with that game of yours, Charlie, you certainly didn't come here to play tennis!" countered Father. "Now sit down and have a pastrami sandwich."

Despite Chaplin's protestations, the match ended with Father and Chaplin munching sandwiches, while Vines and Perry tried to put on a singles exhibition around them.

The Groucho-Chaplin exhibition match marked the beginning of a great change in the character of the Beverly Hills Tennis Club, which had its effect on our family.

Until the remodeling, as I pointed out earlier, the club had been a very *gemütlich,* homey little place, with neither a bar, liquor license nor swimming pool. It was just a club for playing tennis and eating lunch.

But many of its members had grown dissatisfied with what it had to offer and were defecting to the Westside—a new club that had opened in West L.A. The Westside had a bar, a large swimming pool, and in general a more appealing atmosphere for people who wanted to swing.

To counteract this alarming trend, Milton Holmes had to be able to offer his remaining members the same advantages. But business had been bad—many of his actor members never paid their bills—and in order to finance the project, Holmes had to take in two partners, Ellsworth Vines and Fred Perry. Vines and Perry were in the dough, having each made a couple of hundred thousand by turning pro, and together they put up fifty thousand dollars to give the club a face lift.

After the construction job, the old place was barely recognizable.

A second story, with a dining room and a long stand-up bar, had been added to our original clubhouse. Jay stopped doing the cooking, and was replaced by a chef who wasn't very good, and a maître d' with a French accent. The cuisine immediately deteriorated to the level you'd expect of a drive-in on Wilshire Boulevard.

In addition, one of the tennis courts was ripped up to accommodate a swimming pool, gayly striped umbrella tables and outdoor lounging furniture. In good weather you could count on finding a number of scantily clad movie starlets and beautiful actresses lounging around the pool, sipping martinis and trying to catch Greg Bautzer's eye.

In bad weather everyone would be inside the bar room, dancing to a juke box which a small-time hood, who had recently become a member, had donated to the club. There was plenty of boozing, good music and jitterbugging to the records of Benny Goodman, Artie Shaw and Tommy Dorsey, who had a young kid named Frank Sinatra doing the vocals.

Father detested the new atmosphere of the club, and as time went on studiously started avoiding the place. He preferred to spend his afternoons in his study, reading, playing the guitar and practicing his singing. Occasionally he might drop in to schmooze with his good friends Billy Wilder and Norman Krasna, or to case my game to see if I was improving. But that was the most the club would ever see of him.

Mother, however, more than made up for Father's absence. She enjoyed the conviviality of the new Beverly Hills Tennis Club. She loved to laugh, and have a "gay time," as she phrased it. And now that she had two in help permanently and her kids were fairly well grown up, she had few responsibilities to keep her at home.

Consequently, she'd arrive at the tennis club around twelve, play a few sets of tennis, and spend the rest of the afternoon jitterbugging, or sitting on a bar stool, sipping Tom Collinses with the crowd of swingers that was beginning to infest the place—tennis bums and good-looking Hollywood leading-men types who were usually out of work, and therefore available for anything from tennis to sex.

As time passed, Mother discovered that the roadhouse atmosphere of the clubhouse appealed to her more than the life she led at home. What was worse, she was finding out that she liked to drink. Still an abnormally shy person after twenty years of marriage to a Marx Brother, she was turning to alcohol more than ever to help conquer her inhibitions and to be less uptight around Father and his intellectual friends.

Soon, she wound up doing more drinking than tennis playing at our club, and that led to her ultimate destruction.

When I wasn't actually on the tennis court, I used to like to sit around the veranda or the locker room, gulping down cherry Cokes and listening to all the inside movie business talk and Hollywood gossip.

There was plenty of each—in fact, I heard everything a teen-aged boy ought to know about Hollywood, but which he wasn't likely to read in Louella Parson's column.

Frank Capra and Bob Riskin discussing their latest film project—some story with a silly-sounding title, *Mr. Deeds Goes to Town*—and trying to iron out a few stubborn wrinkles in its plot.

Carole Lombard confessing to her best friend that her husband of only a few weeks, Clark Gable, was really a "lousy lay."

Harry Cohn complaining about how Leo McCarey had conned him into making *The Awful Truth*, and predicting what a flop it would be.

Nelson Eddy lamenting to Fredric March that he wouldn't shoot another love scene with Jeanette MacDonald if she didn't stop belching in his face during the filming of *Naughty Marietta*.

Milton Holmes wondering aloud if a certain leading man would ever get another job in Hollywood, so he could pay the club the $7,500, he owed in past due bills.

In the course of my eavesdropping—and eavesdropping I had to resort to, for most of this gossip was not meant for my young ears—I overheard some pretty juicy morsels and racy dialogue. For example, why did a certain handsome actor who belonged to our club never completely disrobe in the men's locker room? Answer: He'd had his balls cut off by the bodyguard of a studio head he'd been cuckolding.

Another item being whispered about concerned one of our most famous actress members. This dish was married to a former silent screen star, who'd been perenially out of work since the advent of talkies. Nevertheless, Mr. Former Star was spending his wife's money on all kinds of necessities, like Rolls Royces, diamond rings (for other women), and four-hundred-dollar suits.

"In one year that bastard's gone through seventy thousand dollars of *my* dough," the actress complained bitterly to Barbara Stanwyck one day.

Stanwyck listened sympathetically, then retorted, "Tell me, Darling, is the fucking you're getting worth the fucking you're getting?"

I saw a few things you wouldn't see at any other tennis club, either.

Paulette Goddard, for example, playing tennis braless, and in a blouse so sheer that all the junior members would line up along the fence just to catch a glimpse of those provocative, dark-nippled protuberances. A few of their fathers enjoyed watching her tennis game, too.

Charlie Lederer, who wrote *Kismet,* was, in addition to being quite a good tennis player, a renowned practical joker. While Charlie was sitting around having a drink one afternoon, Jack Cushingham, a visiting pro, started to kid Charlie about his game. "I could beat you tied to an elephant," boasted Cushingham.

The following day, a truck backed up to the club's entrance, an elephant was unloaded by its keepers, and Lederer insisted that Cushingham make good his boast, and on the center court.

Lederer won the match, but I don't think he thought the victory was worth it. The management insisted he clean up all the elephant droppings on the center court.

With so many colorful show business personalities around the club, it was no wonder that my appetite was temporarily whetted to become an actor.

Father had always tried to steer me away from an acting career, but after hearing, around the club, about some of those six-figure weekly salaries members like Gable, Stanwyck and Lombard were making, I felt that emoting was a shorter cut to big money than learning the craft of writing—the direction in which Father was trying to push me. Consequently, I parted with fifteen of Father's hard-earned dollars to join a little theater group being formed one summer vacation by Hilda Carmichael, a drama teacher from Beverly High.

The group's first offering was *Little Women,* and for some reason I will never understand, I was given the part of Professor Bhaer, an eccentric German, with a station-house dialect, who was courting Jo, one of Louisa May Alcott's precious little darlings in crinoline.

Paul Lukas had played Professor Bhaer in the movie. But I was no Paul Lukas. My dialect was atrocious, even after listening to Lukas around the tennis club.

Opening night—at a community playhouse belonging to the Church of Christ, Scientist in Beverly Hills—the house was packed with well-wishers and relatives.

I probably had a right to feel more nervous than anyone else in the cast, because sitting in front row center were five fairly tough critics—Father, Mother, Miriam, Harpo and the real Paul Lukas, whom Harpo had persuaded to attend, thinking I'd get a thrill out of it.

I got a chill, not a thrill, as I stood in the wings, in a phony mustache and beard, and with white powder in my own hair to make it gray, waiting for my first cue. How could Harpo have done that to me? I'd never be able to remember a line.

But harking back to the days when I rode out on the stage of a real Broadway theater in Captain Spalding's sedan chair, I recalled what Father once told me—that he always would get a sick feeling in the pit of his stomach just before he made his first entrance. Suddenly I lost my fear.

I was a Marx. There was nothing to be nervous about, I told myself as I heard my first cue and strode boldly out in front of the audience.

I don't recall what my opening line was. I just know that the moment after I uttered it, I heard a loud guffaw from someone in the first row. Glancing down, I saw Harpo standing in his seat, pointing at me.

"It's Greenbaum, the landlord from Ninety-second Street!" he shouted, to the bewilderment of the cast and the audience.

He then collapsed into his seat, and doubled up into uncontrollable laughter. Out of respect to a fellow thespian, Lukas managed to maintain a straight face, but the rest of the audience, once they recognized Harpo, started laughing along with him.

It was twenty minutes before the laughter subsided and the show could go on.

I eventually recovered my composure, and turned in what, in my own fantasy world, I considered a fairly creditable imitation of Paul Lukas. That is to say, I didn't forget any lines, or trip on a piece of furniture or lose my beard. I didn't even get flustered and blush when I had to play a love scene and kiss Jo on the lips in front of all those people.

Moreover, I thought the applause for me was thunderous when I took my final curtain call.

How did I know they were applauding because the ordeal was over? I just figured a star may have been born.

Mother, being a wise enough parent not to let her critical objectivity imperil an otherwise good relationship with her son, rushed up to me after the performance, threw her arms around me and said, "You were marvelous, Darling. I was very proud."

Before ducking out to beat the crowd, Lukas and Harpo had said something diplomatic, too.

But all Father could manage was, "You were never better, Big Feet," delivered in a jocular tone. I knew this was a device he frequently employed when he didn't want to be hypocritical, but still was expected to say something.

Nevertheless, I was hoping I'd misread his feelings and that he'd have something complimentary—or at least constructive—to say about my acting on the way home.

But in the car he made no further mention of my performance. In fact, his only comment about the entire evening was that the girl who played the part of Jo "looked exactly like my Aunt Hannah," and that he couldn't see why anyone would want to "get in the hay" with her, let alone marry her.

Father probably would have dismissed my acting debut from his mind altogether if Miss Carmichael hadn't phoned our house the following day and tried to pressure me into parting with another fifteen dollars for the privilege of having a role in her second production that summer.

"You're quite gifted," she used as the clincher. "You should stick to it, Arthur."

When I asked Father for the fifteen dollars that night at the dinner table, he fixed a jaundiced eye on me and growled, "Why do you want to be an actor—just because I'm one?"

I told him that Miss Carmichael thought I had some talent, if only I'd develop it.

"Are you going to listen to me, or to some two-hundred-dollar-a-month teacher?" he shot back. "I thought you were lousy. What's the use of kidding?"

I pointed out to him that he had been no John Barrymore himself when he started in vaudeville as one of "The Four Nightingales," a singing group that, by his own admission, usually got cancelled by the management after its first performance.

"That was different. I had no other way to go. My parents were poor. They couldn't afford to send me to college. But you don't have that problem.

"But you weren't very good either. And you still became a star."

"We were lucky. But most people don't—even those with talent."

He then launched into a speech ("tirade" would be more accurate) about all the people he knew—mostly relatives of successful performers—who were "failures now" because they had gone into acting, when they were really "born druggists." He must have mentioned the word "failure" about twenty times in making his point.

"Did I ever tell you about Uncle Heine—Al Shean's brother?" he went on relentlessly. "A wonderful cabinet maker, and he was making a pretty good living at it, until Uncle Al became a headliner. Then Heine decided he could be a comedian, too. So he gave up his job and stood in front of a mirror all day, practicing how to make funny faces. He wound up a complete failure. The boys and I had to pay for his funeral."

I countered that I thought I could do more than make funny faces.

"That's what they all think. Then you get hooked and waste the best years of your life trying, and then it's too late. Look at Al Shean's son, Larry. He had the makings of a fine commercial artist, but he had to be an actor just because his father was one. So he gave up the art institute and went into vaudeville. He wasn't bad. But then vaudeville disappeared, and all the so-so talents disappeared with it. Now he's selling insurance, and all because he had to be an actor."

I told Father that I hadn't really intended to make any permanent commitment to the muse of Comedy & Drama yet. All I wanted was fifteen dollars to join Miss Carmichael's acting class for a second play. I wasn't planning to give up everything else. It just looked like a long, hot, dull summer coming up, since Father was in the throes of preparing *A Day at the Races* and wouldn't be able to take the family anywhere on a vacation.

"All right, all right, you can have the fifteen bucks to join the group," he acquiesced, suddenly weary of the subject. "I'm just telling you this because I care about you. I don't want you winding up a complete failure living over a fish store in Boston."

As I tried to conjure up an image of how a room over a fish store in Boston would compare with my present luxurious living quarters, I must have presented a rather woeful expression, for Father continued in a much softer tone:

"Don't you think it hurts me to tell you all this, Big Feet? Sure, I could be like your mother and say you were great last night—that you could be another Clark Gable. But what's the use of kidding ourselves? Your ears don't stick out far enough!"

By the time we reached our dessert course, Father was again urging me to be a writer. "Look at Norman Krasna! Two hundred thousand a year, and he's only twenty-five years old. That's where the big money is."

"How do I know I can write like Krasna?" I asked.

"Even if you can't—there are plenty of guys out here with no talent making fifteen hundred, two thousand a week. If the worst comes to the worst, you can always live on that. But an actor who's no good usually starves."

By the time we were getting up from the table I'd definitely made up my mind to say farewell to acting.

Living over that fish store in Boston was a pretty bleak prospect. It would never do for the son of Groucho.

If I wished to make Father proud of me, and not be a fifteen-hundred-dollar-a-week failure, I know I'd either have to win Forest Hills, or the Pulitzer Prize.

CHAPTER 17

SOME PEOPLE ARE BORN SCHOLARS AND SOME PEOPLE ARE BORN TENNIS PLAYERS

FOREST Hills seemed like the logical goal to shoot for first. Not only was it more fun to chase a tennis ball than to sit at a typewriter, but I had a head start in the direction of a tennis career.

I hedged my bet a little by steering my academic ship in a literary direction. I took every elective Beverly High had to offer the would-be Hemingway. English, Journalism, Typing, Creative Writing. Even Print Shop (in case I wanted to be another William Allen White and run a country newspaper).

But though I enjoyed those subjects and did well in them—in my senior year I was one of the editors of the high school paper and wrote a weekly column that won a prize in a national scholastic journalism contest—my heart really belonged to tennis. I could always worry about earning a hundred thousand a year *after* I'd won at Wimbledon and Forest Hills.

That this was more than a wild dream had been inculcated in me by quite a few people and events since I had taken up swinging a racket seriously.

In my first year at Beverly High I won my varsity letter—the first time in the history of the school that it had been done by a freshman, in tennis or any other sport.

After a season of competitive interscholastic tennis, I was knocking at the door to becoming the top man at the Beverly Hills Tennis Club—even though I was only fourteen, and not very tall. I'd already beaten Norman Krasna for second position on the ladder, and now all that stood between me and my goal was Gilbert Roland, who was the recognized champ of the motion picture colony.

Roland had the strength and stamina of a bull, and a powerful top-spin forehand that was as good as any I've ever encountered in big-league tennis. He also had an explosive Latin temper, which he demonstrated by cursing out his opponent in Spanish, or smashing his racket over the net post, when things were going badly for him on the court. It was an unnerving thing for an opponent to witness. On the one occasion when I had a chance to beat him in a non-ladder match, Roland gave me such a murderous look when we were changing courts that I actually threw the set for fear of the consequences if I beat him. At the time I was only a skinny thirteen, and no match for him in a fist fight.

But now that I'd beaten Krasna and was officially in a position to challenge Roland to a match for top position, I was not going to be frightened off by his histrionics.

Unfortunately, Roland felt I could take him, and for a frustratingly long time did everything he could to avoid playing me. At first he'd just refuse to accept my challenge, claiming either that he was too tired, or had another match, or that his favorite racket was broken. When I became too insistent, he started staying away from the club altogether at times when he knew I would be there, like after school and on weekends and Jewish or other holidays. Even when I ditched school and showed up at the club at unemployed actors' hours, I wouldn't be able to find him.

It got to be a club joke that Roland stayed in his hilltop home and looked down at the club through a powerful telescope to find out whether or not I was on the premises.

With the impatience of youth, I was going out of my mind over Roland's behavior. I could not understand such an unsportsmanlike attitude. But at the time I had no idea how much it meant to Roland to maintain his position as best player in the movie colony. In a town where tennis was the favorite sport of Jack Warner, Harry Cohn and Ginger Rogers, being king of the courts gave Roland a certain amount of prestige he was no longer enjoying as a cinema idol.

Roland kept up his various dodges for avoiding me for more than a year, with the club starting to lose money on account of it. Until my appearance on the scene, Roland had been the club's biggest spender. His bills for food, tennis balls and smashed racket replacements usually averaged eight hundred dollars a month. But now that he was staying away—probably keeping up his tennis on private courts—the club was starting to run into the red.

Out of desperation, Milton Holmes decided to hold a club championship—winner take all, including the top-of-the-ladder position. This left Gilbert Roland little choice—either he had to enter the tournament, or not play and forfeit top position to whoever won the event.

That brought him back to the club, and he and I eventually tangled in the finals, where I beat him in a tightly fought three-set match.

Roland took the loss like the good sport that he was. After congratulating me and shaking my hand, he walked over to the net post and smashed all three of his brand new Australian-import rackets.

Everyone cheered, especially Milton Holmes, for with the Mexican actor back on the courts smashing rackets, the club would soon be solvent again.

Following my victory—while Mother and Father were sitting on the veranda accepting congratulations for *their* son-the-tennis-player—Ellsworth Vines told them that if they ever expected me to be a tennis player, they would have to enter me in all the important Junior tournaments in Southern California.

"Don't you think Art looked good today?" asked Father, surprised.

"That's show business tennis," said Vines with a deprecating smile. "I'm talking about big-league tennis."

I was all for Vines's suggestion. I figured if I could win the men's championship at our club, I certainly wouldn't have any trouble beating boys my own age.

How did I know that at that time, in the mid-thirties, there were probably more good juniors playing in Southern California than in the rest of the United States put together?

The tournament draws were peppered with such names as Budge, Mako, Riggs, Hunt, Heldman, Van Horn, Parker, and Kovacs.

In my first year of serious competition I didn't get past the first round in any tournament. Moreover, I kept losing by such embarrassing scores as 6-0, 6-0, or 6-1, 6-0, to youngsters I'd never even heard of—Schroeder, Wade, Olewine, McQuon, Cochill, Levinson.

Compared to me these kids all played like pros. They didn't seem to have any weaknesses. If I rushed the net, the ball would go flying by me, with the accuracy of a rifle shot. If I stayed back and tried to outsteady them, they'd take the net, and I'd be unable to make a passing shot, because their volleying was so effective.

With each ignominious defeat, I was becoming increasingly ashamed to report home to Father. But, understanding parent that he was, he kept telling me not to be discouraged. He'd talked it over with Milton Holmes and Ellsworth Vines, who'd been coaching me between tournaments, and they had assured him—as they had assured me—that these defeats were to be expected, that it was all part of acquiring valuable tournament experience. Everybody tried to salve my bleeding wounds with the usual cliché line—"You learn more by losing than you do by winning."

I didn't know about that, but I did feel that eventually I would run out of opponents who could beat me 6-1, 6-0. Or at any rate, I hoped I would.

By the eve of the Long Beach Junior Championships, I had bounced back from my last battering and was again eager to jump into the fray—so eager, in fact, that I couldn't wait for our copy of *The Los Angeles Times* to be delivered the next morning to find out from the printed schedule and the match listings in the sports section who my first opponent would be. So I phoned the sports department of the paper, and waited breathlessly while the night man on the sports desk searched for my name in the schedule.

I'd been playing tournaments long enough now to recognize the names of the players who could beat me 6-1, 6-0. As long as I didn't have to go up against one of them, I felt I had a chance to reach the second or third round.

I was overjoyed when the night editor informed me that my opponent was some nonentity named Jack Kramer. Mother and Father were finishing dinner with Norman Krasna in our dining room when I brought the news back to the table that my opponent was a nobody named Jack Kramer.

"Kramer," repeated Krasna thoughtfully. "Sounds like a tall, blond Gentile with a big serve and overhead."

Krasna's jibe notwithstanding, I was bursting with confidence as Mother drove me to the Lakewood Country Club in Long Beach the following day.

Some of this confidence vanished when I arrived at the Tournament Desk, and the Tournament Manager introduced me to my opponent—who turned out to be a tall, blond Gentile—and sent us out to one of the back courts. I wasn't, however, going to let this boy Kramer's appearance frighten me. Primo Carnera was tall, too, and he couldn't fight worth a damn. Besides, I was *half* Gentile.

We didn't have to play very many points before I realized that Kramer, in addition to being tall, blond and Gentile, also had a tremendous overhead and serve—to say nothing of his forehand, backhand, volley, drop shot, half-volley and general court presence.

The score was a quick, 6-1, 6-0, in his favor.

Two hours later I was back at the Beverly Hills Tennis Club complaining to Milton Holmes that I was a hopeless case and that I wanted to quit the game.

"Don't be discouraged," said Holmes. "Just remember this—the kid who's a champ at fourteen usually burns himself out before he's eighteen."

It sounded reasonable to a boy who was ready to grasp at any straw.

As I reached my seventeenth year, after playing tournament tennis for the last three of them, I was still waiting for some indication that Jack Kramer was about to burn himself out.

By the spring of 1938, this poor "burnt-out-case" had already won the National Fifteen-and-Under Singles and Doubles Titles, the Southern California Boys' Championships, and the National Interscholastic Singles. He was also winning a majority of the singles tournaments in the eighteen-and-under bracket, defeating with ease most of the boys who defeated me with ease. And in the Beverly Hills Men's Championships he had scored the biggest upset of the year by knocking over Joe Hunt, the fourth-ranking man in the United States and a member of the Davis Cup Team, in the finals.

So phenomenal was this boy-wonder's record that the Davis Cup committee was seriously thinking of putting him on the squad, even though he was only seventeen.

Nobody was thinking of me at all, except Father, who was probably wondering, when I asked him for the entrance fee money to send in with my application to the 43rd Annual Ojai Valley Championships, if it had been a wise move to encourage me in tournament tennis, when he had so little to show for it, except a large bill at the club every month.

Not that I hadn't made some progress as a tennis player, but compared with Kramer's showing, my feats along the tournament trail seemed inconsequential.

I no longer lost 6-1, 6-0 to anybody. I usually reached the second, third, and sometimes fourth round of most Junior Tournaments. I had been ranked thirteenth in my final year in the Fifteen-and-Under. When I was sixteen I upset a seeded player in the Santa Monica Men's Singles Championships.

But I had not won a tournament or even reached the finals of one.

Reaching the finals of a tournament was my own "Impossible Dream"—a dream I usually had as I sat in the stands on the last day of each tournament, enviously watching Kramer playing Olewine, or Riggs playing Hunt, or Budge playing Mako, for the championship and the silver trophies that looked so impressive as they glistened on a table in the sunlight besides the referee's chair.

I'd read *Faust* in school, but it wasn't until I became a tournament tennis player that I knew the true meaning of how it felt to want to sell your soul for something—in my case, one of those trophies. I just had to reach the finals of a tournament some way. I wouldn't care if I lost

6-0, 6-0 in the finals. I'd gladly settle for a runner-up trophy—just so I had something to give to Father when I returned home besides another excuse.

Even Father was starting to become a doubter.

In the beginning of my tennis career, Father would frequently accompany Mother and me to a tournament, if he wasn't busy shooting a picture. After a year of watching me go down to defeat, he'd let Mother do the driving alone, claiming that his presence in the gallery made me nervous. Even so, he'd always be extremely eager to hear the gory details of the loss when we reported back to him, usually around six in the evening, his hour for practicing the guitar.

"Well, Big Feet, what happened this time?"

And then I'd tell him, sometimes with tears in my eyes (if I believed victory had been snatched from me unfairly), and I'd feel like a schmuck for not being another Kramer or Olewine—a son of whom he could really be proud.

"He should have won," Mother, who was a staunch fan of mine, might exclaim indignantly. "But he just kept missing that little shot going into the net." Or, "That linesman really did give Arthur an awful call at point set. Everyone who was sitting around me thought the ball was in."

"Bad calls even themselves up," Father would philosophize.

"But this one was on set point," Mother would insist.

"It's not very important," Father would reply. "Better he should study hard and learn how to make a living."

Make a living! This phrase was enough to strike terror in the heart of any schoolboy raised, sheltered, as I'd been, with nothing much to worry about except how to avoid Kramer or Olewine in the next tournament. But it did help to steel my determination not to be a loser all my life.

Those were just a few of the things that were going through my mind as I drove to the 43rd Annual Ojai Valley Tennis Championships in April of 1938, in my own car, which Father had given me for my sixteenth birthday.

The Ojai Valley Tennis Championships was—and still is—the most prestigious tennis and social event of the Southern California spring tournament season. Since my game had shown considerable improvement since my last tournament appearance, I was hopeful of bringing home a trophy in the Eighteen-and-Under event. But with my usual luck I found my name in the same half of the draw as Jack Kramer's. That meant that even if I should be lucky and reach the semi-finals, I'd still have to beat the greatest junior player who ever lived in order to attain my goal of reaching the finals. And who could beat Jack Kramer? Not even Davis Cup star Joe Hunt, who had lost to him only the previous week in the finals at Beverly Hills.

I could see now that this was going to be another one of those frustrating weeks of play, after which I would have to return home to Father empty-handed, and with another lame excuse.

For some strange reason, all my shots came together at the same time that week—the result, obviously, of intensive coaching by Milton Holmes and Ellsworth Vines, plus three straight years of tournament competition. Except for a lapse of concentration in the second round that saw me down three point-matches before I managed to pull out the deciding set, I played five good matches in a row and defeated five top-notch opponents to reach the semi-finals.

It was the first time I'd ever reached the semis of such an important tournament, and I felt pretty good about it Friday night, in spite of the fact that I knew I had to meet my Armageddon the next morning in the form of "Big Jake" Kramer, who'd breezed through all his matches with alarming ease.

I've always been an optimist, but I figured there was so little chance of this David upsetting Goliath that when I woke Saturday morning and found it was raining, I prayed that it wouldn't clear up until the following day.

Where would that get me? To the finals, believe it or not!

I'd heard that Kramer had another commitment to play in the California State Championships at Berkeley the following Monday. Since few people traveled by plane in those days, Kramer needed a day to get there by other means. So if the play at Ojai was rained out on Saturday, Kramer was going to have to default to me in the semis. Getting to Berkeley on time was more important to him than beating me, because the expense money up there was bigger—and Kramer loved money.

So I prayed to the rain gods—and I prayed—and I *P R A Y E D!* God, how I prayed! Grandma Jo would have been proud of me.

Who cared whether I reached the finals by default? At least I'd have a trophy to bring home to Father and Mother. And who'd know for sure that the reason "Big Jake" defaulted hadn't been because he was afraid to play me?

Around noon it started to clear. But I wasn't finished yet. I knew it would take at least a couple of hours for the courts to dry. By then, I was sure, Kramer would be on his way to Berkeley, because what would be the point of beating me if he wouldn't be able to stick around for the finals? The finals, which originally were scheduled for Saturday afternoon, had now been put off until Sunday. Kramer couldn't afford to wait.

I'm sure that no player who had ever faced Kramer previously had looked quite so confident as I did as I stood at the Tournament Desk at the time of our scheduled match, waiting for "Big Jake" *not* to appear.

After fifteen minutes had elapsed, I casually suggested to Joe Bixler, the tournament manager, that perhaps he ought to consider giving me a default, since I had it on pretty good authority that Kramer was not going to show.

"It's not that I *want* a default," I lied, looking up at the sky, which was beginning to turn gray again. "But you have a lot of matches to catch up on . . . you should use this court before it starts to rain again."

At that point, Kramer swaggered up to the Tournament Desk, stuck out his hand for the balls and said, "Okay, Art, let's get this show on the road. I've got to get up to Berkeley after I win here."

All that praying for nothing! It was the last time I'd put my faith in free enterprise.

Because of Kramer's name we were assigned one of the better courts at the Civic Center. Not the grandstand court, but spectators could sit or stand on the grass and watch, if they chose.

While we warmed up, and during the first part of the match, the sun continued to play hide and seek behind gray cumulus clouds. Between points I kept glancing up at the more menacing ones as they scudded by, trying to assess their rain potential.

Not a drop!

With my eye on the weather, it was a wonder I could see those hard, fast balls Kramer was thumping at me. But somehow I got my racket on them, and returned them for placements. Suddenly I had confidence in everything I tried, and Kramer, for the first time, didn't seem like a superman. I had discovered a weakness—his forehand. I could take the net on his forehand, and he couldn't pass me. Most people played his backhand, which was dangerous.

Miracle of miracles.

I won the first set, 6-4.

Smelling an upset, a small crowd began to gather outside the fence. I did not delude myself, however. I'd won *first* sets before against seeded players, only to have them pull out that little extra something that champions have in reserve, and eventually overtake and beat me. There was no reason to believe Kramer couldn't do the same— especially after he clobbered me in the second set, and got off to a 2-0 lead in the third.

To seal my doom completely, the sun had finally come out for good. No chance of a default now. Believing I was through, the spectators started to leave for other courts.

I wished I could leave with them. At the very least, I wished "Big Jake" would take it a little easy, and not beat me a love set.

That was my thinking as I began rushing the net desperately behind my own serve in the third game. Not to win—I just didn't want to be blanked. And then I discovered what had suddenly gone wrong. In the excitement of winning the first set, I'd forgotten my strategy of playing Kramer's forehand.

The moment I resorted to those tactics again, I forced him into errors, and I started winning points. I took my serve quite easily, and broke Kramer's after a long, deuce game, to even things up.

At three-all I broke Kramer again, and then held my own serve. From a 2-0 deficit, I suddenly found myself with a 5-3 lead.

I couldn't believe it. Neither could Kramer. He got the shakes worse than I did. He started double-faulting and netting easy shots.

I won the set, 6-4, to take the match, and go into the finals against Ted Olewine.

It was a bigger upset than Schmeling over Louis.

I was in a daze as I walked off the court and across Ojai's only street to the Western Union office, where I sent Father a telegram—collect, of course.

I still have a copy of it, which Father, when he was reminiscing lately, pulled out of his desk drawer and turned over to me.

1938 APR 30 PM 7 07

MR. AND MRS. GROUCHO MARX

710 NORTH HILLCREST ROAD BEVERLY HILLS CALIF.
I BEAT KRAMER SEMIFINAL MATCH TODAY I PLAY OLEWINE IN FINALS—

ARTHUR

The headline in Sunday's L.A. *Times*'s sports section read:

SON OF GROUCHO SCORES
UPSET WIN OVER KRAMER

I was hoping Father and Mother would drive up for the finals, but they elected to stay home, figuring their absence had brought me luck, so why change it?

My luck ran out in the finals. Ted Olewine was simply too good for me that day.

But the match was close and hard-fought, the large center-court gallery enjoyed it, and before going down to defeat, I won a set from Olewine—the first time I'd ever done that, too.

And, anyway, who cared if I was only runner-up? At last I had a trophy to bring home to Father. And it was larger than the winner's cup in most tournaments. It was presented to me by Bill Henry, the sports editor of *The Los Angeles Times*, who wrote in his next column, ". . . young Marx, son of Groucho, obviously suffered a let-down after upsetting the great Jack Kramer, but the youngster is definitely someone to be reckoned with in the future."

Even Perry T. Jones, who was the boss of the Southern California Tennis Association, showed up at the center court ceremony to congratulate me. I say "even," because it was a known fact that Jones, who reflected the racial policies of the L.A. Club, where his Association headquartered, never went out of his way to encourage members of minority races to play the clean, gentlemanly sport of tournament tennis. He wasn't openly a racist; his ways of keeping a fellow like Pancho Gonzales out of tournament competition for four years were extremely subtle. But the boys he chose to take under his wing and groom for future greatness were rarely descendants of the tribe of Israel. Almost always they were the tall, blond Kramer or Stan Smith types.

Kramer had been his special protégé for several years, and it did not please Jones to see him toppled by a Jewish upstart from the Beverly Hills Tennis Club.

But he swallowed this bitter pill like the gentleman he made out to be, and as I stood clutching my prized trophy Jones shook my hand warmly, announced he was making me a member of the Junior Davis Cup Squad, and invited me to play at the Los Angeles Tennis Club anytime I wanted.

As I drove down the coast (with my trophy in my lap) I reflected what a damn lucky thing it was that I turned out to be such a lousy rainmaker. If I'd beaten Kramer by default, people might never have known that there was such a person as the Son of Groucho.

At home, Father treated me with a little more respect, too.

He hugged me fondly when I handed him my trophy, said, "Nice going, Big Feet," and carried it into the playroom, where he awarded it a prominent place on our mantel.

What pleased him more than the trophy was the news that I was also being put on the Spalding "free list." This meant he no longer had to pay for my tennis rackets. I could have all I wanted for free from Spalding, simply by turning in my broken rackets and asking for replacements. That saved him a substantial amount every month, since the mortality rate of gut and frames of a tournament tennis player is painfully high.

My uncles—Chico, Harpo and Zeppo—were also impressed with my achievement at Ojai. From the commissary at MGM to the card room at the Friars, they swiftly spread the word that the Marx family had finally spawned an athlete.

No longer was I known around Hollywood as "Groucho's son." Overnight I became "Groucho's son, the tennis player."

A few days after I arrived home from Ojai, Perry T. Jones phoned Father. "Groucho," he said, "your boy Arthur's a fine tennis player—he has the makings of a champ—but he can't play in any more finals looking the way he did at Ojai."

"You didn't like his looks. I think he's a fine broth of a lad."

Jones explained that he was referring to the fact that I had worn shorts in my match with Olewine. Anybody who didn't wear long pants in important matches in those days was considered a pariah by the Southern California Tennis Association.

"What exactly are you getting at, Jonesy, old boy?" asked Father.

Jones said that he wanted permission to take me to the tailor who made Jack Kramer's white gabardines, and order the same for me.

"You mean, you're footing the bill?" asked Father.

"Of course not, Groucho," replied Jones. "But they'll only cost you seventeen dollars a pair—that's a special rate for tournament players. He'll need three pairs."

"What's your cut?" asked Father.

"My cut!?" exclaimed the surprised Jones.

"Certainly. You can't tell me you're going around town hawking pants for the fun of it," said Father accusingly.

Jones told him that his only motive was in wanting "my boys" to look their best.

"If he's your boy, *you* pay for the pants," suggested Father.

"That's out of the question," said Jones. "The Association only does that in certain exceptions."

"I always suspected you were a cheapskate—from the smell of those cheap cigars you smoke," countered Father.

"I don't smoke," said Jones.

"Then you have even less of an excuse for smelling the way you do. Haven't you ever heard of Lifebuoy? Or are you too cheap to spring for that, too?"

"Always clowning, aren't you, Groucho?" said Jones, not really sure if he was or wasn't.

"Don't try to throw me off the scent, Jonesy, old boy. Now come clean. What's your racket? And don't say Spalding. One of us making these bad puns is enough."

Considering Jones's sense of humor—or rather, the lack of it—it's a wonder I wasn't banished from the game for good after the verbal abuse he took that day. No father of an aspiring Bill Tilden had ever spoken so disrespectfully to the Mr. Big of Southern California tennis before. But Jones took every insult Father dished out, and not only didn't ban me, but after persuading Father to spring for two pairs of pants, he personally drove me to Jack Kramer's tailor the following Saturday morning and stood by, supervising, while the tailor measured me.

Receiving V.I.P. treatment from the man who virtually ran amateur tennis in America made me feel that I was finally—and irrevocably—on my way to becoming a champion.

I soon discovered that it took more than the same pants to keep me in the same league with Jack Kramer.

I found I had to concentrate all my efforts in the direction of tennis—at the expense of many other interests, including girls and schoolwork.

During my last year in high school I even developed a chronic case of insomnia, from tensing up and worrying about not getting enough sleep before an important tournament match.

I'd lie in bed with my eye on the clock, and watch the hours I had left for sleep racing by. And I'd panic. Pretty soon I couldn't sleep on non-tournament nights, either.

After six months of this torture, during which I tried all of Father's sure-fire panaceas, to no avail, I was desperate.

Father himself finally cured me by resorting to a very simple psychological trick, which I urge all people suffering from insomnia to try. He made me remove the clock from my bedroom, so that I wouldn't be aware of how many hours I'd lain awake.

It worked, and to this day, I never look at a clock from the time I go to bed until I wake up in the morning.

Father never followed his own advice, however, and when I asked him why he didn't remove the clock from *his* room so that *he* wouldn't have insomnia, he replied testily, "Because someone in this house has to know what time it is."

One of the chief causes of my insomnia was my old nemesis, Ted Olewine, the number two ranking Junior beneath Kramer. I'd beaten everyone else one time or another, but his game had me completely baffled. I'd come close to beating him on a couple of occasions. Once I'd even had him match point, but he managed to pull it out, 8-6, in the deciding set.

I replayed that match over and over in my mind for many months afterwards—while I was in bed trying to get to sleep, while I was day-dreaming in my Spanish class, and while I was supposed to be practic-ing the piano.

I just knew there had to be a way to anticipate those deadly pass-ing shots of Olewine's. One day while I was watching him play a prac-tice match, I thought I detected a weakness.

I could hardly wait to get home to tell Father.

"Guess what?" I exclaimed as I dropped my schoolbooks on the floor of his study and rushed over to his chair, where he was reading *The Nation*. "I think I found the secret to Olewine's game. If you go to the net on his forehand, he'll always crosscourt his passing shot. And on his backhand, he always hits down the line."

I thought Father would be ecstatic over this news, and I went on at considerable length to describe how my new flat forehand, as remod-eled by Ellsworth Vines, would help me facilitate these tactics.

To my surprise, Father cut me off sharply in the middle of a sen-tence, and said, "Big Feet, if you don't watch yourself, you're going to turn into a regular tennis bum!"

"What do you mean?" I asked.

"You know what I'm talking about. You don't think about any-thing else any more. To hear you talk, tennis is all there is to life. You're getting to be a goddamn bore. I don't think you've read a book in weeks or practiced piano or done anything else that'll do you any good. And God knows how you're doing in school, though I imagine not very well. And what about your writing? You claim you want to be a writer, but do you ever write anything?"

I reminded him that I was one of the editors of *Highlights*, the school newspaper.

"Only of the sports section!" he said. "Well, that's not good enough. Hereafter you're going to have to change your ways, and wake up to the fact that there's something else going on in the world besides tennis. If you don't, I'll take your car away, so you won't be able to get to the club as much."

"I thought you wanted me to be the best," I said, hurt that he was taking such an unreasonable attitude.

"I do—but not at the expense of everything else. Just remember, only one man can win at Forest Hills, and the odds are pretty long. There's probably not a hell of a lot of difference between the champ and the ones who don't quite make it. But even if you have what it takes, you could break a leg or get sick along the way and never be able to play again. And then where would you be? How would you support yourself? Only the top man can make a decent living, anyway. The rest, if they keep on playing, starve to death."

I found the best way to handle him when he was angry with me was to say nothing; I was no match for him in a debate. Besides, he was right. So I said nothing, and just stood there staring down at the floor.

He must have felt a pang of remorse for subjecting me to such an unexpected outburst, for suddenly he said, a little more cheerfully, "Now what did you start to tell me about your forehand? You're going to try hitting it flat instead of slicing it when you come into the net?"

It was an old trick of his—to make me feel as bad as he possibly could, so I'd remember his fatherly advice, and then pick me right up again. He had no intention of making me quit. He was getting too big a thrill out of seeing his son's name on the sports page along with his.

He shook me up quite a bit that day, however, because he'd un-knowingly scored a bulls'-eye when he'd guessed that my high school grades weren't what they should be. They weren't bad, but because of "D"s in the two subjects I hated most—algebra and geometry—I didn't have a "B" average. Without that, I stood no chance of getting into Columbia University, where Father—on the recommendation of Morrie Ryskind, a proud alumnus—was determined I should go.

Knowing all this, I had been concealing my grade slips from Mother and Father by cleverly forging their signatures on them and turning them back to the teacher without bringing the evidence home. I even let the Administration office at Beverly High go to the bother of sending my grade transcript into Columbia along with my application.

I believe I secretly nurtured a hope that Columbia might lower its barriers in my case, because I was a four-year varsity letterman at Beverly High, and the captain of a tennis team that was champion of its league.

No chance.

My application came back to me, with a polite letter of rejection, which I immediately stashed under my mattress so that Father wouldn't see it when he came home from the studio.

For a solid month of sheer terror I concealed from Mother and Father the news of what a poor scholar their son the tennis player was.

Every evening when Father returned home from the studio and looked over the day's mail, he would wonder aloud what had become of my application to Columbia. And I'd nervously put him off with some inane comment to the effect that all universities were swamped with applications at that time of year, and that it would probably take a while to process them.

I don't know what I hoped to accomplish by these stalling tactics, for unless I was Merlin the magician, that letter was not going to change from a rejection to an acceptance just by keeping it warm under my mattress.

Each morning I'd wake up determined that this would be the day I'd make my confession to Father, and take my punishment like a man. But I'd always find an excuse to put it off another day.

As graduation time drew nearer, Father forced my hand by announcing that he was going to phone the president of Columbia University long distance and ask *him* why we hadn't heard. Certainly he wouldn't be too busy to talk to Groucho Marx.

This news was about as welcome as a bad call against me on match point. But it rendered unnecessary any more deviousness on my part.

I steeled myself for an explosion, and admitted the truth.

Father studied me through the top portion of his bifocals for what seemed like an eternity. Then he shrugged and announced that tomorrow he was going to Beverly High and have a talk with Mr. Bowhay, the principal. Perhaps, with his influence, something could be done to change things.

The following day Father went to Beverly High, and while I sat nervously on a bench in the corridor, he and the principal conferred for about an hour behind closed doors.

· When Father finally emerged from the principal's office, he approached me with a smile that, while not exactly one of approval, at least stilled my fears that he might do something violent.

"Well, Big Feet, I guess you're not going to Columbia," he said in a resigned tone. "But your principal thinks maybe you can get into USC."

"I'm sorry I made such a mess of high school," I apologized. "If you want to take my car away, go ahead."

And I held out my car keys.

"There's no reason to punish you," he said, reaching out and affectionately tousling my hair. "Some people are born scholars—and some people are born tennis players!"

It was the nicest thing he could have said to me. And in return for such understanding, I beat Ted Olewine in the Dudley Cup the following week.

CHAPTER 18

SHE
COULD HAVE
DANCED ALL NIGHT

WHILE my tennis fortunes were looking up, Mother's and Father's marriage, which had seen fairly smooth sailing since the battle of the *Paris* (at least on the surface), was beginning to founder seriously.

Being an extreme eccentric, and something of a woman hater (which he'll vehemently deny), Father was never what a wife could call "easy" to live with. But as time went by he and Mother managed to iron out, with a minimum of friction, most of the causes of their earlier disputes.

Father, for example, wasn't keeping such a firm hand on the purse strings. He hadn't completely conquered his insecurity syndrome. He'd still grumble mightily (as who doesn't) when the monthly expenditures were climbing higher than he thought they ought to be. But he had bestowed on Mother a generous monthly allowance to spend on herself as she pleased; he was supporting all her relatives (even the anti-Semitic ones); and he allowed Mother to buy anything she needed for the household, within reason, without having to ask his permission.

They'd also reached an armistice on dining room protocol that satisfied Mother's desire to conform to Emily Post while at the same time keeping Father from grumbling that he wasn't getting his meat and potatoes and vegetables at the same time. They had wisely invested in one of those compartmentalized silver serving trays on which meat, potatoes and vegetables could be passed simultaneously by the maid.

Father had acquiesced on another key issue—dinner by candlelight, which he claimed was just another female ruse designed to keep men from getting a good look at their girlfriends or wives. His feelings on female wiles notwithstanding, he eventually agreed to candelabras on the table *provided* Mother kept the main crystal chandelier burning.

So for a number of my formative teenage years there was relative peace in the Groucho Marx family. If there were arguments, they were no more frequent or serious than what went on between most supposedly happily married husbands and wives.

In retrospect, there was one indication that they were not quite so blissful as Burton and Taylor—they were sleeping in separate bedrooms, each with the door locked.

As sexually naive as I was, I remember wondering how Father could stand to sleep so far away from such an attractive, sexy-looking young woman as my mother was. If she'd been my wife, I knew there'd be no such thing as separate rooms or even beds (Shades of Oedipus, but why should I be different and make a fool of Freud?).

Still, I was gullible enough to accept Father's explanation that the only reason he and Mother occupied separate bedrooms was because he had insomnia and needed the freedom to turn on the lights and read if he couldn't fall asleep.

At any rate, I *wanted* to believe they were happy, because I liked both of them; they were a "fun couple" to be around, when they weren't fighting; and I did not look forward to the prospect of ever having to decide which one of the two I preferred to have custody of me.

From time to time when I was growing up I'd been disturbed by vague but sinister feelings (as I'm sure my sister had, too) that someday

I might have to make that decision. Times, for example, when we'd be on a trip or at a resort without Father, because he was working, and I'd see Mother sitting at the bar and becoming awfully friendly, I thought, with some handsome, single guy with whom we'd all played tennis during the day, and who was now buying the drinks, or perhaps dancing with Mother to the piano music. But since Mother made no attempt to conceal these liaisons from Father when she came home, and Father, in turn, would simply kid her about her "boyfriends," I assumed these relationships were precisely what they appeared to be—resort friendships.

"We played tennis with a very nice dentist from San Francisco," Mother might say when the family was all together again. "He promised to show us around Chinatown the next time we go up there."

"Maybe he can take a look at my teeth at the same time," Father would kiddingly reply.

Or if her resort boyfriend happened to be a doctor (it seemed as if her admirers were either dentists or MDs), it would be a medical joke. "Maybe you can get him to take out your appendix wholesale," he'd rib her.

But Father never said anything to indicate he was bothered by these relationships. And since it didn't bother him, I tried not to let it bother me. I figured that was the way life was supposed to be lived by a sophisticated couple. Noel Coward had nothing on them. So I'd dismiss these feelings about divorce almost as quickly as they occurred to me.

But by my senior year in high school, the detente Mother and Father had managed to keep—apparently for Miriam's and my sake—was beginning to show the strain of two personalities (with totally different ideas of what they wanted out of life) pulling against each other in a sort of marital tug of war.

A turning point in the worsening of their relations was, paradoxically, another ocean voyage—this time to Hawaii.

Before leaving for Hawaii, Mother and Father had their usual argument over whether or not to take Miriam and me. In this instance, Father lost out, acquiescing to Mother's pleas that she be given a vacation free of all responsibilities—including children. So they sailed off on the *Lurline* without us.

They were barely speaking when they returned three weeks later.

According to Mother, Father had been in a miserable mood for the entire trip. He had been his usual lousy company on board ship, suffering from one attack of seasickness after another, even though the Pacific was glassy calm. Furthermore, and even though they were given the royal treatment by Duke Kahanomoko himself, Father hated everything about the Hawaiian Islands—the stench of gardenia leis that were always "being thrown around my neck"; luaus; fat women from Pasadena doing the hula; the native girls ("Their mouths are full of gold teeth!"); Hawaiian music; and even Waikiki Beach itself, which he claimed was too narrow and couldn't compare with the beach at Atlantic City.

Father admitted that Hawaii had been somewhat of a disappointment, but he confided to Miriam and me that he could have taken the whole phony milieu a little better if he'd had his children along to keep him company while Mother was getting loaded on Mai Tais and learning to do the hula.

"After all, it's basically a children's resort. What's there to do for a middle-aged Jew who wants to read *The New York Times*? I could do that in my comfortable house in Beverly Hills. At least you kids would have enjoyed the swimming. I could have kicked myself for not bringing you."

It sounded reasonable.

But years later he admitted the real reason why he and Mother weren't speaking when they returned.

On the return voyage, Mother had followed her usual shipboard pattern of wanting to "be gay" and dance until the ship's musicians played "Good Night Sweetheart" and started packing their saxophones and electric guitars back in their cases.

By the same token, Father followed his usual shipboard routine of announcing to Mother, every night around eleven, "Well, you stay up if you want—I'm going to bed." Following which he'd return to his cabin, leaving Mother in the company of whomever they happened to be spending the evening with.

One of the group with whom they'd made friends was a personable man around Mother's age who ran the Arthur Murray Dance Studio on the *Lurline*. He liked to dance with Mother because she wasn't the usual klutzy housefrau he usually had to push around the floor, and

she enjoyed being his partner because they performed so smoothly together that all the other dancers stopped and watched. Being in the
spotlight obviously stirred up Mother's memories of her days as a professional dancer in vaudeville, and at the same time rekindled dormant
desires of being on the stage again.

Instead of resenting him, Father was pleased that the Arthur Murray instructor kept Mother entertained on the dance floor. It meant he
could sit at the table and smoke his cigar.

The night before they were to dock, Father retired to his cabin at
his usual witching hour, leaving Mother and the instructor on the
dance floor. When Mother hadn't returned to their cabin by three A.M.
Father started to worry, threw on some clothes, and went up on deck
to look for her.

He found Mother with the instructor, out by the lifeboats, and he
was not teaching her dancing. They were locked in a tight embrace,
with their lips glued passionately together.

Father, refreshed from three straight hours of insomnia, gathered
his strength, socked the interloper on the jaw, and dragged Mother
back to their cabin.

Mother wasn't a promiscuous woman by nature, but she'd had
more than she should to drink, which undoubtedly had lowered her resistance and steamed up her libido.

Drinking was beginning to become a serious problem with
Mother, anyway, by then. And it was unquestionably compounded by
another problem not uncommon in beautiful women approaching
forty—she was afraid of growing old and losing her looks. And since
she realized that she was still enormously attractive to men, she was determined to make the most of her life while she still had her youthful
face and trim figure.

Father, on the other hand, was equally determined not to spend
what he called his "declining years" nightclubbing and consorting with
the kinds of people who frequented the night spots—café society
phonies, actors and actresses on the prowl for cheap publicity; big
drinkers; and Arthur Murray dance instructors.

At the age of fifty, Father was a good thirty years away from
being on the decline—either physically, mentally or professionally.
He'd always lived a life of extreme moderation: one drink before din-

ner, none after; two cigars a day plus a few puffs on a pipe. He watched his weight, and, as you've obviously gathered, he kept regular hours. He couldn't sleep, but he spent a good deal of his life supine.

Consequently, he was in excellent health, except for a mild case of low blood pressure, and a mysterious affliction that he referred to as "a grippy feeling." A grippy feeling was characterized by icy feet and a general lack of energy, which he felt was the precursor of the flu or a cold, neither of which ever actually came on. No doctor has ever been able to find the slightest shred of medical evidence to support his grippy-feeling complaint. But despite its psychosomatic overtones, it was enough to incapacitate Father and confine him to his room a couple of times a week—usually when he had something unpleasant facing him, like having to escort Mother to Ciro's or the Mocambo, or attending one of those large Hollywood parties (generally given in a cold, damp tent in some celebrity's back yard), where the beef stroganoff wouldn't be served before eleven, and he'd have to dance whether he liked it or not—if only to keep warm.

If Father had a desire to stay home that was more compelling than the average husband's, it was understandable.

After years of appearing in vaudeville and on Broadway, when he *had* to be out every night, what greater luxury could a man have than the opportunity, which making films afforded him, of spending his evenings with friends or family in the comfort of a beautiful home? Everything he needed to keep him content was right there—his books, his guitar, his Capehart phonograph, a large collection of classical recordings and even a professional-sized pool table.

Father was an expert pool player, thanks to his many years in vaudeville, when there'd be nothing better to do between shows than to hang out in the local billiard parlor. He wasn't as handy with a cue as Chico or Zeppo (who were close to being hustlers), but on a good night he could run the table a couple of times without missing.

Until I was a grown man he could spot me fifty points and still win. From the time I was twelve on, I spent most of my evenings trying to beat him, and rarely did.

When he wasn't entertaining his friends, Father liked to read or listen to classical music after he'd successfully fended off my nightly challenge at the pool table. In addition, he was turning into a Gilbert &

Sullivan buff, having been introduced to the operettas by his good friends Ira Gershwin and Newman Levy, the poet.

Father liked nothing better than to invite a few friends over for an entire evening of Gilbert & Sullivan. Everyone would have to sit around with the librettos on their laps, pay strict attention, and sing along with the D'Oyly Carte Opera Company.

Mother liked nothing worse. She hated having to pay strict attention to anything, because it reminded her of school. Besides, she liked the songs of Rodgers and Hart much better. "At least you can dance to them," she'd say.

When Father wasn't playing Gilbert & Sullivan, he was reading about them. He had enough biographies of the pair to fill an entire wall of our library. There were no intimate details of either of their lives with which he wasn't totally familiar, and he delighted in regaling both friends and relatives with his newly acquired Savoyard lore.

"Did you know," he might say to Mother at the dinner table, "that Gilbert hated Sullivan?"

"That's nothing," Mother would retort. "I hate the two of them."

"If you'd just give it a chance," Father would implore her, "you might learn to like them. Now why don't you sit down with me this evening, and we'll listen to *Trial by Jury* together?"

But Mother would either go out to a movie by herself (or with me), or over to a friend's for a game of gin or backgammon. If she were really desperate, she'd retire to her own bedroom, and read. But never—". . . no, no, nevah!"—would she spend an evening listening to Gilbert & Sullivan.

Things finally reached a stage where she was even rebelling about spending an entire evening with Father's friends, even without Gilbert & Sullivan. Father rarely traveled in the same circle with other actors, finding them boring, uninformed and often a little bit on the phony side. His friends were of the Hollywood intellectual establishment— writers mostly, because he admired the men who put the words down on paper, feeling that without them there could be no theater or movie business. Norman Krasna, Harry Kurnitz, Nunnally Johnson, Arthur Sheekman, Dore Schary, Bob Riskin, Moss Hart, George Kaufman and Sid Perelman (when the latter three were in town), and any other people who made a living punching a typewriter, were likely to be invited by Father to dinner.

Of course, everybody who came to our house wasn't a writer.

Bobby Sherwood, the guitarist, brought his niece, Judy Garland, when she was sixteen and not yet a star, to our house one evening for an informal musicale.

Andres Segovia, the great classical guitarist, was a frequent visitor when he was in town; so was George Gershwin.

Harpo introduced Father to Gershwin first, bringing him along to a party one evening. Father was dying to have Gershwin play for his guests, but feeling the composer would think he was being imposed upon if Father asked him, he refrained for a good part of the evening. Meanwhile, Gershwin fidgeted nervously in his chair, and occasionally scowled in the direction of the piano.

Finally Harpo came over to Father and whispered into his ear, "Listen, Grouch, if you don't ask George to play pretty soon, he'll go home."

"But I was afraid he'd be insulted if I asked."

"He'll be insulted if you *don't*," Harpo informed him.

Gershwin sat at the piano for five straight hours—until all the guests felt they were being brainwashed by his music.

As George Kaufman used to say, "An evening with Gershwin is certainly an evening with Gershwin."

Don't let me give you the impression that Mother *disliked* Father's friends. She admired them, and was fond of many of them. But they were cut out of the same bolt as Father. They'd rather sit around and crack jokes about the picture business, or discuss the horrible things that Hitler was doing to the Jews in Nazi Germany than go dancing at the Trocadero.

Mother was swiftly acquiring her own coterie of friends: people she'd probably met at the tennis club or Lake Tahoe—people who liked to drink and dance, and whose idea of fun coincided with hers.

Father, quite understandably, couldn't stand her friends, and would usually treat them cooly when she brought them around, if not outright insult them.

As a result, Mother and Father would usually argue about whom to invite to dinner. He'd want Morrie Ryskind; she'd want one of the instructors from the Arthur Murray Dance School in Beverly Hills, or perhaps the Murrays themselves.

Father and Mother had become friendly with Arthur and Kathryn Murray through Ed Sullivan, who had brought them to dinner one night. Later, the Murrays sent for one of their instructors, who came to the house and proceeded to give us all rhumba and tango lessons, free of charge.

Mother was hoping that if Father could master the art of ballroom dancing, he might not object so to taking her nightclubbing. But sensing what her scheme was, he retired from serious terpsichore after the first lesson, although he swore it was an arthritic hip that made him give up the rhumba.

Because it was a form of advertising their business to be seen on as many dance floors around town as possible, the Murrays often went nightclubbing after dinner. They'd invite Father and Mother to accompany them. Father liked the Murrays, except for this mania they had for dancing. But usually he would elect to stay home with Gilbert & Sullivan and me. And in this case, the Murrays would invite one of their instructors along to be Mother's date. This suited Mother fine, and in her eyes, made the Murrays the perfect dinner guests.

Occasionally Father would acquiesce and take Mother out on the town, on his own, but usually when Mother asked him, he'd have "that grippy feeling." She'd then accuse him of malingering, and they'd have another big fight—very often at the dinner table in front of Miriam and me—and she'd storm out of the house.

"I don't want to stay home here night after night and watch you read or listen to that damn phonograph," Mother would scream.

"Your trouble is you have nothing to do all day," he'd point out calmly. "You need something to tire you out when I'm working, so you'll be willing to stay home when I'm too tired to go out."

"I'd have something to do if you hadn't made me quit the act," she'd reply. "I could have been a great dancer—now it's too late."

This would generally evoke a peal of derisive laughter from Father, who would tell her that she was damn lucky she didn't have to support herself with the little talent she had.

Following a crack like that she'd generally call him a son of a bitch, and run out of the house again.

As the front door slammed, Father would shake his head sadly, and say to Miriam and me, "Your mother's a nice dame. Her trouble is she's bored. I've tried to get her to do charity work, or have another hobby. Anything to keep her from running over to that damn club seven days a week. But she won't listen to me."

She must have listened to him at least once, because I remember being called out of school one day, in the middle of a class, handed an address by the principal, and told to pick up my mother there.

The address turned out to be an abortion doctor's mill, in a run-down section of Los Angeles. But it wasn't until Mother—pale and troubled-looking, and clad only in bathrobe and slippers—got into the car, and we were on our way home, that she confessed what she had been doing in such a place.

I wasn't easily shocked, but somehow *that* shocked me. I guess because an abortion, in those days, wasn't something you just ran over to your friendly neighborhood doctor's and had done. It was a jail offense, and I couldn't see the reason why a respectable married woman, and a mother, would risk one.

"Like a damn fool I let your father talk me into getting pregnant," she explained. "But after I was two months gone, I knew I couldn't go through with it. I wasn't going to be stuck at home with a baby like a sweet little Ruthie, while your Father's listening to Gilbert and Sullivan every night. I want to live and be gay—while I'm still young enough to enjoy it."

It was one of those times when I realized that life with Groucho wasn't quite so much fun as a barrel of monkeys. Still, it wasn't Father's fault. He was doing his best to hold the family together. Frequently he took over the family responsibilities normally reserved for women, but which Mother refused to shoulder.

Like the time he went to the May Day Festival sponsored by the Hawthorne Grammar School PTA.

Miriam was dancing in the festival, and very much wanted Mother to come to Hawthorne to watch her and her classmates perform. And in fact she exacted a promise from Mother that she would attend. But as much as Mother loved her children, she could not bear to waste an afternoon on anything so typically average-American as the Girl Scouts or the PTA when she could be at the tennis club having fun, and at the last minute she found an excuse not to attend the May Day Festival as well.

Being a very sensitive thirteen, Miriam burst into tears, so Father gave up a business appointment to go in Mother's place.

Mrs. Pogson, the Principal, was delighted to see someone as famous as Father standing among the assorted Helen Hokinson types in attendance. At one point in the entertainment she invited Father to step to the mike and say a few words.

Obliging, Father surveyed the young ladies gamboling around the May Pole, and said, "It's hard to believe that in ten years most of you girls will be collecting alimony." The few laughs that line got were muffled and embarrassed. But to Mrs. Pogson's way of thinking, Father had done no less than poison the innocent. With as much dignity as she could summon up beneath her rage, she insisted that Miriam escort Father home.

Miriam, of course, was humiliated and angry. She refused to speak to Father until her allowance was due.

I'm pretty sure that, secretly, Father enjoyed playing the role of both parents, because that gave him the freedom to run the household the way *he* wanted, without female interference.

At the same time it angered him that Mother took so little interest in the house and family that she frequently remained at the tennis club, drinking and dancing, until seven P.M.—our usual dinner hour.

What started out to be a sociable cocktail after tennis would frequently wind up being two, three and possibly even four. After a few drinks, Mother completely lost her sense of time. Very often she wouldn't arrive home until seven-fifteen or seven-thirty. When this became a habit with her, Father would tell the maid to start serving dinner without Mother, to teach her a lesson.

Drinking would always make Mother extremely argumentative and vituperative with Father, when she finally did arrive home. "What's the matter?" she would ask. "You couldn't wait five minutes for me? God knows, I've held dinner up plenty of times for you when *you* weren't home from the studio."

"I happened to be working. I wasn't at the tennis club, boozing with a bunch of out of work actors."

"Are you implying that there's anything—?"

"I'm not implying anything. I'm only saying it wouldn't hurt you to get home a few minutes early after you've been over there all day."

"What am I supposed to do here—sit and twiddle my thumbs while you're taking a nap?"

"You could drop into the kitchen and see if everything's all right with dinner, or maybe take an interest in Miriam's homework."

"Why should I? You won't let me run the house the way I want to, anyway."

"Oh, for Christ's sake. You're too drunk to make any sense."

Not wanting to face the truth, Mother would heap more verbal abuse on Father, and the battle would rage on.

It would usually culminate with Mother jumping up and leaving the table, or else the four of us would have to sit and finish our dinner in hostile silence.

"I don't know how much more of this I can take," Father would complain to Miriam and me when we were finally alone with him. "I could be a lot happier with nobody. The only reason I'm not doing anything about it is because of you kids."

We really felt sorry for him. Mother was being impossible.

After a major battle, Mother might get hold of herself for a few days, not drink quite so much at the club, and even pretend to take an interest in the house by arriving home prior to the dinner hour, as Father had suggested.

But her reformation would be short-lived, and things would soon revert to their former wretched state—only with a little more bitterness added, and a lot more booze.

The incident that made us all realize that Mother had finally developed into a true alcoholic occurred one Saturday night, when she and Father were having a few close friends in to dinner.

Father, being the instigator of most of their social activities, had issued his usual combination invitation and warning: "If you want to drink, get here by seven. But we're eating at seven-thirty, regardless."

Knowing Father, the guests were extremely punctual. But Mother still hadn't arrived home by eight o'clock. At Father's behest, I called her at the club to remind her of the time. She sounded a little giggly as she said she didn't realize it was so late, and promised to leave immediately.

Ten minutes later I heard Mother's car roar up to the front of the house, and the screech of tires as she attempted to turn into our driveway without slowing down. I glanced out the window just as her car missed the entrance of our driveway and slammed into a palm tree.

The car was completely demolished. But Mother—more smashed from alcohol than the actual collision—merely broke a leg and sustained a few black and blue marks on her face.

While the doctor, who rushed right over, was setting Mother's leg in her bedroom, Father turned to me grimly and said, "Well, there's one good thing about this evening—at least your mother won't want to go dancing."

Following Mother's recovery and eventual return to her life of total irresponsibility at the tennis club, no day passed without a major argument between her and Father—arguments of such grave proportions that they must portend divorce.

Although we weren't looking forward to such an eventuality, Miriam and I were beginning to *wish* Mother and Father would get divorced, if this was the best they could do. For selfish reasons alone, it was becoming just too damn uncomfortable to have to live in the same house with them, especially when one or the other would expect us to take sides in their arguments.

More and more, I'd take Father's side, for he was generally right in criticizing her behavior. And as the situation worsened, I even urged him to get a divorce and have some peace of mind, and to forget about staying together for the sake of his children.

But Father was a family man in that respect. He hated the thought of breaking up the family unit, with the custody battles that were sure to ensue. He preferred to ride out the storm, feeling that perhaps this was just a phase Mother was going through as she approached the change of life.

CHAPTER 19

IF YOU'RE
GOING TO HAVE
A HEART ATTACK,
HAVE ONE

A DRINKING wife, and a son who got D's in Geometry weren't Father's only worries in those days.

He was also having career problems.

Irving Thalberg, the only producer he had ever truly respected in the picture business, had died suddenly in 1937, at the age of thirty-seven, during the making of *A Day at the Races,* leaving the Marx Brothers under the aegis of Louis B. Mayer, who hated them.

Like most men with dictator complexes, Mayer had very little sense of humor. Moreover, he'd never been a Marx Brothers fan. MGM had signed them solely at Thalberg's instigation. With Thalberg gone they had nobody in their corner.

As long as their films made money for the studio, Mayer was willing to stomach their brand of slapstick comedy, which didn't particularly amuse him. What he wasn't willing to tolerate was their lack of respect for him, which manifested itself in a variety of ways when they were working on the lot.

While Thalberg was still alive, Father bumped into Louis B. Mayer on the MGM lot one day when he was shooting *A Night at the Opera*.

"How's the picture going, Groucho?" asked Mayer cheerfully.

"What business is it of yours?" snapped Father in jest.

Unfortunately, Mayer was not in the mood for jest, and he hated the Marx family from that moment until the day he died.

But that wasn't the only incident when the Marx Brothers showed their disrespect for the head of the studio and one of the most powerful men in the industry.

One day, Mayer was scheduled to have a lunch conference in his private dining room with Will Hays, the movie industry's censor. The purpose of the meeting was to assure Hays that it had been entirely accidental that Lana Turner showed too much cleavage in her last picture, and that he, Mayer, was running a clean and moral studio.

Hearing about the meeting, the pixyish Harpo hired a stripper from a Culver City nightclub to strip down to just a G-string and pasties, and then chased her through Mayer's private dining room and across the luncheon table, while Mayer and Hays were having lunch.

On another occasion, the Marx Brothers started a bonfire in Mayer's outer office because they were tired of waiting for a conference with him that had been called for three hours earlier. They had once pulled this stunt on Thalberg, who had gotten the message and never kept them waiting again. But Mayer wasn't amused.

Mayer also wasn't amused at the way Father stood up to him when they didn't agree on how to make a Marx Brothers film.

One issue on which they were continually at odds was the try-out tours.

Father believed the tours had more than proven their value with the successes of *A Night at the Opera* and *A Day at the Races*. But Mayer felt that breaking in the comedy scenes on the road was a complete waste of money and an unnecessary delay in getting the pictures made. "Those two pictures would have been hits without road tours," stated Mayer flatly.

"Thalberg would disagree with you," countered Father.

"Who cares what Thalberg thinks?" asked Mayer. "Thalberg's dead."

Why Mayer bothered to re-sign the Marx Brothers after their original two-picture deal with MGM was up, Father never has been able to figure out. Mayer did everything he could to make sure their next three pictures would be high points of mediocrity—from fighting the road tours to refusing to hire the best writers and directors available.

For two of their next three pictures, *A Day at the Circus* and *Go West*, Mayer finally gave in on the road tours, but only if the Marx Brothers would personally foot half the production costs. To illustrate how strongly Father felt about the value of trying out their comedy in front of live audiences, he consented to the extra expenditure, even though he felt Mayer was treating them unfairly.

Since *Circus* and *Go West* turned out to be neither top-notch Marx Brothers fare nor resounding box office successes, Mayer had a built-in excuse not to approve their requests to road tour their final picture for MGM—*The Big Store*. Moreover, he insisted that *The Big Store* be made on what amounted to a "B"-picture budget.

This convinced Father that Mayer was deliberately out to destroy the Marx Brothers' careers, by putting them in a picture that would bomb at the box office, so that no other studio would want to touch them when their contract with Metro was up.

"Mayer was cutting off his nose to spite his face," recalls Father. "Now that I think of his nose, that's a bad simile. His face would have been better off without it."

Faced with Mayer's unrelenting attitude, Father made up his mind that the picture would be lousy, but that he wouldn't worry about it. The Marx Brothers were on a straight salary; they would get their money whether *The Big Store* was a hit or a flop. Only the studio stood to lose.

With this decision came another idea—to disband the Marx Brothers as a comedy team, to take the money and run, when their contract with Metro was up. This notion had been festering in Father's mind for the past several years—for a number of reasons.

To begin with, he was getting tired of making Marx Brothers pictures—tired physically and emotionally. According to Father, who used to bring home his complaints to the dinner table every night when he was shooting, there was no harder physical work than being a roughhouse comedian.

In the case of the Marx Brothers, he felt he was carrying most of the burden. He did considerable work on the scripts in their preparation stages, despite the large battery of writers and gag men. He had the most dialogue to learn, all of which was filled with tricky non-sequiturs. And during the actual filming he was usually getting doused with water or splashed with paint, or being chased by the heavies.

All of this added up to a good deal of physical hardship.

"I remember once," recollects Father, "I was hanging by my knees from a ladder that was attached to a plane that was in the desert about to take off. As I hung by my knees in the hot sun, while the director was trying to make up his mind what lens to use, I remember thinking, 'What kind of a business is this for a fifty-year-old man to be in? I have enough money to live on if I never work again. Why in hell do I need this?' "

Emotionally, it no longer was a challenge to Father to continue playing the same role in picture after picture. The backgrounds of the various films might be different—circus, horse racing, opera—but the story elements and his character were essentially the same.

Conversely, Father suspected that audiences might be tiring of the Marx Brothers after three Broadway shows and eleven pictures. If not of the Marx Brothers, of the kind of comedy they were doing, which he was beginning to believe was old-fashioned.

To be truthful, Father didn't think much of Chico and Harpo as comedians, anyway. His evaluation of Chico was that he was a fair dialectician and a lousy pianist, and he felt that Harpo was a great pantomimist and very accomplished at the art of making funny faces—if one cared for that type of comedy, which he didn't.

Father didn't want to retire. He was simply itching to strike out on his own. He believed he was a good actor and wanted to try straight comedy roles—roles in which he could play believable characters—not

Doctor Hugo Z. Hackenbush, in a phony painted mustache and hokey red tie and frock coat.

He'd tried his hand at a straight role when he played the lead in *Twentieth Century* in stock one summer, and had been a resounding success—which confirmed his belief that it was easier to get laughs in a business suit than in a funny costume.

"When you come out in funny clothes," Father used to explain to me, "right away you're announcing to your audience, 'I'm going to be funny, so get ready to laugh.' Automatically they set up a resistance, which makes it harder to make them laugh. But when you wear an ordinary business suit, you can be half as funny and get bigger laughs, because it's a surprise to them that you're going to be funny."

He's always believed that Jack Benny was the prime example of underplaying. No costume. No make-up. "He just comes out and talks, and kills the people. Of course, he's built a great character. That's another thing. I had no character as a Marx Brother—I wasn't real. I just talked fast, and the jokes better be good."

Secondly, Father was nurturing another idea—of going into radio. All his contemporaries—Eddie Cantor, Ed Wynn, Fred Allen, and Jack Benny—were making it big in the new medium, which he felt was a much easier way of earning a living. The pay was good. You didn't have to put on make-up or wear a costume. And you didn't have to memorize dialogue. Someone else wrote it, and you simply read it off a page.

By the time the bloom was off his romance with the picture business, Father had already made a couple of stabs at a radio career. In 1939 he'd been a regular on a coast-to-coast variety show called *The Circle*, which was sponsored by Kellogg's Cornflakes, and which featured a very distinguished cast headed by Cary Grant, Ronald Coleman and Carole Lombard. And a few years earlier, he and Chico had played a team of shyster lawyers—*Flywheel, Shyster & Flywheel*—for thirteen weeks on NBC.

Neither of those shows had been successful, but Father was anxious to try again, for he was convinced that radio was the medium of the future.

A final reason Father was considering breaking up the Marx Brothers team was brother Chico.

Father loved Chico like a brother, but if it hadn't been for the sibling tie, he wouldn't have put up with him as a partner for a minute.

Chico had been a thorn in Father's side from the beginning of their professional relationship. Even *before* they were working together, when they were teenagers living in Frenchie's and Minnie's brownstone back on 92nd Street, Chico's irresponsible behavior had caused Father considerable grief.

Father still hasn't forgiven him for a bit of petty larceny he perpetrated one Easter week way back near the turn of the century.

In those days, Father, known to the neighborhood as Julie, was working as a delivery boy for Frenchie's tailor shop. On the Friday before Easter Sunday, Frenchie handed Father a box containing a suit he had just made for Herman Stuckfish, who ran the local candy store, and told him to deliver it promptly, as it was very important to Stuckfish to have it for Easter Sunday.

Obedient, serious-minded son that he was, Julie galloped the two blocks to Stuckfish's Confectionery, and personally placed the box in the proprietor's grateful hands.

Delighted with the efficiency of Frenchie's delivery service, Stuckfish sat Father down at the counter and rewarded him with a chocolate soda, with two scoops of ice cream. While Father was finishing off the soda, Stuckfish ducked behind a screen to try on the suit. To his dismay, he discovered that the trousers were missing. Angrily he appeared from behind the screen in his undershorts, yanked the unfinished soda away from the startled Julius, and chased him out of the shop without paying for the suit.

When Father reported home with the sad facts, Frenchie held him responsible for losing the trousers, whipped off his belt, and gave him a sound thrashing. The money for the suit was to have been used to pay the rent.

The day after Easter, Stuckfish's trousers turned up in the window of the neighborhood pawn shop. Investigation revealed that Chico had hocked the trousers to pay off a gambling debt. Chico was only sixteen, but that incident turned out to be the pattern of his life.

Temperamentally, Chico and Father had about as much in common as Dean Martin and Marcel Proust.

Father was a worrier; Chico was happy-go-lucky. Chico was a

MOTHER, FATHER, AND MY UNCLE HARPO
ON PARAMOUNT LOT IN 1932, WITH
MIRIAM, ME, AND THE CHIMP, WHO HAS
REQUESTED THAT HIS NAME BE KEPT

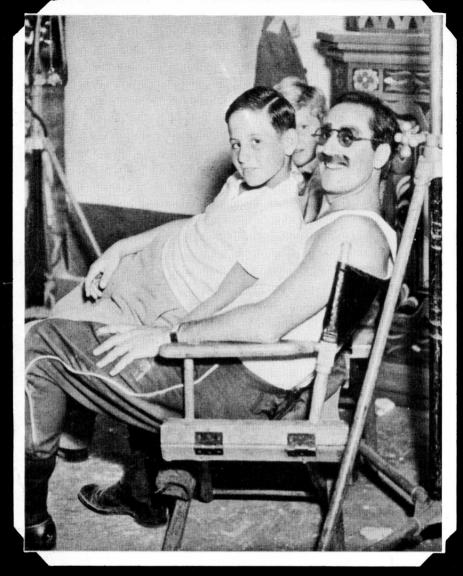

A DOTING FATHER, ON SET OF <u>DUCK SOUP</u>
IN 1932, WITH ME ON HIS LAP.

GROUCHO, RUTH, AND MIRIAM, ON LOT
OF PARAMOUNT STUDIOS, HOLLYWOOD 1933

1939 JUNIOR DAVIS CUP TEAM. FROM LEFT TO RIGHT: SON OF GROUCHO, DAVE FREEMAN, DOUG WOODBURY, JACK KRAMER, THE DAVIS CUP, WELBY VAN HORN, TED OLEWINE, BOB CARROTHERS, TED SCHROEDER, AND BUDGE PATTY. WE ALL HELD NATIONAL TITLES OF ONE KIND OR ANOTHER.

ME AND MY FATHER, STANDING IN FRONT
OF THE PAINTING OF THE MARX BROTHERS.

PHOTO BY SAM PERKINS

FATHER, LOIS, AND OUR BABY POODLE,
ELSIE, THE LATEST ADDITION TO THE
ARTHUR MARX FAMILY.

FATHER WITH CAPTIVE AUDIENCE
PRACTICING FOR HIS ONE-MAN SHOW AT
CARNEGIE HALL, IN LIVING ROOM OF HIS
TROUSDALE HOME IN SPING OF 1972.

PHOTO BY SAM PERKINS

WHO SAYS HE ISN'T AS FUNNY AT
HOME AS HE IS ON THE STAGE?

PHOTO BY SAM PERKINS

gambler; Father handled his money with extreme care, always putting something away for the proverbial rainy day. Chico was a girl chaser; Father was basically a family man. And lastly, and most important, Father took his work seriously, while Chico treated his acting career as an avocation—something to do when he wasn't gambling or in bed with a girl.

Since Harpo was a dreamer, with no business sense, and Zeppo was many years their junior, and not a full partner, early in their ca-careers Father had taken it on himself to shoulder the responsibility of running the team. *He* was the one who showed up at the theater early to rehearse the orchestra and the actors. *He* was the one who dreamed up new material when the old needed replacing. And *he* was the one who made the financial arrangements and argued with the management when things weren't to their liking.

None of which Father would have minded if Chico had just behaved in a professional way.

According to Father, Chico was rarely around when you needed him for a story conference or to rehearse. Sometimes, in their vaudeville and legitimate theater days, he wasn't even around when the curtain went up. They'd have to put on an entire performance without him—because he was either hiding from my irate father, or else he was trapped in a card game with some of the local hoods, who wouldn't let him go until he paid them the money he'd lost.

Chico didn't only mingle with small-time hoods.

When the late Bugsy Siegel was shot and killed in his Beverly Hills home, the investigating police found one of Chico's checks in the gangster's wallet.

"It was a lucky thing for Chico that Siegel never lived to try to cash that check," declared Father, "because if I know Chico, it certainly would have bounced."

Chico, along with Zeppo and Harpo, had great card sense, and was, according to the experts, an exceptionally fine bridge player. So was Harpo. Teamed together in bridge, Harpo and Chico were a formidable combination—on a par with the Culbertsons or any of the great players of today.

Chico, however, refused to stick to bridge, the game he could play best, the one with the least element of chance attached to it. He preferred to try to beat the ponies, or the crap and roulette tables in the professional gambling joints.

In addition, he had an enormous soft streak—never a great asset for a man trying to make a killing at gambling. In bridge, he'd frequently feel sorry for opponents he was beating, and start to grandstand and play carelessly for the amusement of the kibbitzers. Inevitably, he'd wind up being the one who needed sympathy.

But whichever way he chose to lose his money, Chico's addiction to gambling was a constant source of irritation to Father. If he wasn't on the phone with a bookie, when he was supposed to be on the set, he'd be studying the racing form instead of the script. He was the type actor who learned his lines through trial and error. To Father, who had his dialogue down letter perfect and who could generally do a scene in one take, it was sheer torture to have to go through a scene a dozen times or more while Chico tried to learn his part through trial and error.

Even when they were in separate towns Chico found ways to bug Father. A memorable example of Chico's talent for this occurred shortly after the team broke up, back in the pre-Pearl Harbor days.

Chico was in Las Vegas, fronting a band at the Last Frontier. His show was doing good business, too, which made Father and Harpo extremely happy, for it meant Chico could earn a living without them, leaving them free to follow their own pursuits.

A few days after Chico's smash opening, Father and Harpo were shocked to read in *The Los Angeles Times*, one morning:

CHICO MARX SUFFERS HEART
ATTACK AT LAS VEGAS NITERY

Father and Harpo hopped a plane and rushed to Chico's bedside—only to hear him confess, in the privacy of his hospital room, "I didn't really have a heart attack. But I have to get out of this contract somehow. I'm losing more money at the tables than I'm making with the band."

"You're a great brother," Father told him. "You give us a heart attack worrying about your heart attack, which you didn't even have the decency to have!"

Father worried as much about Chico's finances as Chico didn't. He was constantly predicting that Chico would wind up penniless in his old age, and that he and Harpo (who saved his money, too) would wind up having to support him. This is eventually what happened.

In the meantime, however, Father and Harpo did everything humanly possible to convince Chico that it would be wise to get a little nest egg together for his old age. When words proved in vain, Father and Harpo devised a scheme with some teeth in it.

Before agreeing to sign for their last three pictures at MGM, they issued an ultimatum to their errant but lovable brother. Either he would sign an additional agreement giving them the right to handle his money for him—putting some away for taxes, and the rest in a savings account, which he couldn't touch—or they wouldn't sign the new contract with MGM. They would retire, instead.

Chico knew this wasn't an idle threat, for he was well aware that both his brothers had more than enough money on which to retire comfortably, and that they weren't that crazy about working. As a result, he reluctantly agreed to turn over his salary to them every week.

By 1940, when the Marx Brothers were on the final year of their MGM contract, Father and Harpo had managed to bank a sizable amount of cash in Chico's trust account—almost three hundred thousand dollars. On the interest income from it alone, Chico could have lived comfortably for the remainder of his life—if he stayed away from the gaming tables, that is.

But Chico found a way of outwitting them.

While they were saving his money, Chico was gambling and running up huge debts—debts that could not be paid back with the small portion of his salary he was allowed for his personal use.

Chico actually feared for his life if he didn't pay off certain mobsters he owed, and he pleaded with Father and Harpo to release his money.

They tried to be hard-hearted about this, but when Chico retained a lawyer and threatened to sue them unless they turned his money over to him, they threw up their hands in disgust, and told him to take his money and go ahead and die broke.

In a matter of weeks, the money was gone, and with it Father's desire to help his brother. Also any motivation he might have had for continuing as a team.

During the Marx Brothers' waning years as a team, Salwyn Shufro, one of Father's chief financial advisors, asked Chico if he could hazard even a rough guess as to the amount of money he had lost during his lifetime.

"I can tell you to the penny," replied Chico.

"You can?"

"Sure thing." As Shufro looked impressed, Chico asked, "How much money does Groucho have in the bank?"

"Approximately seven hundred and fifty thousand dollars," answered Shufro.

Chico smiled impishly, and said, "That's how much money I've lost gambling!"

CHAPTER 20

A FUNNY
THING HAPPENED
ON THE WAY
TO FOREST HILLS

THE three summers I spent on the tennis circuit between my graduation from Beverly High and the outbreak of World War II may not have resulted in any major tennis championships coming to the Marx family, but at least they gave my life a direction that it wouldn't have had if I'd spent those same summers lying around on a beach, growing hair and smoking pot.

At the risk of being chauvinistic about a sport that's continued to give me a great deal of pleasure and healthful exercise even after I quit playing seriously, I'd like to say there's no better preparation for adulthood than competing in tennis tournaments as a teen-ager. Not only does it keep you in shape, but tennis teaches you to think as an individual as does no other sport (with the exception of golf).

In tennis, unlike team sports, there's nobody to tell you what to do once you step out on the court. You're completely on your own, to devise your own strategy, whether it be stalling, lobbing, rushing the net or cheating. If you find yourself tiring, you can't signal the coach to send in a substitute. And if you lose, there's nobody to blame but yourself, except in doubles, when it's *always* your damn partner's fault.

Tournament play during your formative years also teaches you not to trust many people. Even your own roommate or doubles partner—if the draw happens to pit the two of you against each other—will give you a bad call or do something else equally dishonest to disconcert you if he decides that the outcome of the match hinges on it.

Bobby Riggs, if he found his opponent in a hot streak, would suddenly stop play to tie his shoe, or to take his shoe entirely off and look for a rock that had supposedly gotten inside. By the time he found it and put his shoe back on, his opponent would have cooled off again.

Kramer would walk agonizingly slow between points, to make his opponent nervous. Joe Hunt would intimidate a linesman whose calls he didn't like by purposely mishitting his cannonball serve and nearly maiming him.

Schroeder would keel over with a cramp in his leg, or play with some other mythical infirmity to make his opponent feel sorry for him and let down. Schroeder played the entire summer of 1939 with his stomach taped up, because he had allegedly torn his stomach muscle. He never played or served better. He ended up winning the National Juniors, even though the word was out that he couldn't reach above his head to serve or hit an overhead.

I never felt better, but I lost to Schroeder in the finals of seven straight singles events on our way east to compete in the National Juniors that summer. The shelves of Father's playroom were suddenly so littered with runner-up trophies I'd shipped home that he could hardly find his Gilbert & Sullivan records. I began to rue the day I'd appealed to God to let me reach the finals of just one tournament, and I'd be happy. A couple of times, okay, but seven tournaments in a row—and to a cripple yet—was overdoing it.

With Schroeder as my partner, I won the same number of doubles tournaments, and going into the Nationals, we were seeded second behind Kramer and Olewine.

Schroeder surprised everybody (including the doctor who taped him up) by beating Kramer and walking away with the singles title, and he surprised me by playing like a complete tyro in our semi-finals doubles match, which we lost. (I, of course, was my usual brilliant self.)

Normally Schroeder was a tenacious fighter but after upsetting Kramer that same morning, he played our doubles match as if he were high. He didn't seem to care whether we won or lost the doubles. (Another one of life's valuable little lessons I learned on the tennis circuit: "Never trust a partner, if he has anything else going for him.")

I lost in the quarter-finals, and wound up being ranked fifth in the United States that year. Not spectacular, but no disgrace, either—for it meant that in the eyes of the U.S.L.T.A. there were only four Juniors better than I in the U.S. and two were Kramer and Schroeder, and both of them became Davis Cup stars and Wimbledon champions.

I spent the winter at USC, pretending to be a scholar and waiting for the 1940 tournament season to begin. I'd spend the hours when I wasn't studying working on my game, and according to my coaches, Ellsworth Vines and Milton Holmes, I was capable of "getting hot" at any time and taking one—if not all—of the big grass-court Eastern events the coming summer.

Just getting an invitation to Seabright, Southampton and Newport was difficult—Seabright especially, for its draw was limited to thirty-two entries. This meant that the tournament committee had to consider you among the top thirty-two in the world before they'd send you an invitation.

It also helped if you were white and Gentile, for it was no secret that the Seabright Lawn Tennis and Cricket Club operated under the same liberal set of standards as that other bastion of democratic ideals—the New York Athletic Club.

Of course, my father was a movie star, which probably took a little of the curse off me. But since he was a Jewish movie star, it was unlikely that that could help much.

All the invitations were agonizingly slow in arriving, but the one to Seabright still hadn't arrived by the time I left for the East.

However, I was still young and stupid enough to be an optimist, and consequently believed that if I played well in the tournaments leading up to Seabright, they'd have to send me an invitation.

It was this notion, perhaps, that inspired me to do so well at the Tri-State in Cincinnati, and the collegiates at Montclair.

At the Tri-State, I upset the second seeded player, Johnny Doeg, a former National Men's champion, and reached the finals. I lost in the finals to Bobby Riggs, the current National champion and holder of the Wimbledon title, but it took him five sets to subdue me.

At Montclair the following week I won the National Freshman Intercollegiate title—a victory which merited its own headline and story on the front page of *The New York Times*'s sports section. *The Times*, with typical restraint, didn't mention that I was the son of Groucho until the second line of the lead.

Since both were important tournaments, I have to conclude that my play in them finally influenced the tournament committee at Seabright to send me an invitation.

Whatever the vagaries of the invitation committee, the prized document finally arrived two days before the event, when I was in Baltimore.

Ted Schroeder, who was my roommate that summer, and I bummed a ride to Seabright with Jack Kramer in the latter's car. But because Kramer had been in the doubles finals, we got off to a late start from Baltimore and didn't arrive at Seabright until four o'clock on the morning of the tournament. We were exhausted.

There was one first-class hotel in town, the Sea Girt, an imposing-looking Victorian edifice of the type built along the Eastern seaboard at the turn of the century—all wood and gingerbread and painted white.

It was much too expensive for our pocketbooks. Neither of us was getting any expense money from the tournament, and Father was only giving me twenty-five dollars a week for room and meals. But since all the cheaper places in town had their NO VACANCY signs posted by the time we arrived, we had no choice but to check into the Sea Girt. We might go broke, but we had to get a couple hours of sleep before our matches. But I needed more than a couple of hours sleep, and I was still a little groggy when we checked into the Lawn Tennis and Cricket Club around ten o'clock.

As always, I was happy to find a letter from Father waiting for me at the Tournament Manager's desk. Not only was news from home most welcome, but the envelope contained my weekly expense check.

The letter was important in another way, too, for it gave me my first preview of just how much it meant to Father to have another celebrity—if only a minor one—in the family.

A portion of that letter follows:

> I noticed that you disappeared rather abruptly from the Baltimore Tournament and it must have been the day you played Elwood Cooke. There was no mention of it in the local papers. I've come to the conclusion that it's not so hot being the father of a tennis player. Hundreds of people, to whom I wouldn't talk normally, rush up to me and immediately begin a long, involved tennis conversation, explaining why you either won or lost in the last tournament. As you know, I'm deeply interested in your athletic progress, but not to the extent that I want to discuss it twelve hours a day. Now I have a new answer whenever anyone rushes up and asks me how you're doing in whatever tournament it happens to be. I say, "Don't you know? He's quit the game and taken up squash." This baffles them. A lot of people have only heard of squash in a cafeteria and they can't understand why anyone should want to stand in a restaurant and throw vegetables.

My first-round opponent was Gilbert Hunt, the fifth-ranking player in the United States. What bothered me more, I suddenly felt ill when I was warming up with him. I was faint and dizzy, and my tennis shoes seemed filled with lead weights as I ran around the court. I attributed this to the fact that I was just over-tired, and as the match began, I tried to convince myself that sleep—or the lack of it—was just a psychological handicap. (After all, didn't Thomas Edison invent the electric light bulb on only four hours sleep a night?)

But all this rationalizing didn't help. I could only put up token resistance, and I quickly went down to defeat.

I fell into bed right after lunch, and slept until eight the following morning.

When I awoke I felt weaker than I had the previous day. Not only that, but as I glanced into the mirror when I was brushing my teeth, I noticed strange lumps around my jowls (as if I were storing walnuts in them), and there was a disturbing aching sensation beneath my jaw bone that made it difficult to swallow my orange juice at breakfast.

Immediately after breakfast I returned to bed, and Schroeder sent for the house doctor, who took one look at me and asked if I'd ever had the mumps.

I shook my head negatively.

"Well, you have them now," he said cheerfully, his simple declaration putting an abrupt end to that season.

Having covered myself with glory at Seabright, I returned home to find, among some assorted junk mail on my desk, an envelope from the USC Science Department containing a flunking notice in Botany 1. This, on top of my other scholastic achievements, pretty much convinced me that I was wasting my time at college, when I could apply that same brilliance to earning a living.

A person didn't necessarily need a college degree to become a great writer. There was plenty of evidence to support that rationalization. Shakespeare. Hemingway. Eugene O'Neill. Groucho Marx. So I talked Father into letting me drop out of USC.

Father didn't fight my decision to quit too vigorously—so long as I kept my word and put in the same amount of hours a day at the typewriter as I would have attending classes at USC.

Besides, I think he secretly enjoyed having another grown-up—or quasi grown-up—around the house to talk to, since he wasn't on speaking terms with Mother very much of the time, any more.

He also liked having me available for bicycle riding—his most recent method of keeping physically fit.

Every day, shortly before noon, Father, attired in Bermuda shorts, sweat shirt and a blue beret, would stride into my bedroom where I'd been scribbling away since early morning, and say, "Okay, Hemingway—time to take a break."

With Duke, our German Shepherd, trotting along beside us, we'd pedal through the residential section of Beverly Hills, usually winding up at Harpo's house, about a mile away.

Harpo would generally be in his music room, practicing when

we'd drop in. But, gracious host that he was, he'd never be too busy to stop whatever he was doing to sit on the sofa with Father and discuss their mutual business problems and engage in their favorite pastime—knocking Chico.

After lunch, Father would sit me down in his upstairs study and go over everything I'd written that morning. Father was a tough editor to please, and he wielded the blue pencil with the remorselessness of a network censor.

Being a voracious but discriminating reader, his literary tastes ran high and might even be termed somewhat snobbish. If you weren't a Kaufman, a Benchley, a Steinbeck or some other literary giant, it was difficult enough to impress him. If you were a college drop-out, he could be downright insulting.

His appraisal of my literary efforts would either be the familiar "Amateur night," or "That's not a bad idea—but your English is awkward and you're using too many big words."

Even though Father hadn't gone past the sixth grade himself, I learned a lot from him in these sessions.

Father had been my writing mentor all through my grammar school and high school days. No matter how busy he was with his own work or personal problems, he always found the time to help me polish an essay I was preparing for English class, or a story I might be writing for my high school newspaper.

Frequently he'd be a bigger contributor than I, throwing in bits of inimitable Groucho Marxian humor that a magazine would have paid hundreds of dollars to be able to publish.

He wrote my Hawthorne Grammar School graduation speech, almost verbatim. I had no idea how filled with humor it was until I delivered the speech to an auditoriumful of beaming parents on Graduation Day.

To my astonishment, and bewilderment, I found my speech was getting more laughs than a Bob Hope monologue.

Another time, Father brushed me away from the typewriter and took over the entire writing of an essay on "Americanism" I was supposed to turn into my English class the following day. I didn't mind. I'd been struggling with it long enough, and I was tired from playing tennis all afternoon. But then the whole thing snowballed. My essay (or should I say Father's?) not only got an A, and a special commendation from the principal, but my English teacher thought it was good enough to submit to an essay contest that the American Legion was sponsoring throughout the high schools of America.

It won second prize in the national competition, and a silver medal.

I was so ashamed of myself for allowing this deception to reach such unmanageable proportions that I played sick the day I was supposed to show up on the stage of the Fox Wilshire Theater to have my prize pinned on me by the Commander of the local American Legion Post.

I should have sent Father to accept it for me, but he probably would have insulted the whole American Legion. Which, now that I think about it, might not have been a bad idea.

At any rate, Father could be a tremendous help. His only problem as a teacher was that his own personality was too strong. He wanted to convert everything I wrote into his own style. Which was good, but not me. It took me a few years to realize this, however.

Meanwhile, I kept writing, he kept re-writing me, and together we managed to get rejection slips from every important magazine in the country.

Besides quitting college, there had been another change in my life style since I'd returned from the tennis wars. I had given up my Spartan existence, and had started smoking a pipe and going out with girls.

Smoking a pipe, at least in moderation, wasn't as harmful to a tennis player as you might imagine. Bill Tilden smoked over a pack of cigarettes a day most of his life, and he did all right. Jack Kramer liked to puff on a cigar occasionally. And Ted Schroeder, when he was my roommate, was always sucking on a foul-smelling corn cob in the evenings, which was one of the reasons I eventually gave him up as a roommate.

I didn't, however, take up smoking in self-defense. In my sophomorish way of thinking I somehow believed it would add to my image of being a writer. I needed something to create this image, since I wasn't doing it yet through my writing.

I wasn't sure how Father would react to my smoking, especially since I was using one of his imported English briars and his Dunhill tobacco. But on the afternoon he caught me smoking, he presented me with one of his best pipes, a can of Dunhill for my very own, and these words of advice:

"As long as you do it in moderation, it'll never hurt you," he said. "I've been smoking all my life, and look at the shape I'm in. I can hardly climb the stairs without getting out of breath."

"Moderation" has been one of the key rules of Father's life, and considering the age he's reached and the amount of good health he's enjoyed, there seems to be no arguing with the formula.

Although people believe Father's a heavy smoker, there's rarely a day when he smokes more than two cigars, or fills his pipe more than a couple of times.

When he drinks it's one cocktail before dinner, and perhaps a glass of wine or beer with his meal. He never over-eats. And as for girls, he always has one on his arm in public, but she's rarely still with him at bedtime. He likes to battle his insomnia in complete privacy.

Since it *was* Father's pipe and tobacco, I felt it behooved me to take his advice on smoking. Until I quit playing tennis I smoked very moderately. But I never listened to anything Father had to say about girls. If I had, I probably would have been married six times by now instead of only twice.

The girl I was seeing most often in those days was Irene Kahn, daughter of Gus Kahn, the lyricist of such popular song hits as "It Had to Be You," "The One I Love," "I'll See You in My Dreams," and about five hundred other standards that were the reason Warner Brothers later made a film biography of his life starring Danny Thomas as Gus and Doris Day as his wife and part-time collaborator, Grace.

Irene was a quiet, studious-looking girl, with a sensitive, intelligent face. She wore unbecoming heavy-rimmed glasses and dressed very conservatively in what seemed like a deliberate ploy to keep any boys from knowing she had a good figure for fear they might molest her.

Irene and I had met years before in Chicago, through our respective families, who'd known each other since the golden days of vaudeville.

Later, after the Kahn family moved west to prospect for movie gold, Irene and I found ourselves in many of the same classes together at Beverly High. Since we were both interested in journalism, we also wound up working side by side on the school newspaper. As co-work-ers, we discovered we enjoyed each other's company.

During high school, it was just a platonic friendship, with an occasional movie or dance on Friday nights thrown in. But following my contretemps with the mumps, we started seeing each other steadily. There was no official announcement. We just more or less fell into the habit of not dating anyone else. I suppose you'd call it love, though sexually we hadn't progressed beyond the stage of hand-holding in the movies, and a restrained necking in the front seat of my car when I was dropping Irene off at her parents' house after one of our wild dates at the Fox-Wilshire Theater or the Palladium.

I'm not saying I wouldn't have liked to nail Irene to a bed. After twenty years of being a virgin, I was primed for anyone—even a goat.

But there didn't seem to be the same desire on Irene's part to explore the mysteries of sex—at least, not without benefit of a rabbi. Which didn't make her a great deal different from most of the other well-bred girls from nice Beverly Hills Jewish families. The moment I would put my hand near the top button of her blouse, or touch her leg, she'd stiffen up and become as unyielding as the Viet Cong.

But being a well-bred boy from a nice Beverly Hills Jewish family who didn't give up, even when he was playing Jack Kramer, I didn't stop trying, for there was always that chance in a million that my charm would suddenly turn her into an uncontrollable nymphomaniac. It never happened, of course, but the thought of it kept me necking in the car with her, later and later each night. Pretty soon I completely abandoned my monklike routine of having to get ten hours sleep a night, and I started coming home regularly at two, three and sometimes four in the morning.

Father didn't approve of this change in me, feeling that I couldn't be very creative at the typewriter the next morning if I were half asleep, not to mention what it was doing to my tennis.

If I didn't get home by midnight, Father would bawl me out at the breakfast table. Father could be awesomely vitriolic at these moments, and to avoid his wrath I either had to stop eating breakfast with him, or figure out a way of sneaking into the house more quietly the night before. This latter wasn't easy, since Father's room was built atop a porte-cochere over the driveway.

Coming home late one night from the Kahns', I thought I hit upon a foolproof way to outwit Father. As I pulled my car into the driveway, I turned off the engine and coasted into the garage, for a perfect dead-stick landing. But as I tip-toed up the walk to the backdoor, Father suddenly stuck his head out of his window, wiggled his eyebrows playfully and said, "I still heard you."

Despite the profligate life I was leading, I still managed to win several tennis tournaments that spring, and to be runner-up in three of the big men's events—the Los Angeles City Championships, the Beverly Hills Open and the Ojai Men's Singles.

I'll never forget the finals of the Los Angeles Metropolitan at Griffith Park. I had upset a number of high-seeded players to reach the finals and the newspapers on the morning of the finals were full of glowing reports of how "Groucho's son" was the most improved player of the current crop of Davis Cup hopefuls.

As a result, all the Marx Brothers turned out that afternoon to watch me play Ronny Lubin, the Hearst International Champion.

I suffered a huge let-down from the upsets I pulled off on my way to the finals, and could hardly hit a ball over the net during the match, which turned into a rout. Lubin played exceptionally well, and trounced me 6-3, 6-2, and 6-1, in about twenty minutes flat.

After the first set, I glanced over into the grandstand for some encouragement from my rooters, and saw Zeppo leaving. After the second set, Harpo exited. And in the middle of the third stanza I noticed Gummo sneaking out. Chico hadn't shown up at all; he was at a card game.

The only ones who remained to watch me shake the victor's hand were Father and Mother.

On the way home in the car, Father was furious—not because I'd lost, but because he claimed my mind was no longer on tennis. He blamed the loss on Irene, and the fact that she had kept me out past midnight the night before.

"You can either be a lover or a tennis player," he ranted, "but not both. Now either you settle down and take this game seriously, or I'm not giving you any money to go East this year. You can go to work instead."

I don't think he wanted me to take the game seriously as much as he wanted me to take Irene less seriously.

Although she didn't appeal to him personally, since she was Jewish and not very glamorous-looking, Father liked Irene. He felt she was bright, which was correct; she was a straight "A" student all through school. And he was extremely fond of her parents.

But Father didn't approve of early marriages—his idea of early being anyone under forty—and he feared my relationship with Irene was drifting in that direction. Which, of course, was utter nonsense. I had no more intention of getting married at that time than Irene had of going to bed with me if we didn't marry.

How could I get married on my income? Five dollars a week for dusting the cars, and a three-dollar dividend check every six months from a few shares of General Motors Father had once given me for my birthday.

From my magazine writing efforts I had received not a penny, although all the news hadn't been completely discouraging. Arnold Gingrich, the editor of *Esquire*, had written me a rejection in his own hand, saying he couldn't use the story I'd submitted, but that it showed promise and "to keep at it." And the editor of *Western Tennis*, a West Coast magazine devoted to the sport, had liked a piece I'd written about my experiences on the circuit, and not only published it, but assigned me to cover some of the tournaments when I went East the coming summer.

Western Tennis didn't pay anything, however—it didn't even reimburse me for the stamps I used sending my copy in—so there was little danger I'd use that job as an excuse to marry.

Then, just before I was to leave for the East, I got what seemed like a good break for my career. Dore Schary, an executive at MGM at the time, and a frequent dinner guest at our house, read one of my stories, liked it, and offered me a junior writer's job at MGM, starting at seventy-five dollars a week—which was considerable in those days.

It was a tempting offer, since my ultimate aim in life was to be a screen writer, but with such a large time investment in tennis so far, I wanted to give myself one more crack at the Eastern circuit. So I asked Schary if the job would still be open to me in the fall, and he assured me that it would.

I left for the East, feeling extremely optimistic about life in general. I had a girl and a job waiting for me on my return, and the Helms Athletic Foundation had just voted me "most improved player of the season." With some luck, perhaps I could make up for the grass court experience I'd lost out on the previous year due to the mumps.

But something peculiar happened to me that summer. After a couple of tournaments, I suddenly lost my desire to win. I just didn't care.

I played a couple of good matches. In a replay of our match the previous year at Seabright, I beat Gilbert Hunt, and I was runner-up in a mixed doubles tournament at Southampton. But for the most part my play was uninspired, and I usually got bumped to the sidelines in the second or third round.

In retrospect, I can see several factors that diminished my desire to be a tennis bum that summer.

For one thing, another world war was looming up on the horizon. According to the experts and the newspaper headlines, it was inevitable that the U.S. would be drawn into the European conflict that was currently raging. Roosevelt had already okayed sending destroyers to Great Britain. Ships were being sunk in the Atlantic every day, some dangerously close to our shoreline. And Congress had passed a draft law.

Some of my friends on the circuit were already making plans to go into the various branches of the service, and I knew it wouldn't be long before I'd have to join them. Projecting myself into the future, I could see that after a long stint in the service, I'd be too old to be a professional athlete.

In addition, I was growing sick of life on the tennis circuit. Living tennis twenty-four hours a day, starting early in May with the clay court tournaments in the Midwest and not finishing until after Forest Hills in September, was enough to dampen the enthusiasm of all but the most dedicated and successful. A certain kind of temperament could take it, but I suddenly found I was as bored with traveling from town to town in search of the Holy Grail of tennis as I was with most of the people I was bumming around with. Riggs, Kovacs, Pancho Segura, Van Horn, Bitsy Grant, Wayne Sabin, Frank Parker, Ted Schroeder and Jack Kramer were all nice guys and exciting to watch while they were leaping around a tennis court, but when you had to spend much time in their company—"well, there wasn't a George Kaufman in the bunch," to borrow one of Father's favorite expressions.

Thirdly, I was anxious to put the sporting life completely behind me, and go to work as a junior writer at MGM.

And lastly, and probably the strongest factor, I had suddenly discovered girls during the summer of 1941.

I wasn't getting very far with them, but not because I wasn't trying. Most young girls weren't easy lays in those days before the Pill—especially girl tennis players and the society types who infested such places as Newport and Southampton.

But at Seabright I met a girl named Marge who was neither a clean cut tennis player nor a virginal debutante. She was a Southern belle from Cincinnati, and she was staying at the resort hotel with her family. She was intelligent, beautiful and extremely passionate—so much so that by our second date she was letting me fondle her naked breasts, and by our third date she was jacking me off in the back seat of my car.

She'd never go farther than that, however, although her wanton behavior certainly held out that promise. But she did seem to like me, and she followed me from tournament to tournament.

Having absolutely no will power, I continued to see Marge, always hopeful that my charm would overpower her resistance. But she remained a stubborn hold-out right up until Forest Hills, keeping me up late night after night before important matches.

It was no wonder I wasn't winning any tournaments, but I had so much time invested in trying to get Marge to capitulate that I couldn't give up, even if it was jeopardizing my tennis career.

I couldn't figure Marge out. Judging by her actions she certainly wasn't a prude. I doubted if she was even a virgin.

A few times she even allowed me to spend a night in the same bed with her, but on those nights she wouldn't do anything more sexual than disrobing down to her navel and letting me take a few nibbles on her big boobs. She guarded the entrance to her vagina with the zeal of a goalie for the New York Rangers.

It was damn frustrating to a fellow who had made up his mind not to be a virgin by the time he returned to California.

Finally—the night preceding my third-round match with Vic

Seixes at Forest Hills—I told Marge that she was either going to have to let down the virginal barriers and let me in, or I was going to stop seeing her.

With the moment of truth upon her, Marge finally confessed that she wasn't "exactly a virgin."

"Then what are you waiting for?" I asked with typical teen-aged savoir-faire.

"I just don't want to get laid any more if I'm not married," she said coyly.

When I told her I was in no position to marry, she looked at me unbelievingly, and said she knew that couldn't be true, because I was the son of Groucho Marx, and could give her all the things she wanted, including a trip to Hollywood, where I would help her become a movie star.

That ended our romance. Even *one* person couldn't live on the twenty-five bucks a week expense money I was getting from Father.

She also ended my tennis career.

The next day I lost to Vic Seixes in the third round, 6-2, 6-2 and 6-2, and immediately afterward headed for Hollywood, still a virgin, technically speaking.

CHAPTER 21

SOME DAY
YOU'LL
THANK ME

I **EXPECTED** Father to be pleased over my decision to quit tournament tennis and to take the junior writer's job at MGM. But, returning home, I discovered he wasn't very keen about my working on the West Coast at all. He said that he felt it would be better for me to knock around a big city like New York for a couple of years—the experience would make a better writer out of me.

But what he actually meant was, he was afraid I'd use the MGM job as a stepping stone to marriage. So he was strenuously pushing for me to take a job with a friend of his, Hal Horne, who ran a New York advertising agency in partnership with Richard Condon, who later wrote *The Manchurian Candidate*.

Horne had read some of my tennis articles, and had promised Father when he had visited California that summer that I could join his organization as an apprentice copy writer at twenty-five dollars a week.

Twenty-five dollars a week! Even for those days that was little. Father seemed hell bent on getting me over that fish store yet.

"But MGM will pay me seventy-five a week," I protested. "And I'll be doing what I want to do eventually, anyway. You always said I should work in a studio."

"That'll teach you—never listen to anything I say," he shot back. "Now shall I talk to Horne when I get to New York or not?"

Father was planning a trip to New York with Norman Krasna on the following day, to see about finding a producer for their play, *Time for Elizabeth*, on which they'd just finished collaborating.

"No, I'm going to stay here," I insisted.

"Okay, it's your decision," he said, in a tone meant to make me feel guilty.

It may have been my decision, but two weeks later, Father phoned me from his suite at The Warwick Hotel, and said, "Good news, Big Feet. I talked to Hal Horne, and he's definitely putting you on."

"Look," I told him, "if you're worried about my marrying Irene, forget it. I don't want to get married yet."

"I don't trust you," said Father. "You haven't had enough experience with girls. You fell for the first broad who kissed you."

"Oh, I've been kissed by plenty of other girls," I replied, somewhat evasively. I didn't dare tell him about my red hot romance with the girl from Cincinnati that past summer. He'd have thought *she* was the reason I hadn't won a tournament.

"Well, think it over," growled Father. "And you'd better come to the right decision," and he hung up.

While I was thinking it over, Irene's father, Gus Kahn, died unexpectedly of a heart attack. Irene and Gus had been inseparable, and she took the loss awfully hard—so hard that I found during the days that followed that I wanted to be by her side constantly to do what I could to cheer her up.

That made my decision to stay in California. Consequently I wrote Father that I was definitely turning down the New York job, and that I hoped, under the circumstances of Gus's death, he would understand.

He didn't!

Back came a letter dripping with such vitriol that I won't even quote it. I can't, because I tore it up in anger the moment I finished reading it. But the gist of it was that I was a schmuck for wanting to get married at my age, that I was an ingrate for not listening to anyone so knowledgeable about women as Father, and that Irene didn't need me to hold her hand, because she had a family of her own for that purpose. He concluded by saying he absolutely forbade me to take the studio job, and signed off with, "Writing you this hurts me more than it does you, but someday you'll thank me."

If the thought of marriage hadn't entered my mind before then, that letter certainly helped implant it there. I phoned Dore Schary at MGM immediately, and informed him that I was ready to take the job.

"Okay, kid," said Schary. "Come on out to the studio tomorrow and see me."

Schary greeted me cordially from behind a large desk in his richly appointed, walnut-paneled office. On his desk were the usual accoutrements—a thermos of water, scripts he was reading, and framed photographs of his mother, wife and children. Also prominent on the desk was some kind of humanitarian award from Father Flannigan of Boys' Town—from the picture of the same name produced by Dore Schary.

"Well, kid," said Schary as I sat down across from him, "what can I do for you?"

Right away I had an uneasy feeling that all was not Kosher in Scharyville. What in hell did he think he could do for me—get me an autographed picture of Clark Gable?

I told him I was through with tennis, and that I was there to take the job he had offered me. "If it's still open, that is."

"Oh, that," said Schary. "Well, I suppose I could put you on, but are you sure that's what you really want?"

I told him I didn't know a better way of learning the business.

He then stood up, and in the unctuous tone of a benevolent scoutmaster, delivered a twenty-minute address on how injurious to a budding writer's career it would be to get tied down to a studio job before he'd had a chance to see the world, and mature.

"Go to New York," he went on. "Take a job there. Doesn't make any difference if the pay's no good. See how the other half lives. Tramp up 3rd Avenue—from the Battery to the Bronx." (He sounded like the opening number of *On the Town*.) "Bum around. Sleep in the Bowery. Get some experience. Then when you have something to write about, come back and see me."

"In other words, you won't put me on now?"

"For your own good, no."

I was beginning to get the picture. "Have you, by any chance, been talking to my father?"

"Why do you say that, kid?" he asked, uncomfortably.

"Because you two sound alike."

"That's because we both came from the same school of hard knocks, kid. We know what's best for you." And he stood up and offered me his hand. "Sorry to disappoint you, kid, but some day you'll thank me."

My career as a junior writer at MGM was over.

That night, while I was reluctantly packing for a prolonged stay in New York, Mother expressed concern over the length of Father's absence. He had gone to New York for only a few days, and now over a month had passed, and he was still there, but calling her up every day to say it would be just "a few more days."

"He's probably just having trouble finding someone to produce his play," I said.

"That's what he tells me," said Mother. "But it's not like him just to stay for that. He hates hotels. He could be here just as well while he's waiting for producers to make a decision."

Two days later, when I moved into Father's suite at The Warwick (until I could find quarters of my own), I discovered what was keeping Father in New York.

Her name was Karen Burke. She was about twenty-five, pretty and a Vassar graduate. She also made no secret about the fact that she and Father had been sleeping together.

"Well, what do you think of her?" asked Father, when I was alone with him.

"She seems very nice."

"I met her through Marc Connelly," he volunteered. "I'm probably going to marry her."

"Really?"

"Yes. She's a hell of a dame. Bright. Great in the hay. And she's
stuck on me."

I wasn't shocked; after all, he and Mother should have broken up
years before. But I was surprised that he had a girl.

During his many years of living unhappily with Mother in California, Father had shown a commendable amount of restraint about
cheating on her, despite the opportunities an important star had for
extra-marital affairs around a studio lot where half the young extras or
starlets would do anything in order to get a break in the movies.

Many a time when Father had come home to find Mother drunk,
he had *threatened* to step out on her if she didn't pull herself together.
And occasionally—if the fighting raged on long enough—he actually
would storm out of the house and not return until the next day. Perhaps he was seeing girls on those evenings.

But oddly enough, he remained—at least to my knowledge—remarkably faithful to Mother during the climactic and unhappiest years
of their marriage. Maybe he was too exhausted from fighting, but he
seemed to prefer his books and Gilbert & Sullivan to outside sexual engagements.

Until he met Karen on his trip to New York, that is.

More surprising to me than the entanglement itself was the age of
his new girlfriend. Karen wasn't much older than the girls I'd been
going around with, and Father—well, he was old enough to be my father.

Oh, well, that's show biz.

I wished him luck, and hoped I'd be as fortunate.

For propriety's sake, Karen moved back into her own apartment
while I was staying temporarily with Father at The Warwick. And a
good thing that she did, for Mother surprised Father by showing up
unannounced in our suite a couple of weeks later. She immediately
confronted Father with the fact that she'd heard a rumor back on the
Coast that he had been squiring a young girl around New York, and
demanded to know if it was true.

"It's true," admitted Father, after some hesitation.

"I thought so," said Mother. "You couldn't leave Gilbert and Sullivan this long, otherwise."

After a short but bitter argument, they agreed to get a divorce. But Father never married Karen. Their romance exploded when he discovered that there was hardly a celebrity on the Broadway scene she hadn't slept with at one time or another.

"What did he expect at his age—the Virgin Mary?" quipped Mother, not altogether displeased when she heard the news.

Despite the break up of Groucho and Juliet, Mother hired a lawyer as soon as she was back on the Coast, and divorce papers were served.

Once the decision to divorce was made, Father's and Mother's relationship immediately improved. The two of them continued living in the same house together for the year it took for a divorce to become final in California in those days. In the best Noel Cowardian tradition, they lived separate lives under the same roof, coming and going and dating, as they pleased.

When the spoils of twenty-two years were finally divided, Mother was awarded half of Father's money, the Chippendale dining room furniture, and an antique sterling tea set.

Father kept the house, and unofficial custody of Miriam, for Mother was moving into a small apartment in which there wasn't room for both a daughter and an Arthur Murray dance instructor she was having an affair with.

The United States Coast Guard got custody of me, for by the time Mother's and Father's divorce was settled, the Japanese had already played their little practical joke on Pearl Harbor, and the country was at war.

Early in the war, while I was stationed at a Coast Guard post on the California coast, I received the following letter from Father, giving me the latest news in his marital adventures:

GROUCHO MARX

Beverly Hills   December 1942

Dear Art:

Your Mother moved out today, and the whole thing was kind

of sad. I was sorry to see her go, for I am still fond of her, but obviously this uncomfortable set-up couldn't continue.

I said good-bye to her before she drove off in her car. It was one of those awkward, half-serious, half-comic moments, and I didn't know quite what to say. I put my hand out and said, "Well, it was nice knowing you, and if you're ever in the neighborhood again, drop in." Your Mother seemed to think that was a funny line —so for once in my life I got a laugh when I wasn't trying for one.

The house is pretty quiet now with just Miriam and me rattling around in fourteen rooms. Well, it's better than fourteen people rattling around in two rooms. I'll let things drift along—anyway, for the present.

Love,

Padre

Like Father, I, too, felt a little sad. Because their divorce, no matter how necessary it was, meant that I was saying good-bye to a period in my life that I'd never see again.

CHAPTER 22

THE
BATTLE
OF GAVIOTA

ALTHOUGH I wound up in the Coast Guard, my first choice of a military branch in which to serve was the United States Army Air Force.

When I applied for pilot training in the summer of 1942, I wasn't too sanguine about the Air Force accepting me because I was such a schlemiel when it came to higher math. But I fooled myself. I managed to pass the torturously long mathematical examination without trouble, but was turned down because one of my eyes was a fraction away from measuring the required 20-20.

As an alternative, I decided on the Coast Guard, figuring if I couldn't be soaring through the wild blue yonder, I'd prefer the feel of a tall ship beneath my feet to the mud and jungle the infantrymen were schlogging through on those mosquito-infested islands in the South Pacific. I'd always liked boating and being around water anyway. Before I had become a tennis bum, I had once spent a summer in Maine, putt-putting around Lake Wasserunset in an outboard Father had bought me. And God knows, I certainly had a nautical background, after being brought up on a steady diet of *Pinafore*.

Besides, I'd heard that the Coast Guard was forming an entertainment unit, with a professional band fronted by Rudy Vallee, and that they would be needing professional joke writers. (This was the same unit that later gave Sid Caesar, then an ordinary gob, his start as a comedian.)

My background as a joke writer for Milton Berle had been brief, to be sure—one season between Pearl Harbor and my enlisting in the service—but no one could deny that I was a pro.

A Lieutenant Sturges, who'd been assigned to form the Rudy Vallee Band Unit, welcomed me cordially when I told him my qualifications. He promised me that if I could qualify as a Yeoman, Third Class, I wouldn't have to go to boot camp and he'd see that I was permanently attached to the Coast Guard Base at Wilmington, California, where the Vallee unit was going to make its headquarters because of its proximity to Hollywood.

All I had to do to qualify for a Yeoman's rating, the Lieutenant explained to me, was to pass a simple typing test—forty words a minute. I'd never clocked my speed before, but I was so excited at the prospect of spending the war an hour's drive away from Beverly Hills that I typed eighty words a minute!

I was immediately sworn in, given a seabag full of bell-bottoms, and temporarily assigned to the Personnel Office at the small-boats base at Wilmington. There I was to labor at ordinary yeoman's typing and bookeeping duties until the Vallee unit sent for me.

Four weeks of typing out dull reports later, the Personnel Officer sent for me.

"Marx?" he said.

"Yes, sir."

"I've been looking over your work. You're a first-rate typist. Really first rate."

"Thank you, sir."

"I'll be sorry to lose you. Good yeomen are hard to find."

I figured this was it; I was finally being transferred to the Vallee unit.

"I'll be sorry to go," I lied, "but I guess I can do more for the war effort writing shows."

"Bullshit! We're not going to waste you with that bunch of Hollywood commandos, when the CO of the Beach Patrol needs you. I'm shipping you up to Beach Patrol headquarters at Gaviota."

Gaviota?! Was it a town or a vegetable?

"It's north of Santa Barbara. You'll like it there. Plenty of fresh air and ocean."

"There must be some mistake," I said nervously. "I was brought in specifically to write for the Rudy Vallee unit."

"I know all about that, sailor. There's lots of fellahs who can write that Hollywood hogwash, but there's hardly anyone who can type like you. The yeoman they got up on the Beach Patrol now doesn't know a muster roll from a roll of toilet paper. He's fucking up all our records. You can't win a war without keeping accurate records."

"But I don't know anything about muster rolls, either, I'm just good at jokes."

"You'll get the hang of it—a bright boy like you. Now, how soon can you be packed? They need you up there today."

There was no arguing him out of it, and when I tried to appeal to Lieutenant Sturges, I discovered he was in Washington, D.C., with Rudy Vallee, and nobody knew, or seemed to care, when either of them would be returning.

By the time Sturges did return, I was already stationed in a field of oil wells, on a windswept bluff overlooking the Pacific—about a hundred and fifty miles north of Rudy Vallee.

The Beach Patrol was easy duty—if not for the men who pa-trolled the beaches every night on the lookout for Japanese invaders and possible saboteurs, for me. All I had to do was keep the records of the other men; order the supplies for the station, which was located in a ramshackle bungalow that had formerly been the living quarters of the hardhats who ran the oil drilling rigs; and occasionally walk a beach myself when one of the regular patrolmen was sick or drunk.

The duty was monotonous, for there were no towns for social life in the area, but otherwise not too hard to take. It was a lot better than being on Guadalcanal, though the shortage of girls was just as acute.

About once every three weeks I was given a thirty-six-hour week-end liberty, so I did get home occasionally. But in wartime, Beverly Hills wasn't very much fun. There was a meat shortage, a gasoline shortage, a sugar shortage, a rubber shortage, and a people shortage.

Having divorced parents compounded the discomfort.

Father expected me to eat dinner with *him* on the one night I had in town (Saturday), and would be insulted if I elected to do otherwise. Mother, of course, would be hurt if I ate with Father, especially since I also slept at his house. Satisfying the two of them left me practically no time to see my girlfriend, Irene, who, war or no war, wasn't about to lose her virginity to a sailor who was anxious to lose his.

Without a marriage ceremony, that is.

I didn't believe I could afford a wife yet—not on a third-class petty officer's pay of seventy-eight dollars a month. The notion of succumbing to marriage had, however, crossed my mind more than once since I'd been in the Coast Guard—usually when I'd be lying awake in my bunk, dreaming of those halcyon days on the tennis circuit when my little Southern belle from Cincinnati was doing her topless act in her hotel room in order to tempt me into marrying her.

A great many servicemen who had no more economic right to a wife than I were taking the plunge in those days, feeling that there was a war on in which they could possibly lose their lives, so why not marry and enjoy a little happiness, in case they didn't return.

One thing was deterring me slightly. I wasn't sure if I was in love with Irene Kahn. I enjoyed her company, platonically, and I knew our respective families wouldn't object to being in-laws. But her prim, school-teacherish looks didn't excite me sexually—at least not to the degree that my bunkmates' pin-ups of Rita Hayworth and Betty Grable could.

Still a girl was a girl, and they all had the same basic physical equipment. Proportioned differently, to be sure, but as Father never failed to remind me, "They're all alike in the dark, so you'd better get one you can talk to, as well as hump."

Since Irene and I did plenty of talking, and very little else on the week-ends that I did manage to get back to Beverly Hills, I was vulnerable to just about any suggestion that might lead to an improvement in our physical relationship—including marriage.

Curiously, the one who suggested we get married was not Irene, but her sister-in-law, Lois, who was married to Irene's brother, Donald Kahn.

Lois, a former Saks model, with long chestnut-brown hair, a pretty face and great figure, was only a bride of two weeks herself when I, in my dress blues, turned up at the Kahn household one Saturday in February of 1943, to call on Irene.

Lois and I had seen a lot of each other during the three years that she and Don had been going steady, and I'd grown extremely fond of her. In addition to her good looks, she had a warm, fun-loving personality, and we enjoyed great rapport with each other. She was, in fact, the kind of girl I could have gone for myself, but since I assumed she would eventually marry Donald, I never bothered to cultivate any kind of a relationship with Lois except that which was proper between two potential in-laws.

But we would always gravitate towards each other, whenever the opportunity presented itself, which was often.

The Kahns—Grace, Don and Irene—were a very cliquy trio, and had become even more tightly knit since the head of the family had passed away. They were always excusing themselves and disappearing into another part of the huge house for private family conferences—usually convoked by Grace—leaving Lois and me to shift for ourselves—often for hours at a time.

Mostly we'd sit on the couch in the Khans' oak-paneled library, talking or playing backgammon, but occasionally we'd take a walk in the garden, or around the block. A few times we even held hands.

The Kahns continued their practice of excluding Lois from their summit meetings even after she'd become a member of the family. Thus it happened that Lois and I again found ourselves alone together in the library on a Saturday afternoon when I was home on liberty.

"When are you and Irene going to get married?" Lois suddenly asked me, apropos of nothing.

When I said I didn't think I could afford it, Lois laughed and said, "That didn't stop Don and me."

I pointed out to her that Don, being a civilian instructor of meteorology for the Army Air Force, was earning considerably more than I, and that I didn't think I had a right to ask Irene to marry me on seventy-eight dollars a month. I even questioned whether she'd have me.

"Are you kidding?" exclaimed Lois. "Just ask her!"

I thought about it overnight, finally decided, "Why not?" and on Sunday afternoon, just before driving back to Gaviota, I suggested we get married.

My matchmaker sister-in-law knew what she was talking about. I'd barely mouthed the words before Irene was telling me the china pattern she and her mother had decided on. The wedding date was set for the first Saturday I could get away from the Coast Guard again.

Lois gave our marriage another assist. She forged my signature on our application for a wedding license, because by the time the marriage license office opened the next morning, I was already a prisoner of the Coast Guard Beach Patrol again, and my CO wouldn't let me off for anything so unwarlike as wedding preparations.

My father wasn't much more cooperative, when I imparted the news of the impending nuptials to him.

"Why do you want to get married now?" he snapped. "You can't live with her."

"I can on week-ends."

"If you just want to get humped, there must be a cheaper way."

"We have a lot of other interests, too," I said.

"How can you afford a wife?"

"Irene'll live with Grace until the war's over. She has a big house."

"Then what?"

"I can get another job writing radio."

"You were only making fifty a week with Berle. That'll hardly support a wife."

"Look," I blurted out. "You're not going to talk me out of it. A date's been set, Grace has already booked a rabbi, and Irene's picking out china."

"Well, there's one good thing," said Father, when it finally dawned on him that I couldn't be talked out of it. "At least you won't have to support her parents!"

Father was extremely fond of my future mother-in-law, Grace Kahn.

He had known her and her talented husband, Gus, since 1909, when they, as a young, struggling songwriting team, had called on him in the dressing room of the theater he was playing, and offered him ten dollars of their publisher's money to introduce their first song, "I Wish I Had a Girl," to the theatergoing public in his vaudeville act.

Father agreed. The song turned into a hit. And the Marx family and the Kahns had been friends from that evening forward.

Eventually, after Gus Kahn became successful on his own, Grace retired from show business to raise a family. As a Beverly Hills housewife, she was a very capable manager of her household, a charming hostess and a frequent party-giver. Everybody called her the Perle Mesta of the music business.

Father admired these qualities in Grace, and always wished his own wives could have been more like her.

After Gus died in 1941 and Father was single again, I believe he actually would have proposed to Grace—if she'd been younger, prettier and not Jewish.

But in spite of the fact that he approved of my future mother-in-law, Father sulked right up to the night of the wedding, which took place in Grace Kahn's living room, in front of a small group of friends and relatives (including Harpo and Zeppo) with Rabbi Nussbaum officiating.

Following the ceremony, Father swallowed his disapproval long enough to kiss the bride, hand me a check for a thousand dollars, and kid Nussbaum. "Is it true you fellows breed like rabbis?" he asked him.

After a hasty supper of champagne and wedding cake, Irene and I stole away to a honeymoon suite at the Miramar Hotel in Santa Monica—the only hotel in greater Los Angeles that wasn't full up because of the wartime housing shortage.

With only thirty-six hours of my week-end pass remaining, there was no time to waste traveling out of the city for a honeymoon site. We had to make the most of the hours we had left.

We didn't exactly spend the night orgying, but after several misfires, we did manage to consummate the marriage in the manner prescribed and graphically illustrated in the twelve-page pamphlet *The Physical Side of Marriage: A Guide to Everlasting Happiness*, which Irene's lady gynecologist passed out to all her young bride patients for guidance on their wedding night.

Father remained strangely uncommunicative during my first few months of marriage, and when he did write, his letters weren't very warm. This wasn't like him, so one week-end when I was home on liberty, I made it a point to drop in on Father without my bride.

He studied me as if he wasn't quite sure whether he was happy to see me or not.

Finally, I broke the ice.

"You still mad at me for getting married?" I asked.

"No, just hurt."

"Hurt?"

"Yes. When you moved out of here to move in with the Kahns, you didn't once thank me for all those years I supported you."

"I thought that was understood," I said. "I didn't know I had to do it formally."

"You could have said something," he replied, sounding hurt again.

"Okay," I said. "Thanks for supporting me all those years."

"That's more like it," he said, clasping me to his bosom. "Now, how's married life? You look a little peaked! You're not humping too much, are you?"

I assured him that I wasn't. Which not only was the understatement of the century, but turned out to be the story of our marriage, even though Irene and I were compatible in most other ways, and people thought, because we held hands, didn't fight in public, and had a couple of very nice kids, that we were ideally matched.

CHAPTER 23

WORLD
WAR TWO
SPEAKING

THE closest Father had ever come to going to war was when he made *Duck Soup*. Poor eyesight had kept him out of the first world war, and middle-age out of the second.

Still, trying to cope with the everyday problems of life in Beverly Hills during a war wasn't any picnic. Not on an "A" gasoline ration card, and if you had Father's honest and patriotic nature, which wouldn't permit him to dabble in the black market, as most others in Beverly Hills were doing.

To save gasoline, Father used to pedal to his office in Beverly Hills on a bicycle. Sometimes he'd be so tired from the bike ride that he wouldn't have enough strength left to navigate the flight of stairs to his office. In that case, he'd stand on the sidewalk under his office window and call up to his secretary, who'd lower by rope a wire basket containing any correspondence or checks that required his signature. Frequently he'd dictate a letter up to her from the sidewalk.

Father also did the household marketing on a bike.

Not that there were many left in the house for whom to shop. Its occupants had dwindled down to just Father, a maid, a police dog named Duke, and Miriam, who was fifteen and enjoying enormously her role as mistress of Groucho's manor.

Because his Japanese gardener was in an Internment Camp for the duration, Father was forced to do his own gardening. Father didn't mind this for he'd been an amateur horticulturist ever since his Great Neck days, and he enjoyed the pleasant exercise of weeding a flower bed or nurturing his orchard along from tiny saplings into fruit-bearing trees. He even started a Victory Garden, but gave it up when he found he could only get radishes to grow, and radishes give him a headache.

One thing Father did mind was the steady stream of tourist traffic that flowed past his house when he was working in the flower beds bordering the street. Many of the curious stopped to get his autograph or to kibbitz about his gardening. It wasn't often that people from Prairie Junction or Coffeeville, Kansas, got an opportunity to watch a real live movie star doing his own gardening, and perhaps take his picture. But Father didn't like being civil when he wasn't in the mood.

What put him in a better mood was being mistaken for someone else—like the day a Beverly Hills dowager, obviously on the lookout for a non-Japanese gardener to work her own place, drove by in a Cadillac and stopped in front of Father's house. Father was dressed in old pants and a sweatshirt, and he was down on his hands and knees in a flower bed, working with a trowel.

"Oh, gardener," the dowager called out the window to the crouched figure in the garden, "how much does the lady of the house pay you a month?"

"Oh, I don't get paid in dollars," answered Father. "The lady of the house just lets me sleep with her."

Timewise Father could have accepted the dowager's offer, for he hadn't worked regularly at his own vocation since the break-up of the Marx Brothers as an act in 1941, following the release of *The Big Store*.

Father wasn't out of work in the sense that he needed an income

—he had enough money, in annuities and securities, to last him comfortably for the rest of his life. But he desperately wanted to prove to himself that he could be an important star in his own right, without the reinforcements of Harpo and Chico.

He was appearing regularly as a guest star on the *Rudy Vallee–Joan Davis Sealtest Show*, and doing occasional guest shots for Hope, Crosby and anyone else who'd meet his salary demands. But that didn't satisfy him. He wanted a radio show of his own, and had ordered his agents, Zeppo and Gummo, to do their utmost to find him one.

When Zeppo bowed out of the Marx Brothers act after *Duck Soup*, he had started a theatrical agency, and had taken in Gummo as his partner. In the agency's formative stages, the Marx Brothers were the nucleus of Zeppo's client list, but by the early forties, the enterprising baby of the family had built the Zeppo Marx Agency into one of the most successful in the business. Clark Gable, Carole Lombard, Robert Taylor, Fred MacMurray and Barbara Stanwyck were just a few of his clients.

But the Marx Agency wasn't strong enough to come up with a radio program for Father. After the disappointing showings in the ratings of his first two radio attempts—*Flywheel, Shyster & Flywheel*, and *The Kellogg Corn Flakes Show*—potential sponsors weren't exactly beating a path to Father's door to sign him up. Not when they had such favorites with radio audiences as Jack Benny, Bob Hope, and Red Skelton to sell their products.

Father'd seen bad times before, however, and as he wrote me in a letter, he was ever hopeful that one of the reigning comedians would die and have to be replaced. And when that happened, a sponsor would be forced to hire him.

While he was waiting, Father formed a troop entertaining unit consisting of himself, singer Fay McKenzie, guitar player Joe Carioca, and his friend, song writer Harry Ruby. Together the four of them toured this country's Army, Navy and Marine camps and hospitals, helping to maintain our fighting boys' morale.

In the course of these troop entertaining hegiras, Father managed to get quite a few laughs off the stage as well as on.

While playing Camp Pendleton, the Marine base near San Diego, Father was invited into the private office of the Commanding Officer,

General Beadle Smith, for a drink and a little socializing between shows. When the phone rang imperiously, Father grabbed the receiver before the General could reach it, and exclaimed into the mouthpiece, "World War Two speaking!"

At one point in the war, the Treasury Department sent Father and a number of other celebrities—Bob Hope, Bing Crosby, Dorothy Lamour, Charles Boyer, and Desi Arnaz, among others—on a train tour of the country to publicize a Victory Bond campaign, and to sell bonds. The final stop on the junket was the nation's capital, where Father wound up at a reception for the show business luminaries on the White House lawn, chatting with the First Lady, Eleanor Roosevelt. This was a special treat for Father, who had been a Democrat and liberal all his life, and who felt that Eleanor Roosevelt was one of the greatest women of the century.

While Father and the First Lady were making small talk, the U.S. Marine Band struck up an extremely loud Sousa march. Father hates military band music almost as much as he hates mayonnaise on sandwiches, and after a few bars, he turned to Eleanor Roosevelt and said, "Now I know why you travel so much."

During the show that some of the performers put on a little later for the White House staff, comedienne Charlotte Greenwood tore loose with one of her famous eccentric high kicks—the one where she literally wrapped one leg around her neck.

Father leaned over to Mrs. Roosevelt, and said, "You could do that if you'd just put your mind to it."

Bob Hope, who was also along on that Victory Bond train junket, told me an anecdote about Father that I thought particularly revealing. And so did Hope, or he wouldn't have told it to me.

Father always claimed that he doesn't have a typical actor's ego—that he doesn't have to be "on" all the time, or recognized by the general public. This was why, for many years, he remained clean-shaven in private life. He could go down among the common folk incognito, and nobody would bother him for autographs, or expect him to be funny. With so many other stars along, Father had no difficulty maintaining this pose during the first week of the bond junket.

The train stopped at a number of whistlestops across the country, and at each station the other stars would alight, sign autographs, and pose for pictures, while attending to the main business at hand—hawking Victory Bonds. Nobody ever recognized Father. According to Hope, he was left standing with egg on his face while the other celebrities reaped all the attention. Eventually this started to bug Father.

When it happened again at the depot in Washington, D.C., Father decided he'd had his bellyful of anonymity. He hopped back on the train, then reappeared on the station platform moments later with his greasepaint black mustache smeared under his nose, a cigar in his mouth, and doing the famous Groucho walk.

"Doesn't anybody want little old Groucho's autograph?" exclaimed Father, wiggling his eyebrows as he scurried up and down the station platform in his inimitable half-crouch. "You know, I'm somebody, too, even if I am out of work."

While Father was mingling with the brass in Washington, I had a chance to become an officer myself.

In the summer of 1943, the Commandant of the Eleventh Naval District sent word to the COs of all Coast Guard stations to submit names of men they deemed worthy of being sent to Officer's Training Academy in New London, Connecticut.

Since by then I was getting pretty sick of having to unbutton thirteen buttons every time I had to go to the john, I applied for Officer's Training.

Lieutenant McGuire, my CO, approved my application, and several weeks later a white-haired Coast Guard Commodore and one or two of his aides arrived at our Beach Patrol Station to interview the prospective officer talent.

My interview seemed to go along smoothly until the Commodore asked me if it was true that my father was Groucho Marx.

I answered rather proudly that it was.

"Are you Jewish?" asked the Commodore.

I confessed my guilt, and then added, a trifle uneasily, "but what difference does that make—sir?"

The Commodore regarded me critically, but assured me that it made "none at all."

Perhaps he was sincere, but when the names of those men eligible to take the exam were announced, mine wasn't among them.

I immediately complained to McGuire about this, and he interceded on my behalf, threatening to blow the lid off the whole establishment if his superiors couldn't come up with a reason why they had excluded me.

Since they couldn't, they bowed to my COs pressure, and I was allowed to take the exam along with the others. When the results were posted, I was among the top scorers.

According to a bulletin that came through from Washington, D.C., all personnel who had passed the exam were to be held at their present bases until orders came through transferring them to the Academy at New London.

"No exceptions!"

Four weeks later when I received orders to report to Coast Guard Headquarters in Long Beach "for further assignment" I was thrilled, and quite understandably assumed I was being sent to New London. But in Long Beach I was informed by the Personnel Officer in charge that my orders read. I was to be transferred to the Coast Guard Base at Alameda, California, for temporary duty while awaiting assignment to sub-chasing duty in the South Pacific.

When I complained to the head travel agent who was arranging this trip, he went to the files, dug out my service record and said, "You want to know why you're not going to New London, sailor?"

"Don't tell me," I said. "Let me guess. Is it because I'm a Mormon?"

"Don't be childish," said the officer. "This is America. You're not going because you got a speeding ticket—sixty miles an hour in a forty-five-mile zone, during a dim-out."

This was true. Under orders to make the trip as quickly as possible, I once had to drive a handcuffed prisoner—a deserter—from Gaviota to the brig at Long Beach, using my *own* car, and my *own* gas. The reason for the speed was that the entire West Coast was on an "alert" status.

I had volunteered for the job, and on the return trip a cop stopped me and gave me a speeding ticket, in spite of the written orders I whipped out of my pocket. The Commandant fixed the ticket because I had been on official Coast Guard duty.

But peculiarly enough, this didn't matter when I pointed it out the day I received my traveling orders.

My "temporary duty" in Alameda lasted over a year. Shortly after reporting there, I was assigned to be the personal yeoman of Commander Simpson, the officer in charge of forming the crews for the sub-chasing frigates the Coast Guard was manning.

Commander Simpson, a regular in the Coast Guard, had a reputation for being a tyrant. In fact, Walter Winchell had once labeled him in his column "the only dictator in the United States." And in some ways Simpson was a martinet. If you didn't keep your uniform clean, or if you reverted to landlubber language and said "upstairs," instead of "topside," or "floor" instead of "deck," he'd chew you out and take away your liberty.

I could never get used to saying "topside" or "deck" even aboard ship, but Simpson liked me, anyway—I believe because I took over all his letter writing chores (both official and personal) for him. Free of these responsibilities, he had more time to study the racing form and try to beat the ponies at Bay Meadows.

In return Commander Simpson allowed me to keep regular office hours, and to live off the base with my bride of less than a year. He even freed me every week-end.

Because of gasoline rationing and stringent wartime priorities on air travel, Irene and I didn't get back to Southern California more than once during the year I served in Oakland.

But I managed to keep abreast of Father's activities through his letters. From these I learned that war in Beverly Hills may not have been exactly hell, but that it was putting obstacles in the way of leading the good life.

Because his Cadillac ate up so much gas, Father was finally reduced to traveling on a bus.

And because there was very little butter to be had in the markets, Father decided to make his own. He bought an old fashioned butter churn at Sears, Roebuck, and presented it to his cook, who promptly put a damper on the whole venture by informing him that sour cream was required for churning butter, and sour cream wasn't available during the war, either.

When he wasn't coping with household crises, or entertaining troops, Father was still waiting for that comic to die, so he could snag a sponsor.

It never happened. All of his comedian friends remained disgustingly healthy.

Nevertheless, in the spring of 1943, Gummo brought Father good news. The Pabst Blue Ribbon Brewery was willing to sponsor him in a weekly half-hour radio variety show. Which goes to prove if you hold the right thought, God will reward you.

Father spent the next year trying to make a success of the *Pabst Show*, entertaining servicemen and insulting everybody in general.

Since he realized that if he failed again he would be *persona non grata* in the broadcasting industry, he worked doubly hard on the show. Nevertheless, by the winter of 1944, the *Pabst Show*, starring Groucho Marx, was what is known in *Variety* as "a doubtful pick-up." There was something about Father's brash personality that was not getting through to radio audiences—or perhaps it was.

Regardless of the rumors, Father traveled with the show to Milwaukee to celebrate the hundreth anniversary of the Pabst Brewing Company. Among those on hand for the festivities was Edward Pabst, whose father had founded the brewery. By 1944, Edward was almost eighty, and just a figurehead in the company, but was nonetheless slated to make the main address at the Centennial Celebration.

About an hour before he was supposed to appear, Mr. Pabst confessed to father that he was so nervous he didn't think he'd be able to go through with the speech. To calm him down, Father took old man Pabst to a nearby saloon, where they both ordered beer.

"What'll you have?" asked the bartender.

"Miller's High Life!" exclaimed Father. "And Mr. Pabst'll have the same."

Father isn't sure if this incident had anything to do with the fact that the Pabst company finally made the decision not to pick up his option and to replace him with Danny Kaye. But however they arrived at it, he was unemployed again, and didn't break back into broadcasting until 1948, with *You Bet Your Life*.

In the meantime, I was getting fed up with being a land-based sailor in a town as dull as Oakland was during the war, and bored by the monotony of doing straight clerical work.

So when Commander Simpson was put in command of a repair

ship named the USS *Duluth* that was bound for the South Pacific, I volunteered to go along as his yeoman.

Father traveled to Oakland for a good-bye week-end. When I met him at the train station there was no one to help with his luggage, so I picked up his two heavy suitcases and a guitar and started carrying them towards the cab stand.

On the way to the curb, I found myself face to face with an admiral who had just stepped out of a cab. The gold-braided old gentleman looked at me expectantly—obviously waiting to be saluted. But both my hands were in use, grappling with Father's luggage. Luckily I had a quick-thinking father.

Still steeped in the military tradition drummed into him in *Duck Soup*, Father immediately sucked in his own belly, drew himself up to his full five and a half feet, and gave the Admiral a snappy salute. As the Admiral looked at this short Jewish man somewhat bewilderedly, Father indicated me with a jerk of his thumb and exclaimed, "He pays me to do his saluting for him!"

CHAPTER 24

WHERE THE HELL ARE YOU, RUDY VALLEE? OR, SOUTH PACIFIC WITHOUT RODGERS & HAMMERSTEIN

THE vessel on which I sailed out of San Francisco's Golden Gate one foggy morning in August of 1944 was a twenty-five-year-old former Great Lakes freighter that had been converted into a repair ship at a cost to the taxpayers of three million dollars.

Paradoxically the *Duluth* was not a Coast Guard vessel, but belonged to a huge fleet of small tugs and inter-island freighters under the command of the Army Transportation Corps, which—just as paradoxically—had a larger navy than the Navy.

The Coast Guard merely supplied the crew to man her; the GI's on board—approximately one hundred—were to handle the actual repair work of the war-damaged vessels.

The first ship that should have been repaired, if not scrapped, was the *Duluth*. While she was still in dock being converted, her rusty, ancient hull had split under the extra weight of a new superstructure that had been added on the main deck to house its complement of soldiers.

When our skipper, Commander Simpson, called this to the attention of the ATC, the General in charge assumed a most puzzling attitude. He accused the Coast Guard of being hypersensitive, and ordered Commander Simpson to take the old bucket to sea, regardless of her infirmities. Being a man who loved life, Commander Simpson refused. The Army then accused him of holding up the war effort, and threatened to have the Coast Guard Commandant relieve him of his command. Simpson stuck to his guns, knowing no other sane sea-going man would take over the vessel under such hazardous conditions, and the Army reluctantly had the split rewelded. But it was a haphazard job, and according to Simpson, "one good storm and we'd all have gone to the bottom."

If we didn't go to the bottom that way, we were certain to get torpedoed.

The *Duluth* had a top speed of seven knots an hour—not very comforting when you had to travel eight thousand miles through sub-infested waters to reach New Guinea. The Army thought so little of us that we weren't even sent in convoy; our only protection were eight forty-millimeter anti-aircraft guns, and a three-inch cannon on the stern.

The enemy evidently thought even less of us than our own side. Not once were we bothered by subs.

I shared a cabin—about the size of a prison cell—with ten other sailors. With no air conditioning, and the portholes sealed tight because of blackout conditions, there was nothing to breathe, as we sailed through the heat of the equatorial zone, but the BO of my bunkmates.

I felt as if I'd at last wound up in the equivalent of that room over a fish store. It may not have been in Boston, but there were plenty of fish beneath my feet. And if I were unlucky, I might even wind up sleeping with them, through eternity.

We sailed for thirty-four days before we sighted land. I knew how Christopher Columbus felt. When we finally dropped anchor in Hollandia Bay, I was sure we had reached the end of the world.

It had to be the drop-off point that so many ancient mariners had feared, because it looked as if every other ship in the world had anchored there for the same reason—because they could sail no farther without falling over the edge.

The hundreds of warships, LST's, freighters and carriers that I saw bobbing up and down under the glare of the tropical sun turned out to be the armada that General MacArthur was planning to use to retake the Philippines.

Six weeks later, the invasion fleet hit southern Leyte. The *Duluth* was part of MacArthur's vanguard, only we brought up the rear, about two days after the General waded ashore.

I figured the Philippines had to have been retaken by then, otherwise MacArthur wouldn't have sent for us. But as our convoy sailed into Leyte Gulf one morning, we were attacked by a squadron of Japanese aircraft.

As the General Quarters alarm sounded, I reached for my helmet and life jacket, cursed the day I had become such an accomplished typist that I couldn't be wasted on the Rudy Vallee unit, and tried to remember where my General Quarters post was supposed to be (beside the Captain, on the bridge, you schmuck).

The raid went on for several hours. A number of ships in our convoy were hit. And one vessel—an ammunition ship filled with high explosives—literally disappeared before our eyes in one giant flash after taking a torpedo in her side.

We survived our baptism under fire, and though none of us aboard the *Duluth* were gung-ho types, we were grateful for the experience, for we were now entitled to wear battle stars on our overseas service ribbons. (If we ever got back to a port where we could put on a dress uniform, that is.)

Thereafter we were subjected to daily and nightly air attacks, until the southern section of Leyte was completely secured, approximately six weeks later.

After the fighting ceased, the *Duluth* was assigned a permanent anchorage in Leyte Bay, about a mile off the village of Tacloban, and there she settled down to the tedious business of repairing ships.

There was plenty of work for the GI's doing the repairing, but we of the Coast Guard had nothing but time on our hands. We soon sank into a kind of *Mr. Roberts* existence in which the only exciting events in our lives were mail call, sightseeing excursions on foot through the muddy, hut-lined streets of Tacloban, and beer ration days. Unlike what I've read about GI's during the Vietnam war, we enlisted men were completely starved for any kind of sex life. Local Filipino girls were all Catholic, prudish and unavailable for dates unless carefully chaperoned. There were plenty of Army nurses in the area who weren't very prudish, but they only slept with other officers, or Supply Sergeants and Chief Store Keepers, who could give them all the cigarettes, whiskey and nylons they needed. For the rest of us, there was a whorehouse on one of Tacloban's side streets. But it was "out of bounds," and besides, its occupants were so diseased-looking that even this sex-starved yeoman couldn't be tempted. Anyway, I was married, and didn't believe in cheating.

To keep my mind off the subject, I started to write a novel about the Beverly Hills Tennis Club, but was forced to give it up when it became too sexy. I also ran out of typing paper.

After six months in the South Pacific, I had finished reading every book I'd brought along from the States, plus all the reading matter in the ship's meager library. There was nothing left to read except the overseas editions of *Time*, which didn't arrive through the mail too regularly.

Things finally became so monotonous that I even began to long for the excitement of another air raid.

One day, at mail call, I received a box of cigars from Dunhill's in New York. The card simply read, "Max Gordon."

I was puzzled. Why would an important Broadway producer, whom I hadn't seen since I was twelve years old, be sending me expensive cigars?

After the war, Father supplied the answer.

It seems that during the war Father had gone to New York on business, and had run into Max Gordon on the street.

Gordon, as was his wont, promptly launched into a twenty-minute monologue on his own problems in producing plays for Broadway —the critics, the high-handed practices of the stagehand unions, lack of good playwriting talent, etc.

Father listened as long as he could, then lashed out at Gordon with "Max—what kind of a selfish bastard are you? There's a war on.

My son, Arthur, is in the South Pacific. Any minute he could get killed. If you don't want to send him a box of cigars, I'd think you'd at least have the decency to once ask me, 'How's your son, Arthur?' "

Gordon made no immediate comment, finished burying the Broadway theater, turned to go, then spun back again, "Oh, by the way, Groucho, how's your son, Arthur?"

Father needn't have feared for my safety—at least not at the hands of the enemy. The war had moved past us—up to Luzon, and then on to Iwo Jima. Even the last of the Jap snipers on Leyte had been smoked out of their hiding places and imprisoned in stockades. The only thing that could have killed me was the 190 proof medicinal alcohol we were drinking, mixed with grapefruit juice, in the evenings.

I thought that was the only thing, anyway. But one morning I woke up with a headache that was more severe than the ones I normally incurred after our 190 proof cocktail parties on the fantail. Nevertheless, I assumed it was a hangover until the pain persisted into late afternoon, at which point I reported to the Pharmacist's Mate. We had no M.D. on board.

The Pharmacist's Mate took my temperature, and promptly informed me that I had 105—two more degrees and I'd be dead.

I was hastily packed off to an Army hospital on shore, where I was told I had malaria.

During the month I spent in a ward recuperating, I grew to enjoy being a landlubber again. I also grew to enjoy my nurse, a Lieutenant Joan Mobley, who would continue to hold my hand long after she had finished taking my pulse.

However, I was just a Yeoman, First Class, and she was a full Lieutenant, so we broke up the romance the day I was discharged.

My orders, strangely enough, did not read that I was to report to the *Duluth*. Instead I was to report to Coast Guard Headquarters in Tacloban. C.G. Headquarters consisted of a few desks and typewriters on empty packing crates on the second floor of a rat-infested waterfront warehouse.

When I told the Commander in charge that someone over at the hospital must have made a mistake in my orders, he said, "No—I sent for you." And then he explained that because there were so few USO shows coming through Leyte, and so many homesick servicemen, the

Coast Guard was forming an entertainment unit to combat the boredom.

He said that he was putting me in charge of the writing, because of my previous experience with Milton Berle, and that I was to work in conjunction with a fellow named Bud McTaggert, a former B-picture Western star, whose idea it was to form the unit.

When I asked Commander Evans what had become of the Rudy Vallee unit, he shrugged and said, "I guess they're too big to come out here."

It wasn't easy to put a first-class show together so many miles from MCA and William Morris. You couldn't exactly phone Jules Stein from there and say, "Send me twelve great jazz musicians," or tell Abe Lastfogel, "I want one Milton Berle, a couple of girls who are built like Betty Grable, and maybe one thin singer like Sinatra."

But after culling the service records of the men attached to the various Coast Guard ships in the South Pacific, we discovered that there was considerable professional talent around—and all willing to be relieved of their regular gob's chores to join our cast.

In a month's time we had put together a variety show consisting of a fifteen-piece swing band, a specialty act featuring a guitar, accordion and hot violinist, a Shortnin' Bread type baritone, a former first violinist from the Detroit Symphony who could play "Flight of the Bumble Bee" faster than Jack Benny, a sexy, eighteen-year-old, Filipino girl vocalist, whom we'd picked up singing in a local theater, and Bud McTaggert handling the emceeing chores.

The only thing we couldn't find was a comedian, so Bud McTaggert drafted me to do a ten-minute stand-up monologue, in the style of Bob Hope.

My last appearance on the stage, if you remember, was as Professor Bhaer in *Little Women*—a role in which I proved beyond doubt that I could make an audience laugh.

What influenced my decision to come out of retirement was something Father had once told me—that if you could write monologue jokes for someone like Milton Berle or Bob Hope, that it didn't take that much more talent to stand up in front of a mike and deliver them.

Nevertheless, it took courage to face a couple of thousand war-weary GI's and pass yourself off as a comedian. For all I knew, they'd take out their carbines and start shooting at me.

I have to admit I was pretty jittery the first time I tried out my monologue—at an Army hospital fifty miles by truck from Tacloban.

To put myself more at ease during my opening moments of trial, I lit one of Max Gordon's cigars and stuck it in my mouth just as I strolled out on stage. Using the cigar as a prop was a trick I'd stolen from Father—and not because I was trying to imitate him. "A stogy's a very handy thing on the stage," he had once explained to me. "If you forget a line, you can always puff on your cigar until you remember what you want to say."

It's no coincidence that many comedians,—Benny, Burns, Jessel, Berle, Danny Thomas—all smoke cigars when they're performing. (Berle is so dependent on his cigar that he once asked permission of me to smoke it when he was starring in *The Impossible Years* in Miami— and one of the plot points was that the character had given up smoking and was fighting the urge to go back to the filthy habit.)

Bud McTaggart introduced me, and, of course, couldn't resist telling the audience that I was the son of Groucho—I guess he figured it added to my credentials as a comedian.

Since I had expressly asked him *not* to mention my heritage, figuring the audience might resent it, I curbed my uneasiness by making a joke of who my father was.

"I notice that Bud told you my father is Groucho Marx," I began nervously. "Well, please don't hold it against me—I had nothing to do with it. As a matter of fact, my mother told me my *father* had nothing to do with it."

That brought down the house, and warmed up the audience for the rest of my routine. I don't remember all of my monologue, but here are a couple of sample jokes:

"About this weather in the Philippines . . . It was so hot today that I saw a dog chasing a cat and they were both walking."

And,

"Now I'd like to introduce our solo violinist, Max Fishbein. Max comes from a very fine Pittsburgh family. His folks are in the iron and steel business . . . his mother irons and his father steals."

When jokes of that caliber had the audience doubled over with laughter, I knew we were in. I also knew just how *desperate* the GI's were for entertainment.

Our show—which was also broadcast weekly over Armed Forces Radio—became an immediate success, and when word of its existence spread through the area, commanding officers from all over the Philippines started contacting us and booking it for their bases.

During the next six months we played every kind of military installation imaginable—from open-air amphitheaters in the middle of a jungle to the decks of battleships and aircraft carriers. Sometimes these warships would be anchored so far out into Leyte Gulf that we'd have to travel by open landing barge for as long as three hours on choppy water, with our clothes and musical instruments getting soaked from the flying spray. And frequently we'd be pelted by tropical rain as well.

To make sure that we'd show up, commanding officers of well-heeled ships would promise us all kinds of booty in advance—cases of beer, cartons of cigarettes, boxes of prime meats, like New York cut steaks and French lamb chops, which were rationed in the States, and even cases of evaporated milk for our Filipino vocalist, who had two babies at home to feed.

Before long, the two-story house in Tacloban that the Coast Guard rented to accommodate our cast was stacked so high with cases of beer that we looked like the South Pacific distributor for Miller's High Life.

But as much as I loved beer—and at the risk of sounding sentimental—I have to confess that there was no pay ever quite so rewarding as the thrill I felt the day I stood on the prow of the battleship *Texas*, and did our show for its entire 3,000-man crew. As far as the eye could see—from the quarterdeck to the mid-section, from the forward gun turrets, where the gobs sat astraddle the sixteen-inch cannons, to the top of the superstructure—there was just one enormous, undulating sea of white uniforms and happy faces. Adding to the thrill of the moment, two destroyers just returning from the battle of Iwo Jima pulled alongside—one on our port, and the other on our starboard—and asked permission to watch the entertainment.

With good entertainment in that theater of war at such a premium, I was delighted one day to hear that the Rudy Vallee Band, together with its entire cast of performers, including Sid Caesar, had come into the bay the previous night aboard a transport. We could use reinforcements. We were running ourselves ragged, trying to service all the bases in the Philippines that needed entertainment.

But when I ran into Johnny Hacker, a clarinet player from the Vallee band, on the street in front of Coast Guard Headquarters several hours later, he informed me that his unit was only going to play one show in Tacloban that night, and then return to the States immediately.

"One show," I exclaimed. "What's the purpose of sending you way out here to play one show?"

"We're making a movie—*Tars and Spars*," he explained. "And the producer wants us to be able to wear some decorations on our uniforms—like the Pacific Southwest Theater of War Service Ribbon, so it'll look like we've seen some action." He winked and added, "It wouldn't be honest of us to wear them unless we'd really been out here, would it?"

I may not have been the comedian Sid Caesar was, but by August of 1945, when the Japanese came to their surprisingly sudden decision to surrender, our show had been honed to such perfection from months of playing and rewriting that most of the servicemen who had seen it agreed it was better than any entertainment that had been sent out from the States.

Moreover, we were beginning to garner a reputation—as far away as Washington, D.C. While we were nervously waiting around wondering what would become of our show now that the war was over, the Treasury Department sent for us to return to the States immediately, for a bond tour.

We were playing the bases around Manila, and living in a C.B. camp there, when our orders came through to board the USS *General Altman*, a troop transport anchored in Manila Harbor.

To reach the *Altman*, we had to load all our gear—personal belongings, musical instruments, trunks containing musical arrangements and stage props—into two trucks, ride thirty miles over a dirt road to the waterfront, reload into a landing barge, and travel two hours out into the bay.

When we reached the transport, the officer in charge of our unit hailed the bridge for permission to come aboard. After sixteen months in the South Pacific, this was a big moment for us.

But the Captain of the transport strode to the bridge and informed us that he wouldn't take us aboard—he was only carrying "fighting men" home.

Dejectedly we retraced our steps back to the C.B. Camp, and waited for new orders, which came through the following day. They again read, "Proceed to the USS *General Altman* for transportation back to the United States."

Once more we loaded all our gear in the trucks, rode to the harbor, clambered aboard the landing barge, and sailed out to the transport. And again the Captain refused to take us aboard.

Four days in a row this happened—until the Commandant in Washington finally had to threaten to court martial the Captain of the *Altman* for insubordination if he wouldn't accept us.

The Captain of the *Altman* acquiesced—but reluctantly. He wouldn't permit us to come up the gangway. In a heavy sea, this Queeg-like tyrant forced us to climb aboard via a rope ladder hanging down from the *Altman*'s stern, and carry all our heavy equipment, like bass fiddles, drums and music trunks, up with us on our backs.

When we finally flopped down exhausted on the fantail, we were informed by the *Altman*'s executive officer that the Captain had no intention of giving us a "free ride" home. We were to work for our passage, chipping paint, mopping decks, cleaning heads and performing other unpleasant tasks.

We did just that until our transport reached Okinawa, where she was to take on four thousand combat-weary Marines. Luckily for me and the other pariahs in our cast, the Commanding General of the Marine base capriciously decided, shortly after we anchored off Okinawa, that he wouldn't be ready to load any troops aboard our ship for another week or ten days.

This sent a shiver of fright up our Captain's spine, because the weatherman had predicted that a major typhoon was heading toward Okinawa, and he desperately wanted to get his ship out of the area before it struck.

To cajole full cooperation out of the Marine General, the Captain of the *Altman* made an offer: He said he'd send our show ashore to entertain at the Marine base, provided the General would get off the dime and start loading his troops immediately.

The General agreed, and the Captain, relieved that he and his ship might be able to escape the fury of the typhoon called on us personally to tell me and the rest of our cast about the deal he'd made.

At the time, we were on our hands and knees, chipping rusty paint off one of the passageways in the bowels of the ship, where the temperature was about 110 degrees in the shade. But we were not so far out of the mainstream of shipboard life that we weren't very much aware that the Captain needed our cooperation if he expected to get the hell out of Okinawa before the typhoon struck.

So when the Captain said he wanted us to go ashore to put on a show for the Marines, we could afford to play it cool.

"That's very nice of you, sir," I said, continuing to chip paint away from the deck around the Captain's feet. "But we've given up show business. From now on, we're going to be regular fighting men, just like you wanted."

Picking it up from my cue, the rest of the cast joined in and agreed that they'd rather be just "plain, ordinary gobs." The Captain's face went white with rage, he spluttered, and even threatened court martial as we insisted that we were telling the truth about quitting show business. But we knew we had him over the well-known barrel, and before we'd consent to putting on a show, we exacted a promise from the old four-striper that we were to be treated as first-class citizens for the rest of the long voyage home, and that included participating in the officers' beer rations.

So for the three days it took 4,000 marines to board the USS *Altman*, we entertained the boys on Okinawa who were not lucky enough to be going home.

When we climbed back aboard the transport three evenings later, the typhoon was already threatening on the horizon. With all the Marines finally aboard, the Captain hurriedly weighed anchor, pointed our bow toward Seattle, and we rode home as first-class passengers.

We later heard that the typhoon wreaked terrible devastation on Okinawa, but it proved beyond doubt that it's indeed difficult to find a wind so ill that it bloweth no man to no good—in our case, to Seattle and a train for Los Angeles.

Three weeks later, while I was waiting around Seattle for a priority that would put me on a train for the rest of the trip home, I saw some publicity about my recent activities that showed things hadn't changed much since my tennis-playing days.

In an old newspaper, I came across a feature picture story that had been carried by one of the major news wire services, under the heading:

MARXES MAKE NEWS

The first of three boxed head shots, showing me in a pith helmet, with a cigar in my mouth, was captioned:

Groucho's son pictured as he imitates his father in a radio program at a Philippine Coast Guard base. He is heard in most parts of the South Pacific over an Armed Forces Radio Station

The second picture showed a well-stacked but petite blonde, and next to her, in still a third box, was a likeness of Father, in stage make-up, puffing on a cigar.

The rest of the story read:

Groucho Marx, left, mustachioed stage, screen and radio comedian, and blond actress Catherine Marvis Gorcey, center, were married last week. Marx, 54, was divorced from his first wife, Ruth, in 1942. His twenty-four-year-old bride was divorced from actor Leo Gorcey, one of the Dead End Kids, in 1944.

Well, the Marx family had always done things differently. So why shouldn't Son of Groucho have a mother who was younger than he?

CHAPTER 25

MOTHER
NUMBER TWO

▌MUST confess I wasn't totally surprised by Father's leap into matrimony. He had prepared me for it earlier in the summer with a letter he had written while I was still in Tacloban.

"I'm going to marry Kay Gorcey on your birthday, July 21st," he wrote. "This is in deference to you, and the fact that you can't be here to attend the nuptials, as they'd phrase it in the society section of the newspaper. However, I'm sure the war will be over by my third marriage, so you will be able to attend that one."

Father was being facetious about a third marriage, of course. From his letters he was very fond of Kay, and she was "stuck on me," as he so quaintly phrased it. Nevertheless, I think he had a fear—subconsciously anyway—of marrying a girl so much younger than himself.

Age was certainly on his mind.

In between Karen Burke and Kay Gorcey had been another short-lived romance, this one with Budd Schulberg's ex-wife, Virginia. Father had been quite smitten with Virginia, and had told me earlier in the war that he intended to marry her. But soon after I was transferred to Alameda, he informed me that he had broken off with Virginia because she was only twenty-seven while he was fifty-one. That was the reason he gave me, but I don't think it was the only one.

In addition to being physically attractive, Virginia Schulberg had a brilliant mind—perhaps a little too brilliant for Father, who prefers his women slightly on the docile side. He didn't object to her intellect per se; only to the fact that she wasn't afraid to assert her own strong personality around him. In other words, she insisted on being her own person, and would take no male chauvinism from him or any man.

That, I suspect, more than age, was the real thing that frightened Father off. Two strong personalities like his and Virginia's—and one with an actor's ego yet—would be clashing constantly.

There was a greater difference between Father's and Kay's ages. But Kay was more his basic style—blonde, Gentile, tractable, and not likely to talk back to him, or try to top him. In these traits, Kay was somewhat like my own mother at the time she married Father in 1920.

Father had met Kay when he was doing the radio show for Pabst.

Leo Gorcey, one of the Dead End Kids, had been a regular member of the cast, and sometimes his pretty wife would tag along to rehearsals with him.

My sister, Miriam, who acted as Father's Girl Friday, also attended rehearsals, and it was she who first became friendly with Kay—probably because they were more or less contemporaries. It was Miriam, in fact, who had originally introduced Kay to Father.

Father didn't steal Kay away from Gorcey—he's too Victorian ever to pull a thing like that. Kay's marriage to the former Dead End Kid was already pretty shaky when she and Father met.

A heavy drinker, Gorcey used to get smashed and beat Kay up—for no other reason except to prove that he was really a tough guy. Kay didn't like being used as a punching bag, and finally she left Gorcey. This infuriated Gorcey even more, and during the time it took Kay to obtain a divorce, he would harass her, and even threaten Kay's life.

Kay went to the police for protection, but they weren't much help, claiming they weren't allowed to become involved until her ex-husband had either attempted to kill her, or killed her.

Frightened that Gorcey might actually harm her, Kay, at Miriam's urgings, sought advice from Father—a father figure if ever there was one. Soft-hearted sentimentalist that he is, Father has never been known to turn a helpless girl out into the street, especially if she's pretty, blonde and Gentile. Father invited her to move into his house for protection. How fatherly that arrangement was I can't say.

During his first period of being single in more than twenty years, Father was always threatening to eschew a second marriage. He'd lost half his fortune to Mother, and he vowed it would never happen again —which is what he always says when he's single. But from his frequent references to Kay in his letters to me while I was in the Philippines, I suspected that he was fooling no one but himself.

As much as Father hates matrimony, he hates being single more. To him, being single represents phoning and dating girls he really has nothing in common with, plus a good deal of actual physical inconvenience such as calling for them, having to talk to their relatives while waiting for them to finish dressing, and then, after the date, returning them to their homes—provided he can't persuade them to return to his home.

"I've tried being single," Father once said. "It doesn't work. You sit at a table, alone, eating."

As soon as Kay was free of Gorcey, she became Father's bride and moved into his new domicile in West Los Angeles.

In the dark days of the war, when help had been hard to get, and he was convinced he would remain a gay bachelor forever, Father had sold the house in Beverly Hills in which I'd grown up, and purchased a smaller place in Westwood. Miriam shared the new house with him— until Kay displaced her.

By then, Miriam had developed into an extremely attractive eighteen-year-old. She had inherited most of her mother's looks, and much of her father's wit, sense of humor and native intelligence. At Beverly High she was extremely popular and could get any boy she wanted. But in her estimation, none of her boyfriends could possibly measure up to her own father when it came to stimulating companionship. Miriam adored and idolized Father—both as a comedian and a parent—and probably would have been content to remain single and go on living with him for the rest of her life. One thing seems certain. She probably never would have introduced Kay to Father if she had seen her as a threat to her own security. Being a soft touch for anyone in trouble, Miriam was merely doing Kay a favor.

Losing her position as mistress of the house to Kay was something my sister hadn't exactly bargained for. It immediately sent Miriam into a spin from which she hasn't until this day fully recovered—in spite of thousands of dollars' worth of psychoanalysis.

Soon after Father and Kay were married, Miriam renounced Southern California. She said she wanted to live in the East, and she enrolled at Bennington College, Vermont.

Miriam picked a girl's college, because she was through with men forever after being double-crossed, she felt, by one of them—her own father.

For nearly four years, Miriam applied herself seriously to her studies at Bennington and seemed on the verge of a major break-through—she was about to become the only member of our family ever to graduate from college. But a week before graduation Miriam came through like a true Marx—she was expelled from Bennington without explanation from the authorities.

Father, of course, was not oblivious to all of this. But he had more pressing problems—a young wife to satisfy, a whole new group of relatives to support. In addition, there was a pox on the name of Groucho Marx in broadcasting circles. No radio sponsor would touch him.

As a result, Father had to make still another adjustment in his life. He swallowed his pride, and became a member of the Marx Brothers again. The result was *A Night in Casablanca*, for independent producers David Loew and Charlie Einfeld.

Father, in fact, was on the set at General Service Studios, shooting a scene from *A Night in Casablanca*, the day I finally returned home from the wars. Irene, who'd picked me up at the Union Station, and I stopped off at the studio on our way back to Beverly Hills for a quick, between-takes reunion.

Father and his brothers were ebullient in welcoming the wandering half-Jewish sailor home. Father, especially. He bussed me soundly on both cheeks in the manner of a French General, introduced me to the cast and crew as "Admiral Lord Nelson, who single-handedly won the 'Battle of the Coral Sea,' " and bought me an ice cream bar from the Good Humor truck on the lot.

Seeing Father, the movie star, back in action again before the cameras, firmed my resolve to make a name of my own. It also brought sharply into focus my own precarious position in life—that of being a civilian again, with a wife to support, no job, and little prospect of one. Moreover, all I had in the way of money was three hundred dollars in severance pay, plus what Irene had been able to save during her brief tenure as an assistant sound cutter at Paramount Studios—a job she had taken, as a patriotic gesture, to alleviate the manpower shortage in Hollywood during the war.

Of course, we weren't likely to starve—not as long as I had a father who bought me Good Humors, and Irene hung onto her job. But how long her position at the studio would last was questionable, since she was obligated to turn it back over to the man she replaced whenever he returned from the Army.

There was one bright note. We didn't have to look for a place to live. While I was still overseas, Irene's mother had invited us to share her house with her after the war, along with Donald, Lois, and their brand new baby, Linda. And although I had always been warned by Father that it wasn't a good idea for more than one family to live under the same roof, there was a legitimate excuse for it in our cases. The wartime housing shortage still existed—and would for some time to come.

What better place to live out the housing shortage than Grace Kahn's commodious Mediterranean-style villa in Beverly Hills?

Her house had sixteen rooms, beautiful gardens and a swimming pool, a staff of servants, and the price was right (nothing). On top of that, no in-laws ever got along any better than Don and Lois and Irene and I. So we decided to take Grace's offer, figuring it might be fun, as well as economical, to live communally for a while.

Could I know we'd be there for seven years?

CHAPTER 26

HE
ISN'T
CALLED
GROUCHO
FOR NOTHING

ONCE the euphoria of finally being out of uniform wore off, I knuckled down to achieving my ultimate goal in life—that of trying to impress Father with my accomplishments, both as an author and maker of important money.

But as I quickly discovered, this wasn't going to be easy to accomplish in post-war Hollywood. Already the movie capital was beginning to feel the pinch of the first of many recessions whose cumulative effects over the years have gradually succeeded in turning the City of Easy Money into one long unemployment line. By the time I was back in civies, the outlook for work for young talent trying to break into the film business was anything but promising.

In spite of my previous experience as a gag man for Milton Berle,

I couldn't find a radio job because most of the staff writing berths on shows still on the air had already been filled before I returned from the war. And I couldn't get work in a major film studio because all of them had eliminated their junior writer programs in the economy wave that suddenly hit the town, and no sane studio executive would give a regular script-writing assignment to an author who hadn't first made a reputation as a novelist, playwright or magazine writer. Or who wasn't his son or brother-in-law.

In addition, I had a small reputation to live down—being known as "Groucho's son the tennis player." No one could quite believe that anyone who had once beaten Jack Kramer and who was the champ of the Beverly Hills Tennis Club could be any good with a typewriter. An athlete had to be dumb. That was the role assigned to him in days before Arnold Palmer, Rod Laver and Wilt the Stilt were all making two hundred thousand a year.

Furthermore, I knew I couldn't depend on Father to help get me a job. Not only didn't he own a studio or even run one, but at the time he didn't even have his own radio show on which he could have used me as a gag writer. In addition, he was not the kind of father who would go on his son's behalf to any of his friends who *were* in positions of influence. Perhaps he was inherently shy. Perhaps he was trying to avoid the stigma of nepotism that's always been associated with Hollywood and those who labor therein. Or perhaps he still remembered that day in 1943 when I stood before him in my Coast Guard bell bottoms and defiantly told him I was marrying Irene no matter what he thought, and that he need have no fears about my ability to support her after the war.

Even if he had extended himself, I'm not so sure Father could have persuaded any of his friends to give me a chance. In spite of the ribbing about nepotism Hollywood has taken down through the years, it's always been my experience that friends will go out of their way to *avoid* giving you a job. I remember what one producer told my agent when the latter had tried to get him to hire me. "Sure, I'd like to put him on, but I'm a friend of Groucho's. If Arthur doesn't work out and I have to fire him, it'll be embarrassing."

At any rate, Father didn't volunteer to help when I returned from the wars, and I was too proud to ask him—no matter how desperately I needed the work.

No, I was going to do it entirely on my own, and the hard way—via the free-lance-writer market.

All I wanted from Father was a little encouragement. And that's what I got—a little encouragement. Damn little.

For some reason known only to Father, he was always most eager to put in a discouraging word—just when I needed a lift or a small pat on the back.

For example, soon after I returned from the Philippines I wrote a magazine piece called "The Return of the Sailor." It was a humorous account of what it was like to be an unemployed ex-serviceman, who was hanging around the house all day, cooking, cleaning, and sewing, while his wife was gainfully employed and bringing home the so-called bacon.

Through habit, I let Father read it before I submitted it to a magazine—I was still juvenile enough to need his praise.

"That's a nice little writing exercise, but you certainly don't hope to sell it," was his quick verdict.

Nice little exercise! I'd worked damn hard on it all week, and I wasn't about to have it dismissed so cavalierly.

I put it in an envelope and mailed it off to *Esquire*.

Two weeks later *Esquire* sent me a letter of acceptance, and a check for fifty dollars. Not a fortune, but it was my first sale, and I certainly had a right to be proud and excited. I immediately telephoned Father, figuring he'd be as thrilled about the news as I was.

"Well, you certainly fooled me," was his unenthusiastic reply. "Now what are you going to do about making a living?"

I attributed his lack of enthusiasm to a normal parental reluctance to admit he might have made a mistake by underestimating his offspring's ability—that plus his generally pessimistic and lugubrious attitude toward life. He didn't get the name of Groucho for nothing.

Anyway, what difference did it really make what *he* thought? The editor of *Esquire* liked it, and that was all that mattered.

Nevertheless, I couldn't help being bugged by Father's attitude just a little. I didn't expect fifty dollars to mean anything to him, but a little praise certainly wouldn't have given me a swelled head.

Once I was a published author, I found an agent in Hollywood who was willing to take me on as a client. With my *Esquire* credit as evidence that I wasn't an amateur, he talked Columbia Pictures into letting me do a script for one of their *Blondie & Dagwood* series. My epic was called *Blondie in the Dough*. It was no *Best Years of Our Lives*, but for what it was intended to be—the second half of a double bill—it turned out to be a fairly creditable piece of family entertainment. I got my first screen credit, and both trade papers said it was a "better-than-average" *Blondie*. Faint praise, but not bad for a first effort, and my agent said there was talk of giving me a term contract.

I tried to talk Father into driving down to the Pantages Theater in Hollywood with me, figuring he might like to see a full-length feature with his son's name prominent among the credits, but all he said was "I can wait until it plays the Marquis in Beverly."

He never saw *Blondie in the Dough*, however, and I never got the Columbia contract. This was the incident I mentioned in Chapter One, when Harry Cohn, while carrying on some kind of personal vendetta with Father, had threatened to fire me because I was his son. When the picture turned out well and my boss wanted to hire me to write a second *Blondie*, I figured Cohn would forget his feud with the Marx family. But I was not rehired. A Harry Cohn never forgets.

I wasn't the only writer who suddenly found himself unemployed. Another panic had hit the business—this time over a little monster called TV that was looming up on the horizon as a competitive entertainment force to be reckoned with. Experienced screen writers with a lot more credits than my one measly *Blondie in the Dough* were once again finding it impossible to get assignments. Since some of them were offering to work for half their usual salaries, there was little chance for me at any salary.

I wasn't discouraged. I was still young—only twenty-six. And if there were hazards to being Groucho's son I hadn't counted on, I'd just have to overcome them.

The best way I knew was with my typewriter, so as soon as I checked off the Columbia lot, I set up shop in a gardener's shack in Grace Kahn's backyard.

With a sale to an important magazine like *Esquire* already to my credit, I figured other magazines would automatically snap up every-

thing else I could turn out, and before long I'd be as famous as Somerset Maugham, and Father would be satisfied.

Was I in for a shock!

Over the next year and a half, I sold two more humorous articles —one to *Cosmopolitan*, and the other to *Redbook*—plus a short story to a Canadian magazine, for a total income of nine hundred dollars.

It was progress, but nothing I'd ever become wealthy on.

During this period, I'd get a phone call from Father nearly every evening around six. A typical conversation would go like this.

GROUCHO:	Are you working?
SON OF GROUCHO:	I'm writing a magazine piece.
GROUCHO:	Are you making any money?
SON OF GROUCHO:	Only what I can make selling to magazines.
GROUCHO:	That's a tough racket. Why don't you get out of it and become a director?
SON OF GROUCHO:	I don't want to be a director.
GROUCHO:	That's where all the big money is. And you don't need any talent to be a director. Look at all the schmucks out here who are making five grand a week.
SON OF GROUCHO:	Look. You just don't call up Louis B. Mayer and say, "I'm a schmuck—I want to be a director." It's not that easy.
GROUCHO:	Krasna did it.
SON OF GROUCHO:	Krasna had twenty-five major screen credits behind him —plus an Oscar.
GROUCHO:	(doggedly) If I hadn't told him he could direct, he wouldn't have tried.
SON OF GROUCHO:	(exasperated) Okay, I'll tell you what I'll do. Get me a job as a director for five thousand dollars a week, and I'll take it!
GROUCHO:	Go ahead and be a wise guy. But in the meantime, people like Mervyn LeRoy and Leo McCarey are driving around in Rolls Royces while you're still trying to hack out a meager living on a typewriter.

The dialogue might vary with each of our conversations, but the way I'd feel after being assaulted by Father with a few thousand discouraging and deprecating remarks every evening would always be the same. I'd want to dive off Pasadena's Suicide Bridge.

Irene, who wasn't too fond of Father because of his pejorative attitude, would try to bolster my morale by telling me that we shouldn't let him get us down, that we didn't need anything from him. She no longer had her cutting job at Paramount, but we weren't about to starve, for she was now receiving an income from a small trust fund her father had left to her and her brother, Donald. Besides, Grace was paying the rent and grocery bills, and seemed happy to do so in exchange for not having to live by herself. It seemed like a fair trade—company for security, the way we rationalized it—and she needed us more than ever now that Donald and Lois were moving out.

I was sorry to see my brother- and sister-in-law leave, for they were good company around the house.

Donald, who was struggling to emulate his father's success in the popular song-writing field, and I enjoyed good rapport, for we were both striving to overcome the same problem—that of trying to get out from under the shadow of famous fathers, and make names for ourselves in Hollywood or on Broadway. We had even written a musical comedy together, when we were living under the same roof, and Lois, who had once been a professional vocalist, had made the demo record of the songs to play for potential backers, one of whom was Al Jolson. We never got any backers. Jolson said our show wasn't professional enough for Broadway. He was being kind. We'd all worked hard on the project, however, and that naturally brought the Marxes and the Kahns closer together than most in-laws.

Lois and I were better friends than ever, still keeping each other company when the rest of the Kahns were closeted in Grace's room discussing family business. Occasionally, when Donald was hanging around Hollywood and Vine, trying to peddle his songs to some recording artist, I'd sit with Lois in the nursery, while she was tending her baby, and we'd discuss our mutual problems.

Lois's biggest problem was our mother-in-law, Grace Kahn.

Grace may have been the Perle Mesta of the Beverly Hills Tin Pan Alley crowd, but her relationship with her son and daughter-in-law bore the matriarchal stamp of a Sarah Delano Roosevelt. She tried to dominate certain aspects of her son's personal and professional life, and found fault with many things Lois did—from what she spent on clothes (not very much, since her husband didn't have anything), to inviting her parents over to see their granddaughter without first obtaining permission from the head of the oligarchy.

All these things naturally upset Lois, and as a result there was considerable friction between her and Grace. Eventually this culminated in Lois telling Donald that there would be a divorce if they didn't get a place where they could live their lives the way *they* wanted to. So after two years they found a house they could afford in San Fernando Valley, and they moved out.

With her son, daughter-in-law and granddaughter gone, Grace was more dependent on Irene and me than before, and wouldn't have wanted us to leave even if we could afford it.

Once our own baby, Steve, came along, in 1947, considerable friction began to develop between Irene and Grace, too.

Although placid and mouse-like on the surface, Irene had a behind-the-scenes temper that at times was uncontrollable—especially when her mother criticized her housekeeping ability or how she was raising Steve. With two grown women living under one roof, and each wanting to run things her way, conflict was inevitable. They clashed constantly.

The result of these flare-ups would be that mother and daughter would not speak to each other for weeks on end, and I'd be in the middle—a very uncomfortable middle, for each woman would expect me to side with her.

At some time during these running battles, Irene would announce that we were moving out, and then she'd start phoning real estate agents, or maybe she'd even begin to pack, regardless of whether we had a place to go or not.

I was all in favor of moving, too; it seemed the only way to avoid bloodshed. But in the end, Irene would back down, saying resignedly that it wouldn't be right to leave her mother.

I was easily talked into keeping the *status quo,* too. For it didn't take any mathematical genius to figure out that we'd never be able to afford our own house on the nine hundred dollars a year I was currently making free-lancing the magazine market.

I'd have to stop kidding myself. It was obvious I'd have to get some kind of a steady job, and the only one I knew with the power to give me this was Father's old friend and mine, from the tennis club,

Dore Schary, who had recently replaced Louis B. Mayer as production chief of MGM.

Dore didn't play tennis at the club anymore now that he was head of Metro, and I never could reach him by phone when I called his office, so I wrote him a letter, reminding him of the time he had advised me to go forth into the world and get some experience, and to come back and see him about a job after I had.

I informed Schary that I believed I now had the required experience. I allowed I hadn't spent a great deal of time yet pounding New York's pavements "between the Battery and the Bronx," but to make up for this I pointed out that I had been through one World War, in which I had risked life and limb standing up in front of GIs and passing myself off as a comedian; that I was married; that I was a father; and that I'd had much valuable experience changing diapers and fighting with my wife. I concluded with a short résumé of my professional credits—a season with Berle, my name on a *Blondie,* and some magazine sales to *Esquire, Redbook,* and *Cosmopolitan.*

I mailed my letter off, and never expected to hear from Schary again.

But the Scoutmaster of Culver City fooled me.

About a week later I received a phone call from Dorothy Pratt, the head of MGM's reading department, saying Schary had turned my letter over to her with the recommendation that she hire me.

I immediately assumed it was some kind of a writing job. Instead, she said she'd give me a two-week tryout as a reader, replacing someone who was on vacation. The pay would be sixty-five dollars a week, and I could start immediately.

As desperate as I was for a steady job, I wasn't sure I wanted to settle for being just a reader. After I'd already worked as a screenwriter, it was like taking a giant step backwards. I could make more as a box boy at Ralph's Market.

Nevertheless, after mulling it over for a couple of days, I decided to take Dorothy Pratt's niggardly offer. It made more sense to be making sixty-five dollars a week than to be laying off at two hundred and fifty. Besides, there was always the chance that once I got my foot in the studio door, I could make my true worth felt and eventually be promoted to a better-paying job. My father had bought me a copy of Horatio Alger while I was still in a crib, and I still was a firm believer in its philosophy.

But after I'd passed my two-week trial period and I settled down to the tedium of a regular office job, it slowly dawned on me that the all-American success dream didn't apply to studio readers.

MGM readers were treated like the lowest form of animal life roaming the studio lot—and that included sight-seers, the bootblack who hawked shines throughout the Thalberg Building, and the fellow operating the newsstand.

Readers weren't allowed to enter the lot through the main artists' entrance; we had to punch in and out through a side gate, along with the grips, carpenters and other laborers. We didn't belong to any talent guild; our bargaining agent was the Painters' and Carpenters' Union, Local 805; and nobody respected our opinions.

Ostensibly, readers served an important function. We'd sit in a dingy office for eight hours a day and plow through all the written material that agents submitted to the studio—original screen stories, magazine articles, plays, and novels. After that, we'd synopsize each submission and make written recommendations to producers as to whether or not such material should be considered for movie production.

This took much of the burdensome chore of reading off the producers' shoulders, leaving them free for more important things—like going to the races, and chasing their secretaries and would-be actresses around their offices.

It was a tedious and unrewarding job to read some other author's work of, say, five hundred pages, and then have to boil it down to ten. Not to mention the disservice it was doing to other authors. But what producer had time to read a book or screenplay all the way through and still have any sex life?

The disheartening part of all this was that nobody paid any attention to a reader's recommendations—even though most of the readers I knew were better educated and more qualified judges of story material than the producers. Most of them aspired to be writers themselves, but had never quite made it, for one reason or another. They hung in there, however, hoping in their spare time to turn out a screenplay or novel that would sell and liberate them from their eye-straining bondage.

But few ever did, and even fewer got promoted out of the reading department. I knew one reader who'd been sitting in the same office for twenty years, reading, synopsizing and growing older, and he was still making only a hundred and twelve dollars a week—the highest salary paid a top reader.

If this white-haired old man was a typical example, I had a pretty bleak future ahead of me. Twenty years of reading—most of it dreck—to wind up earning a hundred and twelve dollars a week.

I decided I'd better do something to escape falling into that trap, but fast.

One day during my lunch hour I brought some of my published articles to Pete Smith, who, through his dry wit and distinctive voice, had turned making one-reel comedies into a very lucrative and respected entertainment form. His *Pete Smith Specialties* were frequently more amusing than the features they were on the bill with, and he had a number of Oscars on his desk to prove it.

I told Pete that I thought I could write his *Specialties*, and asked him to read my humorous pieces to see if he agreed with me. He said he'd be glad to, and I sneaked back to my office. I use the term "sneaked," because it was against the rules to try to better yourself if you were a reader, and if Dorothy Pratt thought you were trying to promote a better job on company time, even your lunch hour, you were liable to get the axe.

A couple of days later Pete called me back. He said he liked my comedy-writing style, but that he didn't have a place for me on his staff at the moment. However, he would keep me in mind if he ever needed another writer.

Was he just being polite, or did he really mean it?

On my way back to my office, I bumped into Dore Schary on the lot, and since he couldn't very well avoid this pariah's eye, he stopped for a moment to chat with me.

"Well, kid, how do you like it in the reading department? They tell me you're doing very well."

"I'd rather be a writer," I said. "Can't you get me an assignment?"

But Schary shook his head and said that the only way I'd ever get out of the reading department would be to write something saleable in my spare time.

That shook me up, and that evening after dinner, I sat down to begin work on a novel.

I'd been mulling over an idea for one for about a year, but until I'd gone to work in the black hole of the reading department, I'd never had quite enough confidence to tackle such an onerous, long-term task. But after three months of daily exposure to what other writers were selling, I felt I could do as well, and in some cases, better.

My heart to heart talk with the rabbinical Scoutmaster provided the rest of the incentive, and for that I'll always be grateful.

I already had an idea that Ken McCormick of Doubleday had expressed interest in on my last trip to New York.

During the war I had written a novel called *Hooligan Sailor*—the satirical adventures of an ex-tennis bum in the Coast Guard. It wasn't published, but Bennett Cerf said Random House would have bought it if Marion Hargrove hadn't already beaten me to the book stalls with a comedy novel that was similar in feeling, only about the Army. Concurrently, Ken McCormick had written me that he liked the character of Willie Brown and that I ought to consider writing another book about his adventures but to put him in his natural habitat—the hypocritical world of amateur tennis.

So that I wouldn't procrastinate writing the novel until I, too, was hoary with age, I set myself a schedule for my moonlighting that was so restrictive to a normal social and family life that today I wouldn't dream of attempting the same thing for fear my wife would divorce me.

Irene and I made no social plans for weekday nights. Instead, I locked myself in my study immediately after dinner and remained there chained to the muse of creativity until I had completed my minimum quota of three pages a day. I had decided not to set a higher minimum, for fear I wouldn't be able to stick to it. Besides, three pages a day add up to quite a few at the end of a month's writing—nearly a hundred.

Except on week-ends, when I was free to work on the book during the day (if I chose to give up tennis, which I did for nearly a year), there was no deviating from my nocturnal writing schedule, no matter how tempting the invitation might be, or who asked us over to dinner —even Father, who gets insulted quite easily after a few rebuffs. ("You mean you can't work on that damn book some other night? What difference does it make if you finish it a few days later?")

For a solid year, while all our friends and most of our relatives were beginning to wonder if Irene and I had turned into a couple of hermits, I maintained this schedule.

Sometimes, when Dorothy Pratt wasn't keeping too close an eye on me, I'd be able to sneak in a few pages at the studio, too.

Working an eight-hour day at MGM plus another five or six at home was an exhausting schedule. Every morning I'd wake up with a splitting headache from staying up late the previous night, chain-smoking and straining my eyes, which were already overworked from reading garbage all day at the studio.

Over the long haul of a year, it was hard enough to shake off the normal periods of self-doubt that any creator experiences. Was it worth it? Would any publisher really want to publish it? Was TV, which was just coming in, going to kill off the publishing business to the point where publishers would be afraid to take a chance on unpublished authors? etc., etc., etc.

At the same time I had to contend with regular nightly telephone calls from Father, advising me not to waste my time on a novel that would probably never get published, and to stop being a schmuck and become a director.

Just what I wanted to hear after staying up until four the previous morning, trying to scratch out my daily quota.

Besides having to cope with a father who was trying to undermine my confidence—and sometimes nearly succeeding—I had to contend with a mother who was rapidly turning from just a heavy drinker into as big a drunk as W. C. Fields, only she wasn't as amusing. At sundry times of the day and night—but usually when I was in the throes of writing—I could expect a call from either my mother, who was at some stage of intoxication in her chic Wilshire Boulevard apartment, or from my Grandma Jo, exhorting me to drop whatever I was doing and rush over to Mother's place and see what I could do about sobering her up, or getting her into a sanitarium, or into A.A., or at least off the floor and into bed.

If the calls sounded desperate enough, I very often did have to drop my work to dash over to Mother's apartment, where I'd generally find her bloated, black and blue body crumbled on the floor in a night-gown, with an empty bottle of Scotch beside her.

It was as unsettling as it was sad to see a woman who'd once been as beautiful and vivacious as my mother in this condition, and I did everything I could—from sitting through A.A. meetings with her to chauffeuring her to sanitariums, where I hoped some expert would magically effect a cure—to try to prevent these incidents from repeating themselves.

But it was all in vain.

California laws make it practically impossible to commit anyone with money to a sanitarium against his or her will. No psychiatrist would accept Mother as a patient, claiming she was already too far gone. Private sanitariums wouldn't hold her against her will. And Alcoholics Anonymous refused to become involved until she'd admit to being a drunkard. She never would—even when she was dying of cirrhosis.

Ultimately, I realized that no matter how many S.O.S. calls I got from relatives, I was virtually powerless to do anything about Mother's condition, except worry a lot, and occasionally confiscate her liquor supply, or perhaps send for a doctor to get her on her feet, if only temporarily. So I'd put her out of my mind. Callous as that may seem, it was the only way to preserve my own sanity.

Looking back on that period, with all the distractions I had to contend with, I've often wondered how I ever managed to struggle through to the end of my book. I guess it was the incentive of graduating out of the reading department that spurred me on in my worst moments of self-doubt.

At any rate, there eventually came a time when I typed "The End" on the last page of *The Ordeal of Willie Brown*, and pulled the sheet from the typewriter. My period of enslavement was at an end, I hoped, as I had the whole four hundred pages retyped clean, and eagerly mailed them off to my agents in New York—Edith Haggard and Naomi Burton of Curtis Brown.

When they wrote me back that they liked *Willie Brown* and thought it was saleable, I felt it was safe to give it to Father to read. He'd seemed most interested in knowing what I'd been working on so diligently all those months, and I felt a filial obligation to let him read my manuscript.

Knowing my father, who subsisted on a diet of pure Lardner, Benchley, Kaufman and Perelman, I truthfully didn't expect him to say that *The Ordeal of Willie Brown* was as great as *War and Peace*, or even his own book, *Beds*. But I did expect him to agree with my agents that I'd done a professional job, for a first novel. Whether a publisher would want it or not was strictly up to the gods. But when he finally finished reading the book and summoned me to his house to discuss it, Father remained true to the name of Groucho.

"You want me to be honest, don't you?" he said, glumly, preparing me for the mortal blow he was about to deliver *The Ordeal of Willie Brown*. And then he went into his critique. After all these years, I don't remember what reasons he gave for not liking my book, but I'll never forget the feeling of complete devastation that numbed my sensibilities when he confidently predicted that no publisher could possibly want *Willie Brown* in the amateurish shape it was in, and that I ought to heed his advice and not submit it to anyone before I'd rewritten it completely, according to *his* ideas of what a novel should be, starting from page one.

And it mattered little to him that two such knowledgeable people in the book business as Naomi Burton and Edith Haggard, who handled, among others, Daphne du Maurier, Sinclair Lewis and Ogden Nash, felt otherwise. If I didn't accept his judgment as the Gospel, I was merely deluding myself.

I was in no frame of mind to rewrite the book even if I had agreed with him. But when my wife thought I might be wavering under a cloud of self-doubt, she quietly reminded me that Father had said the same thing about the first piece I sold to *Esquire*, and that it was quite likely he didn't know what he was talking about in this case, either.

Even though I was a grown man, it was difficult for me to stand up to Father in those days, because he was such a forceful personality. At the same time I wasn't going to throw a year's work into the trash because of one person's opinion, and I finally told him so.

"Well, you asked what I thought," he said, sulking a bit as he handed me back my manuscript. "You wouldn't want me to lie about it, just to make you feel good."

Subsequent events made me realize that Father would do just about anything *not* to make me feel good.

Although Doubleday, after much vacillating, including making an offer and then retracting it, eventually turned *Willie* down, the late Jack Goodman, who was running Simon & Schuster at the time, loved the book and sent me a thousand-dollar advance and a publishing contract. He didn't even want much of a rewrite.

Naturally I was overjoyed, and Goodman's enthusiasm for the project confirmed my belief that I'd be foolish ever again to ask Father's opinion of anything I'd written *before* it was accepted for publication or production. I also made up my mind that I wasn't going to rush right to the phone to tell Father that Simon & Schuster had vindicated my own judgment. I was too mature to throw that in his face. I'd play it cool, and wait until the subject came up naturally. It was the only way to treat a kill-joy like Father.

As coincidence would have it, Father phoned me the evening of the day the contracts arrived from Simon & Schuster.

"What's new with you?" he asked. "Are you making any money?"

What a cue for a piece of earth-shaking news.

"Simon and Schuster is taking my book," I said, trying not to sound too smug. "The contracts just arrived today."

Long pause. "Really? That's wonderful! You must be very excited."

"Oh, I am."

"Well, don't get too excited. Just remember—thousands of books are published every year by authors who are starving to death."

CHAPTER 27

DON'T BE
A SCHMUCK—
PLAY TENNIS
WITH JACK WARNER

I WASN'T naive enough to believe that simply because Simon & Schuster was publishing my book, I'd become independently wealthy overnight. But getting a first novel published is a prestigious event in the life of any author, and I felt there was a good chance I'd at least reap some of the residual benefits of publication—a movie sale, or some magazine assignments, or maybe my agent could get me a film writing job.

However, as the new year, 1950, began, I had to think seriously about what I was going to do to make a living until publication date, which was probably a year off. I no longer had my paltry reader's salary. Shortly before Christmas—while I was anxiously waiting for some publisher to take my book—I had been laid off in a sweeping economy wave that swept only me out of the reading department. It was all very mysterious and Kafka-like, and nobody, including Dore Schary, could give me a satisfactory explanation as to the reason *I* was being let go while at the same time they had just hired two new readers.

Any three-year-old would know it had to be something personal, and at first I felt it was because a very petty minor executive who was Dorothy Pratt's immediate superior and the department's hatchet man had heard via the reader's grapevine that I'd written a novel—and he was convinced I'd done it on studio time; he'd implied as much to me. But at the same time I've always had a hunch that my position at the studio wasn't particularly strengthened by a run-in Father had with Dore Schary and his wife about a month before my dismissal.

Father had just recently terminated his second marriage, and he was celebrating the occasion by spending the week-end at Alisol Dude Ranch, outside of Santa Barbara, with one of his string of available single girls. Her name is unimportant, but she was in her early twenties, Gentile, and, in a bikini, quite an eyeful.

The Scharys were also spending the week-end at Alisol, and whenever the four of them would get together around the pool, Miriam Schary would eye Father and his roommate rather critically. For three days she seemed to be dying to say something about it, but reserved comment until one afternoon when Father's girlfriend left him for a moment to go inside their bungalow to change into a dry swimming suit.

As soon as the girl was out of earshot, Miriam leaned over to Father and said, "Groucho, can't you keep your hands off those young *shiksas?*"

Father eyed Miriam Schary rather balefully, and then replied, "And can't you mind your own fucking business?"

Father himself told me about this incident. He told it to me one evening at the dinner table, shortly after he had bawled me out for not playing the Hollywood social game to further my career.

Father, of course, can't be faulted for reacting the way he did. It really *was* none of Miriam Schary's business, and he was certainly justified in telling her so, whether his son was employed at her husband's studio or not. I just mention the incident to illustrate one of the dangers of having a father so firmly established in his business that he doesn't have to worry about what he's saying or to whom he's saying it.

In this case, if Father's choleric retort was in any way responsible for my abrupt dismissal from MGM's reading department I will always be grateful to him for it, because everything lucky started to break for me immediately after I picked up my last paycheck.

Simon & Schuster accepted my book, and a few months later Pete Smith (who had his own unit and was completely autonomous) gave me a job as his staff writer, at the princely salary of $250 a week.

I was now good enough to enter MGM through the same entrance that Liz Taylor and Clark Gable used, and to eat lunch at the writers' table in the commissary.

Over the next year and a half I wrote a dozen *Pete Smith Specialties*. It was a fun job, and Pete taught me a good deal about comedy writing.

One of the most valuable lessons I learned from Pete was the importance of "audience identification" when choosing the subject you want to be funny about. "Don't try to be too esoteric or clever," he warned me. "Write about something the audience can understand without a lot of explanation—like children, or a husband and wife's most annoying habits, like always stepping into a pail of water your wife always forgets to put away, or your mother-in-law, or household appliances, or always getting behind the guy in line at the bank with the most complicated transactions."

A classic example of audience identification was a *Pete Smith Specialty* called *Movie Pests*. In this little gem (which I had nothing to do with), Pete satirized all the people you come across in a movie theater who annoy you: the six-foot, two-hundred-and-fifty-pounder who crawls across your knees and blocks your vision at the most important point in the picture; the kid who sits behind you and kicks your seat; the slob who never stops eating and continually rattles his popcorn bag and candy wrappers; the woman who has to explain the plot to her companion; etc., etc.

What made this short the epitome of audience identification was the fact that, simultaneous with the action on the screen, you in the theater were being annoyed by those same movie pests in the seats all around you.

As much as I enjoyed working for Pete Smith, there finally came a time, as it must to all people in creative endeavors, when I couldn't write another prat-fall or mother-in-law joke without wanting to retch. I had to move on to bigger things.

Clever as a writer had to be to please Pete Smith, he didn't engender much respect from other creative people on the lot. To the big-name feature writers—Dick Brooks, Isobel Lennert, Leonard Spigelgass—who pontificated at the writers' table in the commissary every lunchtime, I was still just a guy who knocked out "one-reelers."

Not surprisingly, my feeling of dissatisfaction over my lowly status overtook me about the same time *The Ordeal of Willie Brown* reached the bookstores. In my ecstasy of seeing my first novel in print all done up in bright yellow cover, with my name prominent under the title (and only a very small mention of who I was "son of" inside the dust jacket)—I could envision a much more lucrative and glamorous life ahead of me than the one I was presently leading.

When I received my author's copies, I autographed one and presented it to Father, who read it again and allowed that he now saw a lot of good things in it. I must have changed it, he said. This was after a number of his writer friends—Nunnally Johnson, Arthur Sheekman, and Billy Wilder—all phoned him up and told him how much they had enjoyed his son's book.

But he had been right about one thing. The book was having a disappointing sale, in spite of a number of pretty good reviews, and my frequent appearances at Book and Author luncheons and on local radio and TV shows.

The speeches I made at Book and Author luncheons, in fact, were a big hit among the ladies. I got more laughs at my book-plugging appearances than an author who wasn't a performer had a right to expect —especially when I related how I'd written a book expressly for the purpose of making a name for myself so I wouldn't have to be known as Groucho's son all my life, and what did I find on the program card of my first luncheon? The misprint I mentioned earlier:

THE ORDEAL OF GROUCHO MARX
by Willie Brown

Laughs I got, but at the end of these luncheons, when the speeches were over and the books were put up for sale, there was no great rush on the ladies' part to buy *The Ordeal of Willie Brown*. If my section of the book-selling table was approached at all, it was usually to inquire if my father was really as funny at home as he was on his new television quiz show, *You Bet Your Life*, which had suddenly turned into a nationwide sensation. And did he *really* ad lib all those funny lines or did he *secretly* have writers?

When I'd get home from one of these affairs, weary from answering three or four hundred questions about Groucho and his brothers, but not having sold a great many books, I'd be damn discouraged. Also curious about what was lacking in my book-selling charisma. Why did they laugh at my jokes, but not want to buy *my* books? It certainly had a nice cover. (Pete Smith could have told me. A book about a tennis bum had no audience identification, especially to the group of establishment ladies attending those luncheons.)

During my moments of despair, when it was obvious I'd have to go on knocking out *Pete Smith Specialties* if I hoped to keep my income at least equal with my wife's trust fund money, I had to field more phone calls from Father.

"How's the book selling?" he'd ask, as though he didn't know from looking at the best seller lists that *From Here to Eternity* and *Caine Mutiny* were doing better.

"Fair," I'd lie, trying to save face.

"You ought to get out and plug it," he'd say. "It's not going to sell if you just sit at home."

Plug it? I could have killed him.

I'd spent every minute Pete Smith would give me off from the studio plugging it, including appearing on a TV show with a chimpanzee, who was photographed with a tennis racket, reading my book. (Did Somerset Maugham or Ernest Hemingway ever do as much for the cause?)

"I'm doing everything I can," I'd reply, curbing a desire to blast him off, but not really daring to because I was still hoping he'd give *Willie* a decent plug on his quiz show. He'd mentioned it once, in kind of a half-hearted way that was so casual the audience thought he was referring to a bottle of Brown's Celery Tonic.

"Why don't you sell it for a movie?" he'd then ask.

Sell it for a movie!!!

My agent—Nat Goldstone, who was the hottest literary agent in Hollywood at the time—had been trying to sell it to a studio since before it was in galley form. But studios were wary of stories about tennis players, and still are. Just count the amount of films about tennis players made in the last twenty years—none.

So I'd tell him all that.

"Agents don't sell stories," he'd say. "You have to get in there and do it yourself. Play the Hollywood social game. Don't be a schmuck. Take advantage of your tennis. Sell it to Jack Warner between sets. All the producers want to play tennis with someone as good as you."

It was true. They wanted to play tennis with me but nobody took me very seriously as a novelist. My reputation as "Groucho's son the tennis player" was still hounding me.

Nevertheless, I decided to take Father's advice and try to sell *Willie* the Hollywood way.

Ever since he had once been my doubles partner at the Tennis Club, Jack Warner had been after me to play up at his court on Sunday afternoons. Lunch was included in the invitations, so I figured, what could I lose but a couple of Sundays?

In addition to me, Warner would invite about ten other top tournament tennis players up to his court, and because he was so lousy, we'd all take turns having him for a doubles partner. Then after we'd nearly gotten coronaries trying to cover the court for Jack, who generally stood in one spot and made derisive remarks about his guests, we'd have what was laughingly referred to as lunch at Jack Warner's.

Warner would sit regally at a beautifully set table under the lanai, while a butler served him a New York steak, French-fried potatoes and a Caesar salad. We tennis players would be treated to moldy salami and Gentile rye bread. In addition, we were expected to laugh raucously at Warner's bum jokes and atrocious puns, of which he seemed to have an endless supply.

What was worse, he never stopped talking about himself long enough to give me an opening to try to sell him my book. Once, when he was choking on a piece of steak, I quickly mentioned to him that I

had written a novel about a tennis player that would make a good
movie. I figured if he couldn't talk he'd have to listen. But when he
finally cleared his windpipe, he merely said, "If people want to look at
tennis, they can go to Forest Hills," and he never even asked to read
Willie.

It was as if he refused to believe a man with my serve could have
possibly written a book—that I was hallucinating or something.

After several Sundays at Warner's, I finally decided I'd rather
continue working for Pete Smith forever than have to play the "Hollywood Social Game" with movie moguls who ate steak while their servants threw salami to the peasants who were their doubles partners.

But the gods repaid me in full for refusing to lead a sycophantic
existence by getting me my first big break in the magazine business.

One afternoon when I was thinking that it really hadn't been
much of a boon to my career to get a book published, the phone rang in
my office at the studio, and a secretary on the other end of the line said,
"Just a minute, please, for Ted Strauss."

Ted Strauss introduced himself as the West Coast Editor of *Collier's*, and said he was wondering if I'd be interested in writing a piece
about my father. They'd pay me seven hundred and fifty dollars.

It was twice the amount I'd ever received for a single magazine
piece before, almost as much as I would probably make from the publication of *Willie Brown*, and the equivalent of three weeks salary writing *Pete Smith Specialties.*

Nevertheless, my immediate reaction was to say "No." I thanked
Strauss but said I'd spent most of my life trying to avoid being known
as the son of Groucho so people wouldn't accuse me of trading in on
my father's name, and I didn't think I ought to change my policy now.

But Strauss begged me to reconsider. He said Father was very hot
copy as a result of the success of *You Bet Your Life*, and he felt a piece
written from his son's angle would have a wide audience appeal.

"Look at it this way," he continued. "Who else but you could
write this particular piece? You're not only his son, but you're a professional writer."

I told him that flattery would get him nowhere, but that on second
thought I would do the piece.

I had an ulterior motive. I figured that if *Collier's* liked the job I did on Father, they might throw other assignments my way. And even if nothing else came of it, I'd at least have picked up seven hundred and fifty bucks for a few nights' work.

Besides, I was sure I could write a better, more revealing article about Father than anyone else, for the obvious reason that no other writer knew, or was likely to find out, the things I already knew about him *without* an interview.

When being interviewed by the average newspaperman or magazine writer, Father can be terribly witty, knowledgeable, and incisive in his observations on the world scene. If his Boswell also happens to be a girl with big breasts and nice legs, he'll be exceptionally charming, and she can be certain he'll get off some clever innuendos about sex, and a number of quotable wisecracks on the hopelessness of any two people living happily together as man and wife. ("Marriage is the chief cause of divorce." "The trouble with marriage is you have to marry a woman—the last person in the world you could possibly have anything in common with.") Chances are, he'll even try to get a date with his lady biographer.

But it would take a Jack Anderson, or at the very least, a superspy equipped with a whole bagful of sophisticated bugging equipment to worm anything out of Father but the most superficial information about his personal life. Groucho the performer just doesn't believe the public has a right to know anything about Groucho the human being.

In his autobiography, *Groucho and Me*, Father divulges less about himself than you could learn by looking up "Groucho" in *The World Almanac* or *Who's Who?* In fact, in Chapter 22 he admits receiving the following note of chastisement from his publisher:

"Up until now you've written 80,000 words and your readers still don't know a damn thing about you."

At his publisher's insistence, he then confesses to being the father of three children; he also admits he has a wife. But except for a few lines about my tennis career, and a plethora of anecdotes illustrating Melinda's precocity as a moppet, you wouldn't know he had a family, a sex life or any other normal emotions. You couldn't even find a picture of Miriam or me in the book, although there were five of him and Melinda.

That's the kind of fellow Father is. He'd rather have a smart wisecrack attributed to him than a kind word or a humanistic deed. As I wrote somewhere earlier, the real Groucho persists in hiding behind a smoke screen of jokes.

I'm not knocking him for that. Most actors live in a world of illusion. Few will own up to their correct ages (even to themselves), or reveal anything about their lives that might detract from their superstar images, even though it might be of interest to readers or theatrical historians. I'm just pointing out that very little of what you read about a celebrity in print bears any resemblance to the truth.

Bernard Shaw once said, "No man is bad enough or good enough to tell the truth about himself during his lifetime." That certainly applies to Father. And it may even apply to me, though I'm at least not denying I have a father named Groucho.

At any rate, I didn't set out to do a hatchet job on Father for *Collier's*. I just wanted to show him as he actually was—amusing, eccentric, lovable, difficult, impossible, and completely unpredictable. At the same time I wanted to be informative. Plenty of things had happened in Father's life since he'd last been the subject of an important magazine article.

An important change was his divorce from Kay. After five years of marriage, and one daughter—Melinda—he and Kay had agreed to a divorce in 1950. It was an amicable parting, for they were both still fond of each other. But the disparity in ages, plus an enormous difference in temperaments, made it impossible for them to live together harmoniously. Highly neurotic and emotional, Kay was given to hysterics and childish temper tantrums when she couldn't cope with Father's dictatorial ways in a more rational manner. Father, on the other hand, was as peace-loving as he was difficult. Result: many arguments and door-slamming exits.

In addition, Kay was, if we can believe there is such a thing, a "night person." She liked to stay up all night and sleep most of the day. This was completely the opposite of the way Father wanted to live.

"I never see her," he used to complain. "When I'm awake she's asleep, and when she's awake, she's always washing her hair. I might as well be single."

The denouement to this pair of star-cross'd lovers' stormy life together occurred as a result of an argument they had one night at the dinner table. Kay, in a fit of pique over the fact that Father insisted on Miriam spending her summer vacation in their house, hurled a filled, sterling-silver gravy boat at him.

She was wide of her mark, giving Father the opening to retort with the perfect curtain line to their marriage. "When I asked you to pass the gravy," he said, standing and preparing to walk out on her, "I wasn't talking about a *forward* pass."

The divorce settlement itself was amicably arrived at. Father got to keep the house he bought after Melinda was born, and though Kay was given official custody of Melinda, Melinda did most of her living with Father, since Kay was busy traveling. Eventually he got official custody, and Melinda moved in permanently.

Father said he'd never get married again. Twice was enough for any man. And this time he sounded as if he meant it.

The other change in Father's life involved his career.

Following *A Night in Casablanca*, he'd appeared in three bomb pictures in a row, all *without* his brothers—*Copacabana, A Girl in Every Port*, and *Double Dynamite*. He co-starred with Jane Russell and Frank Sinatra in *Double Dynamite*—a picture that nearly succeeded in finishing off all three of their movie careers, to say nothing of RKO, the studio that released it.

Howard Hughes was running RKO at the time, and Father's always held him responsible for the picture's failure, because it was Hughes who insisted on naming it *Double Dynamite. Double Dynamite* had nothing to do with the story, but Hughes felt it was a clever way of alluding to Jane Russell's big boobs, and thereby capitalizing on them at the box office without having censor trouble. "With thinking like that, it's no wonder Hughes is just a billionaire," Father complained bitterly. "He'd have to be a billionaire, otherwise how could he make a living?"

In addition to appearing in bad movies, Father was also doing guests shots on radio for just about any show that would have him.

He couldn't get a sponsor of his own, however, until he made an appearance one night with Bob Hope on a program called *The Walgreen Show*—a once a year radio special sponsored by Walgreen Drugstores, and produced by Mannie Manheim, my first boss.

During a sketch with Hope, Father suddenly started ad-libbing.

Hope joined in. The pace became faster and dirtier, and to the producer's dismay, the two comics literally threw away their scripts and started making up their own dialogue.

But the sketch was hilariously funny, and it had the audience in the aisles.

Watching from backstage that evening was a man named John Guedel, who specialized in producing game and audience-participation shows, and who was responsible for a good deal of Art Linkletter's success. Linkletter, in fact, was also appearing on *The Walgreen Show*, which was the reason for Guedel's being there in the first place.

Guedel was impressed with Father's ad-libbing ability, and asked him if he'd be interested in doing a quiz show. "That way you can take advantage of your ad-libbing ability, and you won't have to be confined to a script."

At first Father felt it would be a come down for the former Toast of Broadway to be a lowly quizmaster—like Phil Baker on *Take It or Leave It*. But having no better irons in the theatrical fire, he decided he'd try it.

What could he lose but a few hours of his time, and his reputation as a sophisticated comedian among the people he most respected— George Kaufman and himself?

Nobody in the business expected *You Bet Your Life* to be the success it turned out to be. In fact, for many months Guedel couldn't even get a sponsor—in spite of the fact that the show was budgeted at a paltry $7500 per week, including Father's salary. A real bargain when you consider that one segment of a thirty-minute TV comedy today runs in the neighborhood of $200,000.

Eventually the Elgin-American Compact Company rose to the bait, and agreed to sponsor the show for one season.

Overnight *You Bet Your Life* caught on. Furthermore, it sold so many compacts that the sponsor took advantage of a small-print option clause in his contract to take the show off the air in May rather than wait for June, the accepted time for the summer break, because he had no more compacts left to sell.

All the wise guys around Vine Street thought the show had been cancelled, and that Groucho had flopped again. But the sponsor was merely being thrifty, figuring why should he advertise if he had no more product left to sell?

Elgin-American picked up *You Bet Your Life* for the entire next season, and Father was suddenly a hotter item in show business than he'd ever been before—and making more money.

His impudent brand of insult humor had finally found a radio audience. People *loved* to be insulted, he discovered. Even off the air, when they weren't getting money for it.

Father had bought a new house in Beverly Hills around the birth of his new success, and one morning, when he was standing on the stoop, supervising the painting of the front door, a middle-aged married couple alighted from a car at the curb, and approached him timorously.

"Groucho, this is my wife, Matilda," began the gray-haired gentleman. "Matilda's just dying for you to say something insulting to her."

"You ought to be ashamed of yourself," Father scolded the husband. "With a wife like that, it should be easy to think of your own insults."

The remarkable part of the quiz show's success was how easily it converted to television when the new medium came in strong at the beginning of the fifties. No additional sets were required. All Guedel's production staff had to do was set up cameras and film the radio broadcast.

Other radio shows of stature—Jack Benny's, for example—couldn't switch over to television so easily or inexpensively. Sketch comedy not only required sets, but more writers, because it takes longer to write visual scenes than just dialogue. And in addition, dialogue had to be memorized. So while many of those starring in high-rated radio shows delayed tackling the new medium, Father was already a hit on TV and radio simultaneously.

It was enough to make even a pessimistic soul like Father believe there was a Santa Claus.

And if nothing else, it proved his contention that he could be just as funny without a black mustache and comedy clothes.

When I finished writing the article about him and turned it into *Collier's*, the editors were so delighted with it that they sent me a check for fifteen hundred dollars instead of the agreed upon seven-fifty. They felt I deserved a bonus.

Even then I debated about showing the piece to Father before publication, but since it would be necessary to have his cooperation if we expected to feature him in the picture layout, I had no choice but to let him read it.

I didn't expect him to object to any of the material. I'd done a humanistic piece on him, showing Groucho as an eccentric but lovable, if sometimes misunderstood, martinet around the house, and a doting parent and good provider. In appraising his talents, I'd been as laudatory as I could without seeming unduly prejudiced for a son.

In spite of the kindly way I treated Father in my *Collier's* article, I never dreamed I'd be lucky enough to escape without making substantial revisions in the text to please him. But Father did a complete turnabout.

"It's quite good," he admitted, handing the manuscript back to me with just a few minor pencil notations in the margin. "It's not full of that cliché formula Groucho banter everyone thinks is me. I don't come off as a caricature."

It had been a long uphill battle, but as I left Father's house that day, with most of my manuscript intact, I truly believed I'd finally impressed him with my ability. From now on, I thought, maybe he'll treat me with a little more respect.

But I still didn't know Father very well.

A few days later I phoned him to say that *Collier's* had assigned Bob Landry—one of the really fine photographers in the business—to do the picture layout, and that he wanted to know when he could come over to the house for a photo session with Father, me and Melinda. Landry would need a couple of hours, I explained, because the pictures were to be in color, and he thought he could get better quality with regular studio lights instead of a strobe.

"I'll give him fifteen minutes," barked Father. "Those guys never use half the pictures they take, anyway."

Landry, who was already suffering from a bad case of stomach ulcers from dealing with temperamental talent, went white when he heard about the time limit imposed by Father. He said he couldn't even get his lights set up in fifteen minutes.

But Father stuck to his intransigent attitude when I relayed Landry's message back to him. He abhors picture-taking sessions, and could not be persuaded to be any more cooperative, even when I pointed out that it was his own son he'd be helping.

Because he couldn't afford to give up the assignment, Landry finally settled for snapping just a few informal poses of Father, me and Melinda around the house with his strobe.

The quality of the pictures wasn't up to Landry's usually fine standard, but fortunately the big-whigs at *Collier's* didn't hold it against me. They immediately assigned me to write pieces on other West Coast personalities and institutions—at $1250 a shot, which was more than they started the other writers at.

At those prices I couldn't afford to keep on working for Pete Smith, so I walked into his office one day and informed him I was quitting, as much as I enjoyed him as a boss.

"I figured you would," he said, reaching for one of the many pill bottles that were lined up like toy soldiers on his desk and popping a tranquilizer into his mouth. "Everyone does, after I give them a start." And then he reeled off several important names in the business, including George Sydney and John Huston.

For several years after quitting MGM, I wrote almost exclusively for *Collier's*, on assignment. Between stints for them, I also free-lanced a few humorous articles to *Redbook*, *Good Housekeeping*, *Women's Home Companion* and *Saga*.

After I'd been with *Collier's* for about a year, the Eastern editors prevailed upon me to ghost a piece for Father, called "What I Told Lippy About Baseball."

It was to be in the form of a letter from Father, a fan and armchair baseball strategist, to Leo Durocher, pointing out the various managerial mistakes he had made the previous season which had resulted in his team's blowing the pennant, and advising him how to win the flag in the race ahead.

The whole idea of ghosting a piece for anyone—particularly Father—was anathema to me, but since the editors felt the article would lose some of its punch if it didn't look as if it had come from Father's

pen alone, I acceded to their wishes and agreed to be a ghost this once
—especially after they upped my usual price.

When I completed the article and turned it in, *Collier's* offered to
fly Father and me to the Giants' spring training camp in Phoenix for a
couple of days, so Father could pose for an action picture layout with
Durocher and a few of his stars, including Willie Mays and Sal Maglie.
He would, of course, be expected to pose in a Giant uniform.

Father agreed. If he's feeling well, he will go anywhere or do anything for a free trip. Or for a free anything, for that matter. Ditto most
actors. They rarely pay for anything out of pocket, from refrigerators
and clothes to trips to Europe and expensive automobiles, which is the
reason most stars have the first dollar they ever made, while the rest of
us suckers have to struggle to sock a few dollars away in the bank.

A typical example: Last year, I was notified by letter that *The
Chic Life*, a play that I had written with Bob Fisher, had won the Straw
Hat Award for the best new play of the 1970 summer stock season.
The award ceremony was to take place at the Fabergé Town House in
New York City, and Cary Grant was to hand out the awards. Would
we please be there—and on time?

I was honored, but nevertheless not anxious to spend a thousand
dollars to fly back East just to have my hand shaken by Cary Grant, a
lovely fellow, but I'd shaken hands with him before. I immediately got
off a letter to the Awards Committee, asking them if they would pay
my way. I figured Fabergé could afford it. The answer came back negative—they didn't have the money for that sort of thing, but of course,
my own vanity eventually got the better of me, and I ended up paying
my own plane fare, and my wife's. Also, our poodle's, because we had
no one to leave him with.

None of which I'd be bleating about if Fabergé had given the actors and actresses who were picking up awards the same treatment. But
during the cocktail hour before the ceremony, I happened to be talking
with Audra Lindley, who was there to pick up the "Best Actress"
award—for a role she played in *our* play, incidentally. After I'd con-
gratulated her, Audra said, "It was nice of Fabergé to give us all a free
vacation in New York, wasn't it?"

"They paid your way?"

"They paid everyone's—even Kathy's."

The "Kathy" she was referring to was Kathleen Miller, who won the award for "Best Newcomer," also in *our* play.

So everybody got free rides except the authors.

To top it off, *The New York Times*'s account of the awards neglected to mention that *The Chic Life* had won the "Best Play" honors.

Oh, well, that's show biz—and the difference between the way actors and writers are treated.

Though the free trip to Phoenix had to be an important consideration, Father greatly admired Durocher, enjoyed his company, and he was dying to see some of the Giants' spring training games. Besides, what better way for a ball fan to spend a vacation?

Nevertheless, when we arrived on the playing field at the ball park in Phoenix for the picture-taking session, Father suddenly announced he would not put on a Giant uniform. The weather was too hot to bother with all that paraphernalia, he said, and he was tired from the previous day's plane trip.

"The pictures will be just as good if I wear street clothes," was his final pronouncement.

I urged him to reconsider, for not only would he ruin the picture layout by not posing in a uniform, but he would be jeopardizing my position with *Collier's*. I also reminded him that my bosses were footing all the bills for his little junket.

"Who cares?" he said. "I don't need anybody to pay my way to Phoenix. I can afford my own fare."

Bob Landry, again paling the color of newly fallen snow, took me aside and asked me if there wasn't something I could do to persuade Father to change his mind. He couldn't go back to *Collier's* without a layout, and the pictures just wouldn't be amusing if Father weren't in the garb of a New York Giant.

I relayed all this to Father, who retorted promptly, "Maybe tomorrow. I'll see how I feel."

But Landry couldn't put it off another day; he had to fly to Chicago to photograph another celebrity.

As the three of us stood by home plate, having reached a veritable impasse, Durocher came up out of the dugout with a Giant uniform in his arms.

"What's the rhubarb?" he asked.

I explained to him that Father refused to pose in uniform.

"Why the hell not?" asked Durocher, who was aware of the importance of publicity—even to a baseball manager.

"I'm tired," explained Father. "I didn't sleep very well last night."

"Don't be a fucking prima donna, Groucho," railed Durocher, hurling the uniform, complete with heavy cleated shoes, into Father's arms. "Now go downstairs to the locker room and put that outfit on. And if you don't have it on in five minutes I'll come down there and personally put it on you."

Father looked at Durocher in shock, then replied weakly, "Okay, but I'm not wearing the spiked shoes."

"You're wearing the whole thing, including the aluminum jock," said Durocher. "Landry didn't come all the way to Phoenix to photograph you in that lousy Eddie Schmidt suit."

Father not only put on the shoes, but he was as meek as Caspar Milquetoast for the rest of the afternoon. He posed for every baseball set-up Durocher and Landry could devise, no matter how arduous, and this included one where he had to slide into homeplate head first.

Durocher taught me a valuable lesson in the art of handling Father that afternoon. He's a bully, and if you don't bully him right back, he'll trample all over you.

It was a lesson that was to prove valuable to me through the really difficult times with Father I still had facing me.

CHAPTER 28

NEVER TRUST YOUR FATHER

IRENE and I were still living in my mother-in-law's house when our second son, Andy, checked into this world at Cedars of Lebanon Hospital one morning in 1951, weighing a record eleven and a half pounds (I'd finally outdone Father at something).

A combination of guilt about leaving her mother on Irene's part, and inertia plus frugality on my part, had kept us continually procrastinating about leaving the place that had been our only home since we'd been married. And we probably would have gone on living with Grace for the rest of our lives if fate hadn't stepped in and forced us to make a change.

A few weeks after Andy was born, Irene had a nervous break-down. Her illness—diagnosed as schizophrenia—came on without warning, and nobody discovered the exact cause of it. But Doctor George Wayne, who was responsible for Irene's eventual return from her schizophrenic never-never land, hinted strongly that her reluctance to move out of her mother's home, combined with an understandable desire to have a place of her own, might have caused the breakdown. And he tactfully suggested that we find our own house as soon as Irene was fully recovered.

We could almost afford our own house now that I had a regular income from *Collier's*, so as soon as Irene was well enough to run her own establishment we bought a small bungalow in Pacific Palisades, and immediately proceeded to become one of those typical all-American families you see in a television series: young father, struggling to keep up with the Joneses; community-involved housewife, who screams at the children a lot; one kid with no cavities, and the other with no teeth; a Collie that looked like Lassie (only she wasn't making any money); a garage full of bicycles, toys and other things too un-sightly to keep in the house; and two medium-priced cars with scratched fenders, and a box of Kleenex in the back seat. We even did our own gardening.

One thing we didn't have a great deal of was living room furni-ture. That, plus some badly needed decorating, would have to wait until our ship came in. So far only a small tug had tied up.

Our ship came from an unexpected direction.

Jack Goodman flew out to the Coast early in 1953, and over lunch asked me to write a full-length biography of Father for Simon & Schuster.

On first impulse, I turned him down, for the same reason I once shunned Ted Strauss's offer to profile Father for *Collier's*—I didn't want people to think I could only write about my father.

"Once I might have agreed with you," argued Goodman, "but now, between *Willie* and your *Collier's* articles, you've already proven you can write about other things, so how can it hurt you? And you might make some money."

Between his persuasiveness, and the fact that a novel I'd been fool-ing around with in my spare time wasn't really panning out, I finally consented to write the book. At least it was a definite committment, with a contract and an advance—$2000.

That evening I phoned Father and told him I had contracted to write a book about him.

"You probably won't make any money on it," he said. "Why waste your time—just to have your name on another book?"

Despite his lack of enthusiasm, Father was extremely cooperative with me during the many months it took to commit his life to paper. He didn't have anything to do with the actual writing—even the foot-notes that were signed "Groucho" and were allegedly his humorous comments on what I was revealing about him were entirely my own work—and he never saw a single page of copy until I'd finished the whole thing.

I'd go to him, however, if I were in need of a bright quote, or per-haps a piece of factual material about his or his brothers' early lives with which I wasn't totally familiar.

During *Life with Groucho*'s gestation period Irene and I would usually dine with Father a couple of times a week at his house. At these get-togethers he'd often relate a funny anecdote I'd never heard before, or drop a piece of character-revealing information that would be good for the book. Sometimes his candor would surprise even me, and shock my wife, who was a bit of a prude.

One evening, when the two of us were having dinner with him and one of his numerous lady friends, I happened to mention to Father that I'd written a passage about his first marriage in my book that after-noon.

"What'd you write about me?" he asked suspiciously.

"I said you were a very good father, and a faithful husband," I re-plied.

"That's not true," he corrected me swiftly, almost proudly. "I was a *good* husband, but never a faithful one. I cheated on your mother all the time."

When I expressed surprise that he had been unfaithful to her even in the early days of their marriage, he got up from the table, and es-corted the three of us into the playroom and over to a wall on which hung a large framed picture of the cast of *Coconuts*, taken in Denver, when the show had played there in 1927.

"See that little cutie," he said, pointing the tip of his cigar at a pulchritudinous blonde, dressed in the garb of a Roaring Twenties flapper, standing in the back row of the photograph with some other ladies of the chorus. "She was *my* girl."

I'd never accuse Father of being a Reverend Davidson. But it was puzzling to me how he could equate being a "good husband" with one who cheated on his wife "all the time" and from the beginning of his marriage.

It was just as well that he was single with that attitude, for he certainly wasn't capable of maintaining a relationship with any member of the opposite sex—in marriage, anyway. He was a man's man, preferring the company of Norman Krasna, Arthur Sheekman, or any other of his male friends.

"What can a man possibly have in common with a girl once you're not in the hay?" he often would exclaim. "And you don't have to get married for that!"

Just what a Gloria Steinem or a Germaine Greer would like to hear.

"Anyone who gets married a second time doesn't deserve to have lost his first wife" was one of his favorite quotes from a long-forgotten vaudeville monologist out of his past.

Paraphrasing it to fit his own circumstances, he used to say, "And anyone who marries a third time doesn't deserve anything at all, which is exactly what he'll wind up with." He sounded sincere, anyway.

Since there was an abundance of material on this one subject alone, I devoted almost a third of the book to Father's bachelorhood, his experiences as a Don Juan, and his espousals that he was content to live out his life as a single man.

One of my favorite stories concerned Father and Melinda and a couple of bit-part actresses who doubled as hookers on week-ends.

Melinda was six, but because she loved to horseback ride, Father often took her to the Alisol Dude Ranch in Santa Barbara for the weekend. One Saturday, according to some pre-arranged plans, Irwin Allen, a close friend of Father's, brought the two actresses up to the ranch for him and Father to play with when Melinda was out horseback riding. Allen arrived at the ranch a few hours after Melinda and

Father had checked in, and knocked on Father's bungalow door. At the sound of the knock, Melinda raced for the door and opened it.

Seeing Allen with two stalwart, vacuum-faced blondes, Melinda quickly turned to Father and asked, knowledgeably, "Which one is yours, Daddy?"

So how else could a six-year-old find out about sex in those unenlightened days before Doctor Reuben?

Between his second and third marriages Father was a good bet for hostesses with single women on their hands. Often this resulted in some unlikely pairings.

The hostess of a party once prevailed upon Father to squire Clare Booth Luce, who was then Ambassador to Italy, to her home in Bel Air.

Under ideal weather conditions, Father's always had a difficult time finding his way around Bel Air, which isn't laid out very geometrically or sensibly. But it was extremely foggy the night he was chauffeuring Mrs. Luce to the festivities, and soon after he drove through the main gate of Bel Air, he and the Ambassador were lost.

He and Mrs. Luce finally had to get out of the car and fight their way through some dense shrubbery in order to find a street sign. As the pair emerged from a thicket of oleander at the corner of Stone Canyon and Capriccio Drive, they found themselves face to face with Charlie Brackett, who was out taking his nightly constitutional.

"Well," quipped the writer, eying them speculatively. "I never thought the day would come when I'd catch Groucho Marx in the bushes with the Ambassador to Italy."

"Why not?" retorted Father. "Isn't Chico an Italian?"

Writing approximately 100,000 words about a man I admired and loved so dearly as Father, and still maintain any reportorial objectivity wasn't the easiest assignment in the world, despite my familiarity with the material. But when I finished the book nine months later, in late November, I believed I had achieved a good balance of warmth and truthful reporting.

When I gave the completed manuscript of *Life with Groucho* to my wife to read, her only criticism was, "It's very good, Dear. I just hope it's not too full of hero worship."

If that was her only comment, I was sure that Father would have no complaints about the job I'd done on him.

Nevertheless, knowing Father's predilection for re-writes (the star's God-given prerogative), I decided not to show him the manuscript until after I'd had a professional opinion—either from my agents, or my publisher. Once I had their backing, I knew I wouldn't have anything to worry about. I wasn't really worried, anyway—he'd been such a doll about the first piece I'd done on him.

So I mailed it off without bothering to get his approval.

My agent wired me the first reaction—

GREAT. AM SENDING IT RIGHT OVER TO
SIMON & SCHUSTER.

NAOMI BURTON

Two weeks later, just as I was walking in the front door one evening, the phone rang and it was Edith Haggard, my magazine agent, informing me that Ben Hibbs, the editor of *The Saturday Evening Post*, loved *Life with Groucho*, wished to run it in eight installments, and had offered to buy the serial rights for $45,000. Was the offer acceptable to me?

Was it acceptable? I'd seen the last of the two thousand advance from Simon & Schuster months before; I hadn't been able to get an assignment out of *Collier's* since July; and I'd just come back from spending most of the afternoon in line at the California State Employment Bureau, picking up my unemployment compensation—which came to a grand total of $27 in those days.

After I gleefully shouted into the phone to take the money before Ben Hibbs changed his mind, Edith went on excitedly, "The funny thing, Arthur . . . Ben didn't even want to read the book when I offered it to him. He didn't think your father was a warm enough personality for *The Post*. But after he read your manuscript, he said you convinced him what a warm, wonderful family man Groucho really is."

The sale, Edith added, only hinged on two conditions: Could I assure Hibbs that Father would cooperate in plugging the book on his TV program once it started to run in serial form in *The Saturday Eve-*

ning Post? And could I possibly persuade Father to write a few more footnotes?

Since I'd written all the footnotes myself, the latter was no problem—I could dash off as many as they wanted in no time. And I was positive Father wouldn't mind plugging his own life story on his television show in return for all that loot his son would be getting—the first really big money of my life.

In fact, I could hardly wait for Edith to hang up so I could phone Father. I knew he'd be bowled over by my success, also very proud.

When I reached him, I said, "Hey, Padre—you know that book I've been writing about a certain TV star? The one you said wouldn't make me any money?"

"What about it?"

"Well, I just sold it to *The Saturday Evening Post* for forty-five thousand dollars!"

"The government'll get most of it," he responded sourly.

One evening, after my deal with *The Post* was made official by the arrival of a very large check in the morning mail, I dropped a copy of *Life with Groucho* off at Father's house, fully expecting him to get back to me the following day (if not that same night) and tell me how pleased he was with it.

But when several days passed without my hearing the sound of his familiar voice, I grew nervous and phoned him.

"You'd better get over here right away," Father commanded, in a tone that boded no good. "I want to talk to you about your book."

My pulse rate must have tripled with anxiety as Irene and I traveled the seven miles between the Pacific Palisades and Father's house.

Father met us at the front door in his cashmere bathrobe and slippers. He looked at my wife as though she were some kind of an intruder, then ordered her to wait in the living room. "I want to talk to Art alone." Whereupon he quickly escorted me to his upstairs study, closed the door and sat down at his desk. On top of it was my manuscript, dog-eared and otherwise looking as if it had been maltreated by the Russian Secret Police.

"You certainly don't intend to publish this?" were Father's first words, shooting a disdainful glance downward at what represented nearly a year's work.

"What are you talking about?" I said. "I just sold it to *The Saturday Evening Post* for forty-five thousand dollars."

"It's scurrilous," he said. "You've made me out to be some kind of an ogre—and a cheap one, at that."

"Where is it scurrilous?" I asked, feeling I could assuage him by rewriting a passage or two.

"No one place. Just the whole tone of it."

Treading carefully so as not to upset him further, I said I felt he was being overly sensitive and that he had to be mistaken, because (1) I really hadn't depicted him any differently in my book than I had in the *Collier's* article, which he liked—I had just expanded the material a bit. And, (2) How could he think I'd made him look like an ogre when the editor of *The Post* bought the book solely because he came off as a warm family man?

"I don't care what the editor thinks—he's not printing a word of my life until I'm satisfied with it. I'm one of the biggest names in show business, and you're not going to make a horse's ass out of me for a few thousand dollars."

"But I just told you what Ben Hibbs thinks—"

"Editors will print anything to sell copies. Now sit down at that typewriter and I'll start dictating to you from the beginning. And the first thing we're going to do is eliminate the footnotes—it's an old-fashioned device."

"The editor particularly likes the footnotes," I said, beginning to tremble with anger—also fear.

"What does he know? Now listen to me if you know what's good for you."

And he pushed the typewriter, on its rollered stand, in the direction of my chair.

"Be reasonable, Padre," I said, trying to appeal to his common sense since it was obvious I could no longer rely on his fatherly compassion to save me. "We can't rewrite the book now after I've accepted a check for $45,000. The most they'll stand for are a few changes—but certainly nothing structural. They bought this book. Not the one you want to write. Do you want me to have to give back $45,000?"

"I make that much in a month," said Father.

"Well, it's a lot of money to me."

"Look here," he said threateningly. "Either you rewrite this book starting from page one, or I'll call my lawyer!"

Lawyer! My own father! I couldn't believe it.

Unbelievable as it seemed, I realized I either had to take a firm stand, or be ground into the carpet under his heel. My whole reputation in the magazine business hinged on the outcome—not to mention my bank account, which had been severely depleted by devoting most of 1953 to working only on the book.

"Call anyone you want," I said, in an emotion-filled voice slightly reminiscent of Patrick Henry in his heyday. "I'm not rewriting my book, and you can't stop its publication."

And on that daring announcement, I picked up my manuscript and walked out of his house, for what could have been our final parting.

I was quivering slightly, but at last I was my own man after all those years.

CHAPTER 29

DON'T
TRUST
YOUR SON,
EITHER

FEELING in my heart that I'd depicted Father affectionately—and not scurrilously—helped me get through a rather sleepless night. And having, through my association with *Collier's*, a layman's knowledge of libel laws and invasion of privacy statutes regarding "public figures," I didn't really believe that Father had a leg to stand on in court.

Awareness of my legal rights, however, didn't lessen the intensity of the emotional pain I was experiencing from Father's unreasonable reaction to *Life with Groucho*. Nor would this knowledge get me off the hook with *The Saturday Evening Post*, the publishers of which expected Father's full cooperation in plugging the series on his highly rated television show.

I suspected that Father was much too aware of his public image ever to sue his son, but I also knew that if I didn't bow to his demands, he wouldn't publicize *The Saturday Evening Post* on the air, as I'd promised Ben Hibbs he would.

What bothered me even more was— How could he do this to me, his own son? Me, Big Feet—the same person he had proudly shown off to the audience in the opening scene of *Animal Crackers*. Me, his former horseback riding companion, who'd been a good enough son to trade horses with him and get thrown off in his place. Me, who used to sit on his knee and listen, somewhat bewilderedly, to his joked up versions of *Little Red Riding Hood* and *Jack and the Beanstalk*. Me, who'd put the Marx family on the sports page with a victory over Jack Kramer.

What was going on?

Did Father really believe I'd written something damaging? Had I simply hurt his feelings by not letting him read the manuscript before I'd sold it to *The Saturday Evening Post*? Or, like most superstars, was he merely being difficult just to call attention to himself?

Knowing Father, I couldn't believe it was a simple case of egomania. He wasn't a typical ham actor (although he was showing signs of turning into one since the enormous success of *You Bet Your Life*.) On the other hand, I knew in my heart I hadn't defamed him in my book, either.

Which led me to still another theory.

I was no psychiatrist, but I'd had enough psychology in college to realize that perhaps Father's objection to my manuscript had all the ingredients of the classic father-son rivalry: very successful father on the brink of old age, son thirty years younger aspiring to make a name for himself in a field related to his father's. Could it be possible that Father had a subconscious desire to keep me in a subordinate position, so that he could go on being the important man in the family and thereby hang onto his youth a little longer?

There still wasn't much danger that he would ever be known as the Father of Arthur. And it was hard to believe he would be fearful of such a possibility rather than be proud of it. Still, it made the most sense, since his behavior regarding *Life with Groucho* was consistent with his negative reaction to almost everything else I'd written without his help. And when I checked it with a psychiatrist I sometimes played tennis with, he allowed my theory could very well be correct.

But whether I'd hit the Oedipal nail squarely on the head or not was no particular help to me in arriving at a practical solution.

I finally decided I had two possible courses of action open to me.

I could either go straight to Martin Gang, the Kahn family lawyer, and ask him to take action to prevent Father from doing something that would endanger *The Post* sale—a move that might very well push Father so deep into a corner that he couldn't extricate himself and still save face. Or I could wait the situation out a few days, and see if Father were really serious about stopping the book. Perhaps if I gave him the silent treatment, his more normal paternal instincts would finally show themselves.

I didn't have to wait long.

The phone rang that evening, and it was Father calling.

"Big Feet?" he began in a penitent tone. "Why don't we be sensible and talk this thing over?"

"Okay . . . what do you want to talk over?" I said, trying not to sound too jubilant, for I figured what we had predicted was already happening. He was beginning to feel guilty.

"You don't have to rewrite the whole book," he advised me. "I just want you to take out the parts I don't like."

"From what you told me," I said, "that's the whole book."

"Well, it does need a lot of work still—don't you think?"

"No," I said uncompromisingly. "If *The Post* likes it, Simon and Schuster likes it, and my agents like it, I'll go by their opinions."

A long pause, and then he resumed in a more ominous tone. "I don't know if you're aware of it or not, but I'm a very rich man. I'm going to leave a lot of money when I die someday—which I hope won't be soon."

"I hope so, too," I quickly interjected.

"So why don't you be sensible and listen to me? In the long run there'll be a lot more money in it for you than a lousy $45,000."

The old will bit! I never thought I'd see the day when a man with Father's sense of humor would be pulling a corny thing like that—and seriously.

"Why don't *you* be sensible, and stop badgering me?" I said.

"You come off in the book like a great guy—everybody who's read it thinks so."

"I guess I'll just have to call up Beilenson"—Beilenson was his attorney—"and ask him to get out an injunction. He says he can do it."

On that note, he hung up.

Whether it was pure gamesmanship or the truth that he had already gotten a legal opinion from his lawyer, I'd probably never find out until I was in jail.

I still didn't actually believe he'd sue, but it was enough of a worry to keep me from thinking about anything else for a couple of weeks. I couldn't even concentrate on the new book I'd promised Jack Goodman I'd get right to work on.

My wife was pretty upset too, for she was counting on using the money from the magazine sale to redecorate the living room and buy some much-needed furniture for the children's quarters. But we were afraid to touch any of the $45,000 for fear *The Post* would make us return it if they got wind of possible trouble.

Irene would walk around the house, shaking her head and complaining, "I don't understand a father like yours. What kind of a family have I married into? Your mother's a drunk, and your father's a *momzer*. I thought fathers were supposed to help their kids."

The bitterness around our house became so acute during that period that when Thursday night at eight o'clock rolled around, and our son, Steve, who was six years old and a big fan of his grandfather's TV show, started to tune in *You Bet Your Life*, Irene slapped his hand away from the dial.

"But Grandpa Groucho's on TV," whined Steve.

"You are absolutely forbidden ever to watch his show again," screamed Irene.

"Why?" asked the bewildered Steve.

"Because he is doing something bad to Daddy, and we don't like him any more."

A few more suspenseful days passed, with no further developments, leading me to believe that Father was just bluffing. Nevertheless, every time the phone rang I jumped. I finally reached the point where I wouldn't answer it at all. I just didn't want to hear any bad news.

One day, however, while I was standing out by our RFD mail-box, collecting our daily allotment of bills, a man jumped out of a car and shoved a subpoena into my hand.

I figured it was finally happening. But when I opened up the document, I discovered it was only a small claims action from a repairman I was refusing to pay because he'd done such a bad job of fixing our washing machine. Even *that* seemed a relief.

A call from Gummo, Father's brother and business manager, came that evening.

"Your father's very upset," he told me in a cajoling tone. "Why don't you be nice to him?"

"Why doesn't he be nice to me?"

"I think your wife is turning you against your father," said Gummo.

"I think my *father* is turning me against my father," I retorted. "He's impossible."

The next day I got the call I'd been dreading—from Larry Beilenson, Father's lawyer.

"You know we can stop publication," he said threateningly.

"I don't think you can," I replied confidently. "I know my rights."

"Okay," said Beilenson. "Your father just wanted me to warn you that we're sending off a letter to *The Saturday Evening Post* today, informing them that Groucho's biography is completely unauthorized, and that we're going to get out an injunction if they don't withhold publication voluntarily until Groucho is satisfied with the material."

I swallowed hard and said, "Go ahead and mail it."

As I hung up, I was sure they were bluffing, otherwise they wouldn't be talking so much about what they were going to do, and they'd just do it.

On the other hand, if they did send that letter, who could tell what *The Post's* reaction would be? I had never guaranteed them that the book was "authorized," but since Father's signed footnotes ran throughout the entire text, and the editors even requested that I ask him to write more of them, and I assured them he would, they evidently assumed he had cooperated with me in the writing of the book.

If they now found out otherwise, they might very well claim I'd put one over on them, and wish to renege on the whole deal.

This panicked me into bringing my own lawyer, Martin Gang, into the case.

After reassuring me that I wasn't in any kind of trouble, Gang said he felt that Father's lawyers were mishandling the whole affair, that they were blowing it up way out of proportion with their talk of "libel suits" and "injunctions."

He said that since the trouble was between father and son, the whole thing should be handled on an informal basis, with both sides sitting down together and talking it over unemotionally.

"We'll ask them to pinpoint the parts of the book they don't like, and then if their demands aren't too unreasonable, so you'll make a few changes. *The Post's* got to accept that if they expect your father to plug the book."

Because I felt that compromise often led to complete surrender, it was against my better judgment to give in on any points. However, in the interest of getting the case settled so I could think about other things, I told Gang that I wouldn't mind a few changes, provided they didn't take the guts out of the book.

"Let's worry about that when the time comes," said Gang. "Meanwhile, the important thing is to settle this in such a way that the book is published without destroying the relationship between you and your Dad."

I was in favor of that, and Gang made the contacts with the Beilenson office, settling on a meeting date for the following Thursday.

Father was so pleased at the news that he invited us to a dinner party at his house Saturday night, and we were so relieved that we accepted.

There was no talk about the book at the party—Father was all sweetness and light. That's one nice thing about Father—he can be suing you, and still not carry his animosity to the dinner table.

Things looked so good for a settlement that we even granted Steve permission to start watching *You Bet Your Life* again.

On Thursday afternoon, Gang and I met with Beilenson in Gang's office. Father being somewhat cowardly, especially when he knows he's in the wrong, had wisely decided to stay home and out of the line of fire.

On the conference table in front of him, Beilenson had an open copy of my manuscript, with a number of suggested revisions penciled in the margins in Father's hand. Many of these were minor, and I agreed to them. But there were two important things I wouldn't change: a chapter showing what an eccentric Father was in regard to his spending habits, and a letter he had written to me, describing the day Mother moved out of his house, and quoting his line, "If you're ever in the neighborhood again, drop in."

Father felt the thrifty bit made him look like a miser, which it did not, and that the letter made him seem cruel, which was also not true. It was warm and sentimental, which even Beilenson had to admit to Gang.

"But he still wants it out," insisted Beilenson.

We reached an impasse on that point, and the meeting broke up, with Beilenson threatening to sue again, and my own lawyer telling me not to worry—just to go home and make the changes I had agreed upon.

Shortly after dinner that night, Father phoned the house and said he understood I wouldn't make any changes he wanted. I said that wasn't true—I just wouldn't make *all* of them. "Well, I guess I just have to turn it over to Beilenson and let him handle this in court," he said with finality as he hung up on me.

"He can *ferplatz* on his best *yontiff*," said Irene. "I'll never speak to him again."

At that moment, Steve turned on the TV since it was now Thursday night at eight o'clock—time for *You Bet Your Life* again.

"You turn that thing right off!" screamed Irene. "We're not talking to your grandfather."

"Oh, guy—not again!" exclaimed Steve, and he hurled himself on the floor in a childish rage.

Relations in the Marx family see-sawed back and forth like this for several weeks, always following the same pattern: first threats, sometimes combined with a little cajoling from Father, Beilenson, or Gummo, then peace overtures, and short-lived detentes, during which

Steve would be allowed to watch *You Bet Your Life* again, and Father would invite us to dinner.

But there was always such an underlying threat of uncertainty that I was as mixed up about where the matter stood as Steve was about his television-watching schedule.

To make the situation even more suspenseful, two men from *The Saturday Evening Post*'s public relations department phoned me from Philadelphia, and asked me whom they should contact regarding the TV plugs Father had promised to film in advance. They had already written the copy, and now wanted to come to Los Angeles, and get Father's okay. "Maybe he'll even throw in a few wisecracks of his own," one of them suggested.

They also wanted me to take them down to one of the filming sessions of *You Bet Your Life* so "we can meet the old gent, and tell him how much we love your book on him. You really made him a whopping good character."

That was what I needed all right, to put them together with Father, who'd spill the whole pot of beans, and I'd be back in the line for unemployment compensation.

On the other hand, I couldn't let on that anything was wrong, so I played it as cool as I could, and put them in touch with John Guedel, Father's producer and partner in the *You Bet Your Life* venture.

Having no idea that there was trouble between Father and me about the book, John Guedel naturally was delighted to cooperate with *The Post*'s PR men. As soon as he heard from them, he started making arrangements for the filming of the TV plugs, and the recording of radio blurbs. A good showman, in addition to being very publicity-oriented, Guedel was well aware that an eight-part serial of his star's life in a magazine with *The Post*'s circulation was certainly not going to hurt *You Bet Your Life*'s ratings. Only two other celebrities' lives—Bob Hope's and Bing Crosby's—had ever rated eight parts in *The Post*, and to be in that company was pretty good for a man who, only a few years earlier, couldn't stay on the air with his own show for more than thirteen weeks without getting bounced by a sponsor.

I just hoped Guedel could handle my father, if and when he started balking at doing the plugs.

I also hoped that these PR men from *The Saturday Evening Post* weren't planning to come out soon. If I could just buy some time, I might be all right. I didn't want the whole thing to blow up in my face before I could work out my problem with Father.

While I was worrying about the PR men, I received a phone call from Gene Lester, the Hollywood photographer who did most of the picture coverage for *The Saturday Evening Post*'s personality pieces, including the Hope and Crosby tomes. Lester was no shrinking violet, like Bob Landry.

Before devoting his time to magazine work, Lester had worked for many years on a metropolitan daily, and as a result had more *chutzpa* than Howard Cosell.

"I've been assigned to do the picture layout on your book for *The Post*," he began. "When's your old man available? I'd like to start off with some shots of him around the pool with some broads. It never hurts to have a lot of tits in a layout."

Knowing how Father hated taking pictures under ordinary circumstances, I shuddered at what his reaction would be to spending any time before the lens of Gene Lester's speed graphic.

"Why don't we put it off a few weeks?" I suggested casually. "It's only the spring. The series isn't scheduled until the fall."

"Are you kidding? I've got my work cut out for me if I start right now. You need a bundle of pictures for an eight-parter."

"He's kind of busy," I said nervously. "And he's not too fond of posing for pictures."

"I know. He's a bitch when it comes to that," said Lester. "I've had to deal with him before. But I can handle him. Just tell me when."

"You're sure you don't want to wait a few weeks? He'll be in a better mood."

"Listen, kid, if you're afraid to ask him, give me his number and I'll set it up. I've got to get going on this now, while I've got the time."

I couldn't let on that anything was wrong, for fear it would get back to *The Post*, so I told him I'd try to arrange a session—preferably for the coming week-end—and I'd be in touch with him after I had.

I had no idea how I was going to manage it. Not only that, I was beginning to wonder if the $45,000 was worth all this agony and apprehension.

Between Lester's insistence that he get started right away on the picture layout, continued harassment from Father's legal beagles, and the likelihood of *The Post*'s PR men showing up in Los Angeles any day now and a possible confrontation between them and Father, I was beginning to show signs of cracking up.

I wasn't sleeping very well any more. When I finally did drop off, I had nightmares about having to return the $45,000 to *The Post*. I had also acquired what had to be a psychosomatic cough, because my ear, nose and throat doctor couldn't find any physical reason for my hacking now that I'd stopped smoking. And I couldn't concentrate on anything else. I couldn't even knock out a 2,000-word article on Jack Benny that the editor of *The New York Times Magazine* had assigned me to write.

In short, I was a real mess, and I knew if I didn't do something soon to break this stalemate myself—the lawyers seemed to be getting nowhere—*I'd* wind up spending the $45,000 on psychiatric bills.

So I devised a plan—kind of Machiavellian and unsonlike in concept—but simple, and well worth the gamble.

The plan was inspired by a letter I received from *The Saturday Evening Post*, informing me that they were sending me galleys of *Life with Groucho*'s eight installments under separate cover, and that I should make my corrections—"if possible, a few more footnotes from Groucho, please"—and return them to Philadelphia as quickly as possible.

I immediately wired Hibbs to send me *two* sets of galleys. "I always like to keep one set for my records," I explained.

When Hibbs replied that he'd be delighted, I phoned Father and said that Gene Lester wanted to start photographing him on the weekend.

"You still refuse to cut that letter about your mother?" he asked.

"It's too late to take it out of the manuscript," I said. "They're already setting it up in print. But as soon as I get the galleys, I'll let you see them, and you can delete everything you object to then."

"Now you're talking," exclaimed Father. "I'll tell Beilenson not to send the letter."

He sounded more relieved than I.

"Now, what about posing for the pictures?" I asked.

"I suppose I can't get out of it," he replied. "Okay, tell Lester to be here with his Brownie at eleven o'clock Sunday. I'll give him fifteen minutes. And, oh, yes, bring Steve and Andy. I might as well get some free pictures of my grandchildren while I'm at it."

For him, Father behaved remarkably well with Lester, and the photographer managed to squeeze in several very fruitful photo sessions with his subject before the galleys arrived several weeks later.

I quickly went over my set of galleys, and dashed off a few more funny "Groucho" footnotes to please the editors.

On the second set, I deleted all the material Father objected to, which amounted to about half the book. Then I took the galleys over to his house and sat there while he examined them.

He made a few more corrections, and handed them back to me with the comment, "I hope this is the end of it. I'm getting pretty sick of my life."

Needless to say, so was I.

I dropped the second set of galleys in a trash can on the way to the Post Office, and mailed my set off to *The Saturday Evening Post.*

By double-crossing Father, I'd bought myself a little temporary peace of mind. It was a dirty trick to play on him, but after what he'd put me through, I didn't feel guilty. Besides, what he didn't know wouldn't hurt him—and he wouldn't know until the magazines were already on the stand.

Between the reading of the galleys and publication date, however, he was to give me quite a few more sleepless nights.

CHAPTER 30

MOTHER
NUMBER THREE

AS mid-summer of 1954 approached, and time for the serialization of *Life with Groucho* grew nearer, rumors were suddenly rife around Hollywood that Father was planning to marry a twenty-one-year-old brunette and former model named Eden Hartford, whose real name was Edna Higgins.

An aspiring actress with no films to her credit, Eden was the sister of Dee Hawks, the skeleton-thin *Vogue* cover girl who was married to movie director Howard Hawks. Eden came from Mormon stock, and except for a few years in New York, where she tried to follow in her sister's footsteps, had spent most of her life in the tiny community of Bell, California.

She had been married previously, to a man from Bell, and not unhappily, she had once confessed to me. But when her sister had suggested that life could be more rewarding in the big city, she simply packed up, walked out on her first husband, and got a divorce.

She had met Father on the set of *A Girl in Every Port*, where her sister had brought her to meet its producer, Irwin Allen. Allen introduced her to Father, and the two had been having an off-again on-again romance ever since.

Eden had everything that appealed to Father. She was young, pretty, Gentile and quiet. But what she wanted with a man who was already a candidate for Medicare, only her conscience could answer. Either she was undersexed or underfed. Or possibly the thought of the glamorous life she was going to lead as Groucho Marx's wife is what finally captured her.

Irene and I had double-dated with Father and Eden on a number of occasions, and they obviously liked each other, judging by the seriousness of their necking in the back seat when I was doing the driving. Mind you, I have nothing against necking. I also realize that fathers have a right to enjoy it as well as sons. Nevertheless there was something about glancing in the rear-view mirror and seeing my own father smooching with a young girl and otherwise carrying on like one of the horny kids in *The Last Picture Show* that always struck me as being a little absurd.

Occasionally, the Groucho of yore would predominate, and I'd hear a line or two from one of his early shows emanate from the back seat. "Edna, your eyes shine like the pants of my blue serge suit," he might exclaim, or "Your scent maddens me!" But for the most part he'd be as dedicated to the pursuit of sex as any Central Park mugger.

Dedicated or not, his conversations with me in private were full of steadfast avowals that he would never marry again. As a result, I'd devoted the last third of my book to relating anecdotes about his experience as a bachelor, and flavored it with many of his outrageously funny theories on sex and marriage, such as "The whole concept of marriage is wrong. It can never work except between two men, both of whom like baseball and have separate incomes."

I knew that he was unpredictable, and that one could never rely on anything he said—especially regarding his relationships with the fair sex. Still, I believed him when he said he wouldn't get married again, until the rumors about him and the kid from Bell became so persistent that I figured they had to be more than malicious gossip.

That worried me, and not because I didn't like Eden, or think Father was old enough to know what he was doing. But if he was intending to marry, I had to know about it long before the magazine hit the stands, and the *Simon & Schuster* hardcover went to press, so I'd have time to rewrite it and bring it up to date.

Being son of Groucho, I was supposed to be the leading authority on his life. I'd look like a fine schmo if I wrote that he was single when he wasn't, or that he was going to stay single, take it from me, his son, Arthur.

Unable to ignore the rumors, I finally put the question to him bluntly. "Do you intend to get married before the book comes out?"

"We're just good friends," he answered shiftily.

"Why do all the gossip columns say you're going to get married?" I persisted in the spirit of true journalism.

"Listen," he said, "don't be so nosey. Do I ask you if you're going to get married?"

"I have to know," I pleaded, "because I don't want the book to be out of date by the time it's published."

But I couldn't pin him down. "Listen, Big Feet, I didn't consult you when I married your mother—and I'm not going to start now."

"But you also promised me I could come to your third wedding," I reminded him.

"There's not going to be a third wedding," he insisted.

In late July he, Eden and Melinda took a trip to Sun Valley, and from there he sent me the following telegram:

IF YOU'VE HEARD ABOUT THIS, PLEASE
REFUND THE PRICE OF THE TELEGRAM.
LOVE FROM US BOTH.

GROUCHO

I can't say that I was surprised, but I was pretty disgusted that he had to be playing this game of One-Upmanship with me so late in the proceedings.

It was back to the typewriter again, for a complete rewrite of the last third of the book. Luckily, it was only the last third, for the first few installments had already gone to press by the time I'd finished a new draft.

In the final scoring, I guess I finished one-up on Father, for he never suspected that I'd double-crossed him with two sets of galleys, or noticed, when his life started running in the September 28, 1954, issue of *The Post,* that the text was considerably different from the one he had approved. I know he read it, because he had all eight issues of *The Post* on the nightstand next to his bed. As a matter of fact, when he was writing his own memoirs several years later, I walked into his study unannounced one day and caught him copying from the hardcover edition of *Life with Groucho,* which was open on the desk in front of him.

Life with Groucho sold well in hardcover, probably as a result of a spate of better reviews than I had ever hoped for. *The New York Times* (Sunday) *Book Review* called it "great." *The New Yorker* said it was "an excellent piece of work." And *The Herald Tribune* wrote, "Many sons of distinguished men have written biographies of their fathers, but none has done so with a greater combination of affection and irreverence than the scion of Julius H. Marx."

This latter convinced me that my Oedipal analysis of Father's behavior had been correct—it wasn't *what* I'd written, but *who* had written it.

And if I needed further proof, it was supplied me by *Confidential Magazine*—a scandal-mongering publication that was popular during the fifties—when it published a real muck-raking article about America's "favorite quizmaster."

Their story on Father was incredibly vicious. Among other things, it accused him of being an old roué, with an insatiable appetite for young girls; it also said that his quiz show was fixed, and that he was meaner to his writing staff than Simon Legree, and more miserly than Silas Marner and Jack Benny combined.

"That's what I call scurrilous," I chided Father after he showed me the piece. "Why don't you get your lawyers after those bums?"

He shrugged, and said, with complete unconcern, "What'd they say that's so bad?—just that my show's crooked and that I like young girls! Well, I *do* like young girls—a hell of a lot better than old girls."

From his pleased tone, you'd have thought the piece was a tribute to his virility.

He never consulted his lawyers, of course. The most he felt compelled to do was to dash off one of his inimitable letters to the editor of *Confidential.*

Dear Sir:

If you persist in publishing libelous articles about me, I will have to cancel my subscription.

Very truly yours,

Groucho Marx

Any man that unpredictable was bound to keep a young bride in a constant state of turmoil and bewilderment. I figured he'd be lucky if his marriage to Eden lasted six months.

But Eden was cut from a different mold than his other wives, and this enabled her to hang in there longer—almost fourteen years.

Extremely phlegmatic in nature—almost torpid at times—Eden was not easily upset by Father's dogmatic home rule, or his idiosyncrasies. She may have been young, but she didn't have the sensitivity usually attributed to youth. Frequently she wasn't even aware that Father was criticizing her. Or perhaps she just wasn't listening.

Intellectually, of course, she was no match for him in an argument. But she made up for this in bulldoggish persistence—until she finally wore Father down, and she got her way.

Either that or Father was finally mellowing—having learned from the bitter experience of paying alimony to two wives that it was really a lot cheaper in the long run, and less taxing physically, to give in on certain issues than to fight them.

In money matters, particularly, he was more malleable, probably because his income was larger than it had ever been (his NBC contract assured him of practically a life-long annuity); he had a very healthy bank account; and the time he had left for spending it all was growing shorter, if you could trust the actuary tables.

As a result, Eden was able to talk him into selling the house he had bought when Melinda was born—an old, large, comfortable but not very glamorous-looking Spanish hacienda in the flats of Beverly Hills —and build her a plush, contemporary dwelling of stone and glass, on a fifty thousand dollar Trousdale lot. The new layout wound up costing somewhere in the neighborhood of $300,000, all cash, of course. He still didn't believe in mortgages.

When I asked Father why he was going to all that expense when his present home was more than adequate, he answered, "Because Eden's a young girl. She's entitled to have a house that an ex-wife didn't live in. Besides, she wants a sunken bathtub and a round bedroom."

"Why a round bedroom?"

"I guess she figures it's harder for me to corner her in it."

Eden not only got her sunken bathtub and round bedroom, complete with circular bed, but after they were in their new palatial home for a while, she also talked Father into buying a second house in Palm Springs, for week-ends.

A second house, purely for recreational purposes, was an extravagance Father had studiously avoided all his life. I remember Charlie Farrell, who was promoting Palm Springs when it was little more than an Indian reservation, trying to persuade Father to buy a house near the Raquet Club, because it could have been picked up for $7500, and would have been a good investment. Father was tempted, because he liked the sun and horseback riding, but in the end he put the money into securities instead.

Father's spending didn't go completely berserk as a result of Eden's influence. He was still a little apprehensive of that proverbial rainy day. Which is the reason the inside of his homes were never as attractive as their outsides (if you're going to spend three hundred thousand dollars you have to cut corners somewhere), and why there wasn't always enough white meat for a second helping, and sometimes even a first.

But the net result was that Father had loosened up considerably.

He was more tractable in other ways, too. Realizing that Eden was so much younger than himself, with the need for a more active social life, he would frequently let her stay on at a party and continue having a good time long after he had gone to bed alone.

If it was a non-party night and Eden felt a need to go out, Father was happy to accept her explanation that she was attending an acting class.

"Look, let her have a good time," he'd tell me. "She's a young girl. If she wants to have an affair with someone else, let her. As long as I don't know about it, I don't care."

It was sad to think that at his age, and with so much else going for him, he had to make such a compromise in his personal life. But at least he was wise enough to realize that material things alone couldn't keep a young girl completely contented.

Years later, Father admitted to me, "I never had an ideal marriage. I guess I always looked for the wrong things in a wife."

For fourteen years, however, he thought he and Eden were happily married.

CHAPTER 31

THE
BROTHER- AND
SISTER-IN-LAW
CHARADE

 IN 1958, Harper's published a book of mine called *Not As a Crocodile*—a non-fiction, humorous work on the problems of living and raising a family in middle-class suburbia when you are a writer who works at home and are always at your wife's beck and call, available to handle any household crisis, from fixing the washing machine to excoriating the manager of a little league baseball team for unfairly condemning your son to a position of perpetual bench-warming.

One problem the book didn't mention was: What does a husband do when he and his wife can no longer get along, and, to complicate matters further, he is in love with his sister-in-law?

Despite outward appearances, my wife and I had never been very compatibly matched. In fact, we were living proof that "opposites make good bed-fellows" is a bunch of hogwash.

I liked to play tennis; she liked to stay indoors and build radios and run an amateur radio station she had set up in our bedroom. I liked sex; she could take it or leave it (at least with me). I liked to go to bed at a reasonable hour; she liked to stay up late and guzzle coffee and try to contact the South Pole on her radio transmitter. I liked tranquility; she had a temper and liked to argue, sometimes just for the sheer fun of debating (she'd have made a great delegate to the United Nations). She could carry on an argument for days, giving me the so-called silent treatment if necessary until she got her way; I prefer to make up quickly or not at all.

Once we drove from Las Vegas to San Francisco, and from San Francisco back to Los Angeles without speaking a single word to each other. Real happiness.

Yet none of our friends suspected we were anything but the most devoted of lovers, because at parties, Irene, who was wanting in self-assurance, used to grab my hand for security.

Father used to say, "Beware of couples who hold hands." And then he'd quote an old vaudeville joke: "They hold hands because they're afraid if they let go they'll kill each other."

Father was closer to the truth than he thought—although my relationship with Irene wasn't one where I wished her any harm. Platonically, I was still fond of her. She just wasn't the person I cared to spend the rest of my life with.

Lois Kahn, my sister-in-law, was that person, and she felt the same way about me.

Lois and I had a relationship and love for each other that very few people find in their lifetime. It wasn't a physical relationship in the beginning—although God knows we had plenty of opportunities for that during nine and a half years of constant association within the family orbit. In fact, until 1952, ours was an unspoken, un-acted-upon love. But we both realized it was there. We felt the comfort of it whenever we were in each other's company, whether we were alone or with the rest of the family. And somehow we felt something lacking in our lives when we were apart, in our respective homes.

Others in the family apparently sensed the chemistry between us. Irene and Donald, in fact, often used to kid us about our closeness. "If anything ever happens to us," they'd say, chortling, "you two can always get married."

We didn't consider it anything more than a family joke, either, because neither of us knew just how unhappily the other was married. Then, in 1952, a series of circumstances that I won't go into now threw Lois and me together one lunchtime at a small restaurant down by the beach. There, with a red checkered tablecloth between us, we admitted how our marriages had failed, and confessed our mutual love for each other.

Lois, it turned out, felt the same way about Donald as I did about his sister. She was fond of him, as a friend, but it wasn't love, and she didn't want to spend the rest of her only life with him. She wanted to be with me.

Now that we had professed our love for each other, we didn't want to have to wait for anything to "happen" to Donald and Irene, as the two of them had so quaintly expressed it. Nor in fact did either of us *want* anything to happen to them. We just wished to be cut loose from them, so we could be together. "But do we dare make such a move?" we asked each other in a series of subsequent trysts over the next two months.

This wouldn't be just an ordinary case of divorce and marriage. This was all in one family. My kids were Lois's nephews—they called her "Auntie Loie." And Lois's Linda was my niece. And she called me "Uncle Artie Boots." And Lois and I had the same white-haired matriarchal mother-in-law, who was given to boasting to all her friends about the wonderful marriages her Donald and Irene had effected with her daughter-in-law the model and her son-in-law the son of Groucho.

Even if Grace was more perceptive about the unhealthy state of our marriages than she made out, we doubted if she was quite prepared for incest—or whatever it was the dictionary called love between a brother- and sister-in-law.

Still Grace sensed what was going on between us before either of her children did, and before we were quite ready to make a decision.

One day, when neither Donald nor Irene was around, Grace

summoned Lois and me to her study, saying she had "something private to talk over with you two."

Before entering the lioness's den, Lois and I had the same premonition—that our mother-in-law suspected, and was going to accuse us openly.

Rather than be deceitful and deny it, we decided to level with Grace, and admit our love for each other. We hoped she would be grown-up enough to take it in a mature way, for we didn't want to hurt the old lady. She'd been nice to us over the years.

We even held out the hope that maybe she'd be understanding enough to wish us well in marriage to each other.

Boy, did we have the wrong number.

I will never forget Grace's reaction to our announcement that we were in love and wished to get married.

Turning on Lois like a lioness whose cubs had just been wounded, our mother-in-law lashed out, "Why don't you pick on Arthur's father instead? God knows, you're young enough for him!"

When we told the news to our spouses, they were stunned, but resigned.

Father took it philosophically. "Well . . . well, I always wondered when your true Marx blood would come to the fore," he exclaimed from his bed, where he was laid up with one of his grippy feelings. "How is Lois in the hay, anyway?"

"I wouldn't know," I replied. "And I doubt if I'll find out until after we're married."

"Married," he exclaimed disapprovingly. "I can understand you wanting to get laid, but for God's sakes, why don't you just cheat on Irene, like other husbands? I wouldn't blame you for that."

The reactions and breast-beating from the rest of our relatives were equally disquieting.

"How can you do that to the children?"

"How can you do that to us?"

"Something terrible will be visited upon you if you go through with this."

Our children, quite understandably, were a big consideration. And before making our decision, Lois and I had talked at great length about them. We both had come to the same conclusion. My kids loved Lois, Linda felt the same about me. They'd be able to adjust. Other children had. They'd just have to be told about it in the right way.

Then some well-meaning but meddlesome relative made the mistake of telling Linda about the break-up before Lois had a chance to get to her. Linda, who was only eight, took the news the way we hoped she wouldn't—hysterically—and Lois suddenly lost her courage.

The next day—a rainy day, naturally—Lois and I met for lunch to discuss the situation, and she confessed to me that after seeing the heartbreak in her daughter's face, she just couldn't hurt her this way, no matter how much she was in love with me. Though disappointed, I was relieved in a way, for by then I had some misgivings, too—not only for the children's sakes, but for Irene's. It hadn't been very long since her nervous breakdown. A traumatic experience like a divorce might bring on a relapse. I didn't want to be responsible for a thing like that.

So, as Lois and I looked forlornly out the window at the pouring rain, we decided to call the whole thing off. And we ordered a second helping of strawberry shortcake, instead.

That took care of our marriage plans for 1952.

To make certain that we wouldn't be tempted a second time, Lois and I vowed never to see each other again—even at family gatherings. It was going to hurt. In fact, it reduced us both to tears, just thinking about it.

Grace cooperated to the utmost by not inviting her son and daughter-in-law and her daughter and son-in-law to her house on the same evenings. Mutual friends of ours might wonder why the Kahns and the Marxes, who once had been almost inseparable, were never seen together at Grace's any more, or why they never accepted invitations to the same parties or social events. Although there was considerable speculation about these things, nobody except the immediate family knew the real dirt.

Five years passed. During this period Lois and I never saw each other once, or even talked on the telephone. This didn't make us any happier in our marriages to Irene and Donald, it just salved our consciences a bit and made it easier to accept not being together.

Otherwise, I was doing all right. Father and I were on good terms. My kids were growing into people. And I'd finally achieved some success.

Partly to make myself forget Lois, I had worked extra hard. In a period of three years I had turned out one play, which Max Gordon had produced for Broadway, but which folded in Philadelphia, and three full length books, one a best seller. I was also writing TV scripts for CBS, and getting top money for them. I finally could afford to have the house redecorated. Only the wrong person was in the house with me.

After *Not As a Crocodile* was published, the ruling members of our oligarchy—Grace, Donald and Irene—decided that it was senseless and inconvenient for the entire family never to be able to get together merely on account of an infatuation Lois and I had for each other five years before. How long could love last if two people never saw each other nor were in contact?

Besides, through Donald, Lois suddenly had a blossoming career in the music business, as a pop singer. She had just recorded the *Gus Kahn Song Album* for Reprieve, and she was also doing a lot of demo records for Donald, who had written a big hit called "Beautiful Friendship" with Stanley Stein (son of Julie).

Inasmuch as Donald and Lois's relationship appeared pretty solid to the rest of the family, the edict was handed down that it would be safe for the five of us to get together.

And so a couple of nights later, Grace invited the four of us to dinner at her house.

The moment I was in the same room with Lois, saw that great figure and those expressive brown eyes, and heard her infectious laughter, I knew that five years of separation had done nothing to destroy my appreciation of her. Unhappily, I didn't think the feelings were mutual. Lois was cordial enough, but strangely distant, and more attentive to her husband than I'd ever noticed before.

I was suddenly sorry we'd ever become lovers, for now it looked as if I'd lost her as a friend as well.

I was glad, anyway, that she had been able to come to terms with her own marriage. And at least now there was no danger that I'd ever have to go through the agony and nerve strain of another emotional and extra-marital entanglement.

C'est la vie.

Several months passed, and Grace invited the four of us to a large tax deductible party she was throwing at her house for the music business crowd—song writers, pluggers, publishers and various other Vine Street characters. Everyone from Johnny Mercer to Dinah Shore was among the guests.

Grace rarely hired a professional bartender for any of her soirées; she knew she could count on Donald and me to take turns sharing the drink mixing honors (after all, a penny saved, is a penny earned, even if you are Double A ASCAP).

During one of my numerous stints behind the bar that evening, I heard the rustle of taffeta near me, and looking around, I saw Lois, in a very décolleté black cocktail dress, helping herself to a second drink.

"Let me do that," I said, grabbing her glass.

"I didn't want to bother you," she said. "You've been so busy."

"Never too busy for you," I said.

As I handed Lois's refilled glass back to her, she gave a surreptitious glance over her shoulder to make certain Donald and Irene weren't around, then quickly leaned close to me and whispered, "You know something, Arthur?—I love you, and I always will." And she brushed her lips lightly across my ear.

That disclosure shocked the hell out of me, for I didn't know how to interpret it. Did she really mean it? Was it only that she'd had too much to drink and was feeling sentimental about our past relationship? Or was that her way of tipping the bartender?

Being a man of high moral standards and great strength of character, I immediately said, "I love you, too, but what are we supposed to do about it?"

"Phone me tomorrow, after Donald leaves for the office."

One of the big drawbacks of working at home that I didn't mention in my book of family stories is that it's almost impossible to carry on an illicit relationship with your sister-in-law over the family telephone when your wife is building a short wave radio in the next room and is apt to pick up the extension any moment to place a call to California Electronics Supply. It is equally difficult to think of an excuse that will get you out of the house and to a phone booth when your wife knows it's inconsistent with your working routine to leave your desk during the day.

I was so rattled that it took me two days to think of an excuse to leave the house in the morning so I could get to a phone booth at a Union Gas Station on Sunset Boulevard. My reason—that I had to have the car wheels balanced—was so unbelievably stupid and unimaginative that Irene believed it.

When I finally contacted Lois's house, the maid answered and I had to pretend I was a rating taker from a TV network before finding out that "the lady of the house" wasn't in. By then the mechanic had started pulling my car wheels off, and I had to walk home if I didn't want to spend the rest of my day sitting around a Union Gas Station.

Three mornings later I reached Lois.

"I thought you'd never call," she said.

"It wasn't easy," I replied. "Let's have lunch somewhere tomorrow."

"I don't think we'd better start this thing up again," said Lois nervously. "It's too complicated. It can never work out."

"Then why'd you ask me to call?"

"Because I love you, and like to hear your voice, and want you to phone me whenever you feel like talking."

As difficult as it was, for several months I communicated with Lois from a phone booth during the day, while we continued to see each other as brother- and sister-in-law at family get-togethers in the evenings. I was beginning to smell like the inside of a phone booth.

Through our phone conversations, we both knew that we were more deeply in love than ever and just as unhappily married. What kept us from actually meeting was that we couldn't stop vacillating over whether we had a right to be in love.

Eventually our resistance broke down, and we started having lunches together and going on long drives on afternoons when we could break away from our families without causing suspicion. There was a writers' strike on, and I wasn't allowed to work even if I wanted to.

During the evenings, we continued to play the brother- and sister-in-law charade. We were friendly, but not affectionate.

It wasn't easy to carry on this way. In fact, it was damn nerve-wracking, for we had to be constantly on guard not to make incriminating slips of the tongue that would tip the others off that we had been talking privately. Like one time Lois told me that she and Donald had been to see a movie, *The Last Angry Man.* The next time I was with the two of them together, I forgot myself and asked Donald how he liked *The Last Angry Man.* He quickly picked it up and said, "How'd you know I saw that?"

"You see all the new pictures," I answered lamely. "I just figured you'd have seen this one."

After two years of this kind of deception I was in a complete funk mentally. My nervous system wasn't ready to lead a double life. I guess I wasn't a "true" Marx.

I couldn't concentrate on my work. I couldn't even enjoy my kids.

One day at a very important Little League game at our ball park in Rustic Canyon, I was assisting the manager of our team by coaching first base.

As usual, my mind was somewhere in the clouds with Lois. It certainly wasn't on the game, which our side was losing by one run late in the proceedings.

With two outs, and the tying run on third in the last inning, one of our strongest batters hit a line drive down the first base line, near me. Unthinkingly, I automatically reached out and caught the ball.

According to Abner Doubleday's hallowed rules, the batter is automatically out if anyone on his team—even a coach—catches the ball and interferes with play.

When our team realized they'd lost the game and the league championship on account of that sappy guy coaching first base, they mobbed me and started chasing me with their bats. I had to flee the ball park for my life, and my son, Steve—whose main contribution to the team was that he led the league in strikeouts—was in more disgrace than ever because of his numbskull father.

By the spring of 1960, Lois and I were no longer content just to have lunch together, or to ride up and down the San Diego Freeway, or to rub legs under the table when Grace seated us next to each other at her dinner parties. Not only weren't we content, but we were so burning with pent-up desire that we could barely refrain from grabbing each other and kissing in front of the rest of the family whenever we all got together.

It was amazing to us that no one noticed our covetous glances, or thought it strange how we always managed to be near or seated next to each other at family gatherings.

But as much as we yearned for complete fulfillment, we kept putting it off because of some strange convoluted thinking that seemed to say to us—if you don't go all the way, you're technically not committing adultery.

But one night the Kahns and the Marxes went out to the movies together, and happened to catch the first sneak preview of Billy Wilder's *The Apartment*.

Lois and I loved what the picture seemed to be saying so much that it gave us the courage to want to consummate our own love affair. And although we didn't know anyone who'd loan us his apartment, we did know of a motel down at the beach that looked like a safe haven for a couple of amateurs.

So the first afternoon that we could sneak away, we slipped down to the beach and checked into the Las Tunas Isle Motel—which promised on its neon sign, "King sized beds and Swimming Pool."

I was so nervous that I even signed my real name on the register.

But once we were in bed, our love for each other quickly overcame our self-consciousness, and we were as comfortable as an old married couple—only a lot more active.

The one thing I'd been slightly apprehensive about—that it might be an anti-climax after all those years of anticipation—proved to be quite the reverse.

By five o'clock, when we reluctantly had to dress for the drive home, the only thing either of us regretted was that we hadn't done it sooner.

As I walked in the front door of my house that evening, wondering when I would be able to see Lois again, Irene met me at the door with, "I invited Don and Lois over to dinner tonight. I hope you don't mind seeing them again."

An hour later I was greeting Donald and Lois at our front door, and shaking Lois's hand with such feigned indifference that I deserved an Oscar, although underneath I was shaking.

Things went on that way—sex in the afternoon, dinner together as brother- and sister-in-law with Donald and Irene or Grace in the evening—several times a month, until Lois and I decided we could no longer bear living out our lives in this deceitful manner. We would have to get married. We were too selfish to want to give up entire nights and long week-ends when we could not be together, just because of this game we were playing. We didn't want to give up one minute together.

We were still very much aware that what we were contemplating wouldn't be the pleasantest thing in the world for Donald and Irene and our respective children to have to live through. But at the same time we also knew that we weren't being very good parents or spouses by continuing to live this double life. It was unfair to Don and Irene, and unfair to the children.

Obviously, divorce and remarriage was the only solution. And this time we wouldn't allow any well-meaning members of our family to talk us out of it.

There was just one problem: How should we go about breaking the news that we wanted divorces? Should we be honest again and admit our love for each other, thereby taking the risk that some puritanical judge would disapprove of what we were doing and pauperize us financially? Or should we seek divorces separately, and then when they became final, quietly get together again and marry? Financially, we'd probably be better off to play it cagily. But since I didn't expect to escape without paying alimony and child support, and Lois certainly didn't want anything from Donald after seventeen years of marriage except her freedom, we opted in favor of complete honesty.

No one could hate us for being in love. Or so we thought.

Despite our brave intentions, Lois and I kept postponing the time when we would break the news to Donald and Irene, because there always seemed to be some family celebration we didn't want to spoil, like a birthday or an anniversary. But one Thursday we suddenly realized we had a long Memorial Day week-end, when we couldn't be together, facing us. We decided that we'd tell Donald and Irene that night when we got home. I did, immediately after dinner when the kids were in bed. Irene said she wasn't surprised, then turned into a tiger and demanded that I leave the house IMMEDIATELY!

I did—with two suitcases full of clothes, and just seventeen dollars in cash and a couple of credit cards in my pocket.

Lois had to tell Donald over the long-distance phone, for he had gone to Las Vegas unexpectedly, and was already enjoying a long week-end of bachelorhood at the crap tables by the time she arrived home.

"Oh, no, not again!" he exclaimed, and then went back to shooting dice.

When Lois phoned the news to her parents' home her mother, on the verge of swooning, warned, "Loie—there's a price to pay for everything!"

"I know, and I've already paid it," was Lois's answer, which I consider one of the most priceless descriptions of an unhappy marriage of all time.

My father, as usual, reacted unpredictably, when I broke the news to him in his brand new hillside spread in Trousdale, Friday morning.

When I arrived, he was in his bathrobe, pajamas and slippers, having breakfast on the terrace, which overlooked his swimming pool and, far in the distance, the poorer flatlands of Beverly Hills.

Father is usually at his grumpiest before he's had his coffee and devoured everything there is to read in *The Los Angeles Times*, but I, in my heady state from having made a decision that I felt was good for me, wasn't particularly worried about how he'd receive the news. I knew he couldn't be shocked after having been married three times and divorced twice (with a strong possibility, I felt, of a third divorce in his future, judging by some of the arguments I heard around his house).

I didn't think he'd be particularly surprised, because as recently as two weeks before I had hinted to him that I was still in love with my sister-in-law, and he had been so understanding that at my behest he even invited Donald and Lois to one of his dinner parties, so that Lois and I could be together.

And I was positive that Father wouldn't disapprove of the switch in daughters-in-law, because, (a) he was attracted to Lois himself, and had even taken her out to lunch a couple of times when she was a single girl of nineteen, and (b) he wasn't overly fond of Irene, because she had a penchant for telling him off, and once, in fact, had embarrassed him publicly by creating a scene in the grandstand during the singles final of the Pacific Southwest Tennis Matches.

Armed with this knowledge, I sat down with Father at the breakfast table, told him to prepare himself for a minor shock, and then announced I was going to marry Lois as soon as we could get divorces.

"There's a lot of expense to a divorce," he said. "Can you afford it?"

"I think so," I answered, not really knowing. "Irene has her own income. She probably won't be too unreasonable."

Father shrugged dubiously. "Lois is a nice girl," he said. "But broads are funny. They change after they hook you."

I told him that after being in the same family with Lois for seventeen years, I believed I knew her better than most husbands ever knew their wives, and vice versa.

"Where are you going to live?" asked Father.

I said I'd probably take a small apartment until Lois and I could be married and rent a house.

"You can move in here if you want," he said. "I have plenty of room."

I told him that maybe I'd take him up on it until I could find a place. But in the meantime, Lois and Linda and I were going to Palm Springs for the week-end—mainly to get away from all the phone calls we knew we'd be getting from well-meaning relatives and friends who'd probably try to talk us out of wanting to be happy.

"Well, you can use my house in Palm Springs," offered Father, and he went to his desk drawer and started rumaging around in it for the keys. "Stay in it together for as long as you want. That's the only way you'll find out."

I told him that Lois and Linda would have to stay in a hotel, since Linda was a minor and it wouldn't be right for the three of us to be living under one roof when Lois and I weren't married. However, I'd use the house as it would save me some money.

"You know, all I'm thinking about is your happiness," he said, as

he handed me the keys. "I just don't want you to make any mistakes."
"Don't worry," I assured him. "This isn't a mistake."
"Say hello to Lois," he said, giving me a warm hug. "And don't
do too much screwing."

It was a pleasure to have Father on my side for a change.

Before leaving for Palm Springs, Lois and I phoned Martin Gang,
who'd been the Kahn family attorney for twenty years, and mine since
my trouble with Father over *Life with Groucho.*

Gang was not surprised or shocked by my disclosure that Lois and
I were going to get married, because he was the only person, outside of
our immediate families, who knew we wanted to make the break seven
years earlier.

Furthermore, he didn't foresee any legal difficulties, even when I
impressed upon him that it was imperative for Lois and me to become
man and wife as quickly as possible because of the fact that Lois would
have a minor living with her.

Gang took a giant load off our minds when he promised us that,
provided we could all arrive at a financial settlement quickly, he could
obtain our interlocutory decrees in about six weeks, and following that
he would arrange for us to fly to Juarez, where we could get a quick
Mexican divorce and a remarriage "that'll be legal enough for you two
to have Linda living with you until your California divorce becomes
final." Then, he added, we could get a California marriage, if we
wished.

It all seemed so terribly simple that as Lois and I drove to Palm
Springs with Linda in the back seat, we wondered why we hadn't gone
ahead and made the break years before.

And this time Linda, who was fourteen, wasn't upset about the
impending divorce.

"I haven't really lost a father," wisecracked Linda. "I've gained an
uncle."

Linda treated our whole escapade as a great adventure that she
was lucky to be sharing with us, and she looked with great anticipation
toward the day when the three of us could live in one house together.

"When will that be, Uncle Artie Boots?"

"According to Martin Gang, not very long," I assured her confidently.

How in hell could I know that even the best divorce plans can go awry in the face of a woman scorned?

HONESTY
ISN'T ALWAYS
THE BEST POLICY

AFTER spending what was probably the most delightful week-end of our lives at Palm Springs, Lois and I returned to Father's house in Trousdale late Sunday evening to find ourselves walking into a climate of complete hostility.

Father could barely growl "hello" to us as he opened his front door and admitted us. He looked at me unwelcomingly as I put my suitcase down on the terrazo floor of his entrance hall. And when Lois started to give him a friendly daughter-in-lawish kiss on the cheek, he pulled away from her in a manner that was so calculatingly cold that I knew in an instant that somebody had gotten to him in our absence and poisoned his mind against us.

The most likely suspect was Grace Kahn.

We had never deluded ourselves into believing that Grace would be happy over what we were "doing to her children." In fact it would have been abnormal of her not to be shaken up. At the same time we thought that she'd be mature enough, at the age of seventy-one, to have some empathy for our feelings.

Her first reaction to the news the previous Friday night was evidence that she was anything but mature.

While I was at Lois's house, helping her and Linda pack for Palm Springs, the doorbell suddenly rang imperiously.

Glancing out the peephole, we saw Grace, in just a robe thrown over a nightgown, standing on the front step. Her white hair was up in curlers, and there was a wild look in her beady black eyes as Lois asked her what she wanted.

"You have Arthur in there," screamed Grace. "I want to come in there and talk some sense into him."

As politely as I could, I told my mother-in-law to forget it and to go on home. Nothing she could say could possibly change my mind about marrying Lois.

"You're behind this whole thing," Grace spat at Lois. "You open up that door. This house belongs to my son, too."

Afraid of what her mother-in-law, in her rage, might do if she opened the door, Lois kept it tightly bolted. Undeterred, Grace stood on the step until four in the morning, ringing the bell and pounding on the door with maniacal determination.

A woman who would do that, would also try to poison a father's mind against his son.

When I pressed Father on the point, he admitted that he had talked to Grace on the phone while we were in Palm Springs.

"What about?" I asked.

"She thinks you should go back to Irene," snapped Father. "And I agree with her."

I never did find out what else they discussed, but I have a hunch his sudden change in attitude had to be based on more than an attempt at a reconciliation, or the fact that he felt what I was doing might jeopardize his long personal friendship with Grace.

At the root of it, probably, were his inherent suspicions and distrust of the female animal. His belief, for example, that they're all alike in bed, and that they're all after nothing but a man's money. So why leave one for another? And since Father rarely knows where his loyalties lie, and he generally listens to the last person who reaches his ear, he could have been susceptible to any propagandizing by the other side.

But at the time I was too stunned by his lack of support to do anything but express my surprise that he wasn't happy for us.

"What do you want me to do—give you a medal for leaving your wife?"

"I guess you'd like it better if I stayed some place else," I said. And I picked up my suitcase, grabbed Lois's hand, and the two of us headed for the Beverly-Hilton, after first dropping Linda off at her father's house.

We checked into separate rooms, on different floors, just so society would have nothing further to kick about.

We had no money, but I had my Carte Blanche card; and in the morning I'd be able to go to a bank and draw out enough cash for Lois and me to live on until I could arrange a financial settlement with Irene.

But I had grossly underestimated the woman I was dealing with.

When I arrived at the Bank of America shortly after it opened the following morning, I discovered that Irene had been there first and already closed our joint savings account, in which we had over twenty-five thousand dollars, and redeposited the money in an account of her own. She'd also beaten me to the Bank of Beverly Hills, where we had our checking account, plus a smaller savings nest egg containing about fifteen thousand.

Being without funds wouldn't have hurt quite so badly if I hadn't at the same time also lost my two chief means of earning a living.

With the Writers' Guild still striking the TV networks and producing companies, that source of revenue was cut off for God only knew how long. And I couldn't write any more funny magazine articles about my family, because I no longer had a family, and besides, what was happening to them wasn't very funny.

I hurriedly phoned an SOS to Martin Gang, and asked him if Irene had a right to do what she did with our bank accounts.

Most of the cash in those accounts had come from my *Life with Groucho* earnings, I explained.

Gang said it didn't matter whether she had a right to it or not—it was a *fait accompli*. And, furthermore, she had told him she had no intention of giving the money back to me ever—unless we went to court and a judge made her.

"If you hadn't been such a schnook," Gang added in a friendlier tone, "you'd have drawn a few thousand out before you left her—just as a precaution."

I had thought of it. In fact, a collaborator of mine on a couple of TV shows who had suspected I was about to bolt my marriage, had advised me to do the same. But I had pooh-poohed the idea, saying that I knew Irene. She would be hurt, but never vindictive, or unfair, or dishonest.

Yep, there was no doubt of it. Son of Groucho was a great assayer of character, as well as a fine tennis player. Also a schnook.

"What am I supposed to do for money?" I asked Gang.

"Don't worry," he said with customary lawyer's optimism. "I'm sure I can persuade her to release a few thousand dollars to tide you over."

A week later Irene came through with a check for five hundred dollars, and a cryptic message not to expect any more.

Meanwhile she was running around town charging at all the stores and gas stations, and running up enormous bills at her doctors' offices.

Between the five hundred dollars, and my Diners and Carte Blanche cards, I figured Lois and I could hold out for a few weeks—or at least until Martin Gang worked out a financial settlement, and we could get our divorces, and go to Mexico for another divorce and remarriage down there.

We were so confident that Gang would be able to expedite these arrangements that Lois and I signed a lease to rent a small vine-covered cottage up in the hills—starting in September. Since this was only the end of June, that would give us two months to wind up our other marriages.

Ample time, according to our new lawyer, Hector Sternwise, whom Lois and I had to engage when Martin Gang informed us, shortly after my last conversation with him, that it wasn't ethical for him to represent both sides of a divorce action. And since he had always been the Kahns' family lawyer, he felt obligated to stick with them.

Hector was the type of lawyer you'd hire if you'd just committed first-degree murder but didn't want to spend the rest of your life behind bars—you wanted to be sure to go to the gas chamber.

It wasn't that this tall, gangling, recent-graduate from law school was stupid; he just wasn't very experienced in divorce cases. But according to Martin Gang, it didn't really matter, because this was going to be a "very simple case" and it would be foolish of us to waste money on a "high-priced divorce attorney."

Martin Gang was right. It turned out to be a very simple case.

Gang summoned Hector and me to his office one day in midsummer for what we hopefully thought would be the final meeting to decide just how much Irene would accept in the way of a settlement. One point that had been holding things up was that I felt I was entitled to at least half the money from our joint savings accounts that Irene had taken it upon herself to confiscate. Irene felt otherwise. Nevertheless, she had agreed to have a conference about it.

Irene had a very smug smile on her face as she belatedly walked into the meeting, shook hands with everyone, including me, and then blithely announced that there was no use talking "settlement" because she had decided not to give me a divorce—EVER!

And in those days she could do just that. Even a Mexican divorce without her assent wouldn't hold up in the States.

"What's the point of that?" I asked. "It won't make me go back to you."

"I just don't believe in divorces," answered Irene.

With that she picked up her purse, smiled victoriously at me, and strode out of the conference room.

This was a ploy I hadn't figured on. Why would a person of Irene's supposed intelligence and perspicacity—and with over a thousand fifty-minute hours logged at Doctor Wayne's—wish to hang on to a husband who didn't want her? It didn't make sense.

There could be only two reasons for this tactic, Lois and I decided at a hastily called emergency meeting with Hector Sternwise in his office later in the day. Either Irene was hoping that by making things difficult I would agree to any settlement terms she cared to dictate, or else she was trying to drive Lois and me apart by not giving me my freedom. Quite possibly she figured that Lois would get tired of waiting and leave me.

Whatever her reasoning, she had us over the well-known barrel. For unless I took the offensive myself, and went to court with a provable case of adultery or desertion against her, I stood little chance of winning my freedom.

And who could I prove she'd left me for—a short wave radio?

The possibility of Lois and me ever becoming man and wife looked pretty hopeless, according to our lawyer. But before we left him that afternoon, the three of us had formulated a plan that we thought might drive Irene to the bargaining table.

As long as Irene contested my divorce, Lois would stall her financial settlement with Donald.

When she first left Donald, she hadn't wanted a thing from him— only her freedom so she could marry me. But after Irene made it impossible for Lois to have a husband right away, and she had no other means of support, necessity forced her to go to court and sue for temporary alimony. Irene, at the same time, decided she would go to court and ask the court to block me from seeing my children in "the company of Lois Kahn," on the grounds that her former sister-in-law was a bad influence on them morally.

Because both cases were related, Donald and Irene and Lois and I all were subpoenaed for the same hearing, at the Santa Monica Courthouse.

Our quadruple case came up before a Judge Landis.

I figured he'd really give Lois and me the works for falling in love with each other and breaking up homes with children.

Instead, he awarded Lois $750 a month temporary alimony and full custody of Linda.

He wouldn't release any of my money, but at the same time he adjudicated that Irene didn't need any more from me, so he ruled that I wouldn't have to pay her temporary alimony or child support.

And then he did something else that I could have hugged him for.

He ordered Irene to stand up and, in front of a packed courtroom, bawled hell out of her for trying to use Steve and Andy as weapons in her fight against their father. "And, furthermore," he concluded, "Steve and Andy can be with the very lovely Mrs. Kahn any time she pleases to be with them."

The upshot of the hearing was that I could see my kids with Lois whenever I pleased, and that Lois would be getting $750 a month until she had arrived at a financial settlement with Donald.

Our tactic was simple—if Lois could keep dragging her financial settlement out long enough, and Donald had to keep paying her $750 a month until she was married to me, then it was reasonable to assume he'd be forced to go to his sister and insist that she stop holding up my divorce. Out of compassion for her own brother's bank account, Irene would have to give in eventually, we felt.

It was a dirty trick to play on Donald, but it was our only ace in the hole.

But as the summer dragged on into September, nothing, it seemed, could dissuade Irene from contesting our divorce. Nothing her brother said. Nothing I said (that it would be better for all three children if this case could be settled amicably, without a bitter court battle).

And nothing her attorney said. Martin Gang, in fact, finally became so fed up with dealing with Irene that he quit the case and advised her to get another attorney. He didn't believe in what she was trying to do.

Meanwhile, Lois and Linda moved into the house on the hill that we had rented in anticipation that we would be sharing it as husband and wife by September. Since we weren't married, and society, plus our frightened mouthpiece, Hector Sternwise, said we couldn't live together, because it would jeopardize our case, I leased a small apartment on Barrington Avenue in West Los Angeles. Barrington Avenue is a streetful of cheap apartments inhabited chiefly by husbands and wives in various stages of shedding their mates. My one room cell was about five miles down a winding hill from Lois's house.

For a while, I commuted, but one evening as I was about to leave for my apartment, Lois and Linda confessed to me that they had been hearing noises in the bushes outside their windows every night after they were in bed, and that they were afraid to be alone in the house without a man. Would I please stay there with them?

I reminded Lois of the trouble Hector said we'd be inviting if we lived together without benefit of a rabbi. But Lois said she was more worried about the noises in the bushes, and Linda agreed, saying she didn't see what harm it could do as long as we slept separately.

So tower of will-power that I was, I agreed, and moved into the spare room. Just to protect them, of course (although I will admit that occasionally I slipped down the hall after Linda was asleep and protected Lois from her bed).

Naively, I believed the noises they had heard had been made by wild life—there were a lot of deer in the hills—or possibly the strong canyon winds. But at deposition proceedings months later, we learned that the wild animals were private detectives put on our trail by Donald and Irene.

Again I'd underestimated the enemy. But who would have suspected they'd bother with detectives?

To snoopy neighbors or other strangers who came to the house, I had to pass myself off as "Mrs. Kahn's live-in gardener and handyman." The role was a bit of a comedown to a man who'd once been the head of his own household in the Pacific Palisades, and assistant manager of a last-place Little League baseball team. And sometimes, as I lay awake nights worrying if Irene would ever give up, I couldn't help wondering if love was worth all this trouble.

I found out it was. It's better to be the right person's live-in gardener than the wrong person's husband.

As if I weren't having enough trouble just shedding Irene, I discovered, soon after Lois and I announced our intentions to wed, that we were being the victims of a smear campaign.

Columnist Ed Sullivan, a friend of the Marxes and the Kahns, led it off with a rather uncomplimentary story about us in his column. I don't recall the exact wording, but the gist of it was that Lois and I were two "beatniks" with no more morals than a couple of rabbits.

Louella Parsons and Hedda Hopper also had equally derogatory and mis-informed things to say about us in print.

My mother, turning female chauvinist, phoned Irene and advised her, "Take Arthur for every cent you can get. He's just like his father."

A good many of our erstwhile friends now averted their eyes when we met them on the street—including several who regularly practiced adultery themselves. One husband, in fact, who was so disapproving of us and of what we'd done that he wouldn't speak to us when we met him and his wife on the street one day, phoned Lois the same evening and asked her to meet him at the Polo Lounge "for drinks."

"I guess you don't know this, you nitwit, but I left Donald because I love Arthur," Lois blasted him back. "Now get the hell off this phone before I tell your wife."

Friends!

To make our disillusionment complete, I heard (through my kids, mainly) that my father was now consorting with the enemy.

Although he was shunning the company of Lois and me, he was exchanging dinner invitations regularly with Irene and Grace. He was even sitting at my place, at the head of the table, at my former house.

This bothered me for two reasons: (1) by being friendly with Irene he was giving silent approval to her tactics, thereby encouraging her to continue them, and (2) if we had to fight it out in court, I'd need a witness, and I was counting on him to testify on my behalf, which he certainly wouldn't do if he was being wined and dined by my ex-wife.

Where was Father's common sense? Where was his loyalty? A few well-chosen words from him to Irene would almost certainly persuade her to stop her dog-in-the-manger tactics.

Out of desperation, I finally asked him to intervene.

"Look, don't bring me into it," he said. "I have nothing against Grace and Irene. They've never done anything to me."

"It'll cost me money if we actually have to fight this thing out in court." I figured the mention of money would add weight.

"You should have thought of that before," he replied with self-righteousness.

"This thing is also hurting the kids," I explained patiently. "The longer it goes on, the longer before we can settle down again and lead normal lives."

But Father refused to become involved, in spite of the fact that several of his close friends, including Norman Krasna and Irwin Allen, told him he was giving comfort to the enemy, at his own son's expense.

I wasn't sure what his motive was, but I gave him the benefit of the doubt—that he wasn't actually against me, but merely too chicken to confront Irene. It was easier to say nothing—the cowardly way.

Okay, I decided, I'd come this far without his help—I could go the rest of the way.

But Father wasn't satisfied to remain neutral. At one point he even tried to drive Lois and me apart.

One evening, after another frustrating day wrangling with our lawyer over how to get Irene to change her mind, the phone rang just as we were about to sit down to dinner. Lois answered it.

"Hello, Groucho," I heard her say.

Figuring it augured something good for him to be initiating a phone call to us, I eagerly put my ear to the receiver, too.

"I don't approve of what you're doing," began Father sharply.

Lois was taken aback by the suddenness of his attack. Nevertheless, she pulled herself together to answer, "I'm surprised, Groucho. I should think that you of all people would understand."

"What does that mean?"

"You're not exactly Mary Poppins," said Lois.

"At least I never screwed around with my sister-in-law."

"Listen, Groucho," snapped Lois, trying hard to control her temper. "We're not just screwing around. Can't you understand? Arthur and I love each other. We want to get married."

"Love by any other name is still screwing," he retorted. "Besides, Grace Kahn and I have been friends for many years. This puts me in a very awkward position."

"If he were my son, I'd be more interested in knowing he'd found someone he could be happy with."

"What in hell does he know about happiness? I told him not to marry Irene in the first place."

"So he made one mistake," said Lois. "Must he spend the rest of his life paying for it?"

"You could be a mistake, too," said Father.

"What does that mean?" asked Lois.

"You're not going to get a penny of my money," said Father from out of left field.

"Is that what you're thinking?" exclaimed Lois. "Well, I have news for you, Groucho. I've lived without your money all my life, and I can get along without it now."

And with that, she threw down the receiver and burst into tears. "I don't know if I can stand much more of this," she sobbed, running from the room. "I just feel like going away and hiding."

I was ashamed—also shocked—that my own father could talk to Lois so cruelly. If it had been at all possible, I would have crawled right through the telephone line to get my hands on him.

But since that was impractical, I simply grabbed the receiver and said into it with as much loathing as I could muster, "Well, Padre, you've really done it this time. As far as I'm concerned, this is the end of the line. I don't want to see you or speak to you again—EVER!"

I didn't hang up, however. With trembling hand, I held onto the receiver in case he felt like apologizing. But I didn't hear anything else from him—just the clicking down of the receiver on the other end.

CHAPTER 33

THE
WINTER
OF OUR
CONTENTED
DISCONTENT

IT was a long winter, and I don't know how we ever would have survived it without (1) our love for each other, and (2) the temporary alimony Lois was getting.

We had one bit of good luck—the writers' strike ended, and I started picking up a few television assignments. But because of the length of the strike, the TV writers' market was suddenly so glutted with writers needing employment that the work was spread pretty thin.

By March, the prospect of Lois and me ever becoming legal man and wife seemed bleaker than ever.

Irene was still contesting the divorce—which meant that because of the crowded calendar, our case couldn't come up in court for possibly a year yet. (Uncontested cases were run through the divorce mill quickly because they didn't require much time in court.)

In addition, Irene was again refusing to let my children come to the house, in spite of the admonishing she'd been given by Judge Landis. Rather than go to court about it, I just stopped seeing them.

Compounding our miseries, Lois had to undergo major abdominal surgery. While Lois was in Cedars of Lebanon recovering, Linda, who we weren't aware had a yen to drive, sneaked her mother's car out of the garage one night and cracked it up beyond repair. When we were at the bank one day trying to borrow enough money to pay for Lois's operation plus the down payment on a new car, our house was robbed and we were wiped out of all our personal belongings—including my electric typewriter, my electric razor and Lois's fur coat.

From writing *Perry Masons*, I immediately deduced that the burglar had to be an out-of-work female TV writer with hairy legs.

It was apparent that Someone Up There was putting our love to the supreme test. If we could survive so much hard luck, and still live happily together (with a teenager yet), then the obvious conclusion had to be that we were right for each other.

And happy we were. We'd never been happier, and had so little.

More weeks passed.

Donald grew so desperate over Lois's reluctance to settle that he dragged her back into court, to complain about the fact that we were living illegally together, with Linda, a minor, in the house. He further shocked us by producing documented evidence from a private detective, to prove it.

The judge was unimpressed, but as a compromising gesture to assuage Donald, sent Linda to live with her grandparents—Lois's mother and father!

Then, in early spring, there appeared to be a thaw in the cold war between the Marxes and the Kahns.

Steve phoned one day and said, "Mom says it's okay now for me and Andy to go out with you."

I took them bowling. Why fathers in the process of getting divorced always take their kids bowling is something I've never understood. Perhaps throwing something heavy at a pin that's shaped like a woman purges husbands of a certain amount of hostility. Anyway, we went bowling. And while we were having Cokes afterwards, Steve let it slip that his mother had been dating his violin teacher for several months.

"Are you sure she's just not learning to play the violin?" I asked.

"No, he takes her out to the movies," snickered Steve. "He even kisses her good night."

That was encouraging; at least it proved she wasn't intending to go steady with her mother all her life.

A few days later I received word from Hector Sternwise that Irene was willing to give me a divorce, provided she could have "everything"—including the car I drove off in the night I left her.

I was so happy to get rid of her that I told Hector she could even have the box of Kleenex in the back seat.

Simultaneously Lois settled with Donald, and the two of us got our interlocutory decrees and flew to Juarez, where we were quickly processed through one of those South-of-the-Border divorce mills in a courthouse that smelled like a tamale factory and looked as if it hadn't been swept out of cigar butts since Pancho Villa's heyday.

"Okay, now where can we get married?" I asked eagerly, as soon as the judge pronounced us divorced in his native tongue. I wanted him to steer us to some romantic little church—where an understanding old padre (probably resembling Gilbert Roland) would tie the knot in a way befitting the climax of our beautiful if hectic romance.

"Señor," said the Judge. "You no comprende. I have just married you, also."

When we returned home, we received another surprise. We learned that Irene had married Steve's violin teacher the day before.

If only I'd known she was that anxious to get married I'd have held out to keep the car.

As I marveled at how she had deceived me all those months, I wondered if the fellow who wrote the line—all's fair in love and war—had ever tried to marry his sister-in-law.

Oh, well, the car needed a valve job anyway. Besides, I had what I wanted. Why shouldn't Irene be happy, too?

There was just one thing preventing my contentment from being quite complete, I realized as we settled down to the routine of everyday living.

As difficult as the old boy was, I missed seeing Doctor Hugo C. Hackenbush's inimitable face, smelling his strong cigars, and hearing those razor-sharp barbs cutting down some defenseless boob, like myself.

Nine months had passed since his infamous telephone call. That was the longest we'd ever gone in our lives without communicating. We'd had many serious fights in the past, always to make up again, because of some ineffable bond between us. You couldn't wipe out nearly forty years of good times we'd shared together, and all the generous things he'd done for me, just with one fight.

But this time when I didn't hear from him, I had a feeling that our differences might be beyond repair.

This wasn't over some stupid thing like a book or an article he didn't like—something where his vanity temporarily overpowered his paternal feelings for his son.

This was more basic. This was over a very simple four letter word called LOVE: whether Father *loved* me enough to want to see me happy, and whether I had a right to *love* and be loved by someone I had made up my mind I wasn't going to lose, no matter how hard I had to fight for her, and no matter which ones of my friends and relatives— possibly all of them—I had to sacrifice in the battle.

Lois and I have always believed that you don't get many opportunities to share real happiness and contentment and understanding with another person in one lifetime. So—like the gold ring on the carousel —if you don't reach out and grab it when it comes along, you might not get another chance.

If reaching for the gold ring meant never speaking to Father again, well, then it would just have to be. I certainly wasn't going to phone him, and return to that same old relationship, where the son apologizes to the father, when it should be the other way around.

I guess I'd finally grown up.

It was a Saturday night. Lois and I were having a drink before dinner and figuring out how many "friends" we'd lost through our double divorces, when the phone jangled.

Lois picked up the receiver. "Oh, hello, Groucho," I heard her say. Then: "Just a minute, I'll ask him." She covered the mouthpiece with her hand and whispered, "It's your father. He wants us to come to dinner tomorrow night."

Smiling as I fought to hold back the tears, I said, "Certainly—if it's all right with you."

"We'd love to, Groucho," said Lois. Then she handed me the receiver. "He wants to talk to you."

"Hi, Padre," I said.

"Big Feet, what would you like to eat?" he asked.

"Pot roast?" I said.

"Fine. Be here at seven."

When we walked into his house the next night, you'd have imagined it had only been a few days since we'd all been together. He kissed us both warmly; there was no mention of the disagreement; and though he didn't come right out and say so, he made it perfectly clear that he wasn't seeing much of Irene or Grace any more.

Just before dinner, he took me aside, and with kind of an embarrassed motion, stuck a folded piece of paper into my hand.

Unfolding it, I saw that it was a check for five thousand dollars. As I stared at it in astonishment, Father said, "I figured you could use it. It costs a lot to get divorced and remarried."

For a moment, I considered handing my check right back to him with a polite "thanks but no thanks."

The only thing this man respected was independence. And I'd made my declaration of independence many months ago over the telephone. What kind of a schlemiel would I suddenly be in his eyes if now—at the age of thirty-nine—I were to take a five-thousand-dollar welfare check?

But visualizing that pile of still unpaid legal bills on my desk, I mumbled my thanks and stuffed the check into my pocket.

Besides, it would have been an insult to refuse his wedding present. How could you insult a man who was big enough to admit he was wrong—especially if he was your father?

CHAPTER 34

A
DAY
AT THE
FUNERAL

A FEW months after Lois joined the Marx family, my Uncle Chico left it.

Chico, the eldest of the Marx brothers, was seventy-four when his big heart finally stopped beating one night when he was asleep in his bedroom in the unpretentious bungalow that he and his second wife, Mary, had been renting in a modestly priced neighborhood of Beverly Hills.

Father had always predicted that Chico's life would probably come to an end in bed—but of shotgun wounds, not angina pectoris; and not in his own bed, but in some other husband's.

When his final breath came, Chico had been ailing with a chronic heart ailment for several years, growing progressively weaker, thinner, and more hunched over by the day. Until, when I last saw him alive—at a gathering of the Marx clan at Father's house—I could hardly believe this wizened old man was the same Chico Marx who never was able to pass a good-looking girl without reaching out to pat her rear, or be in your home for over a half hour without succumbing to the urge to start dealing out the cards.

Chico had many faults—chief among them, a total disregard of responsibility—but his friends will always remember him for his sweet nature and a certain *joie de vivre* that only serious illness could subdue. When, finally, he had to take to his bed for his last few weeks upon this earth, I don't believe he really cared about living any longer. Not that way. What good was life if you were too weak to shuffle a deck or lay the manicurist?

As Father did predict, Chico, who'd earned millions, died broke, having gambled or thrown away foolishly every cent he had worked so hard to earn. Whenever I think of Chico's happy-go-lucky attitude towards money, I'm always reminded of *The New Yorker* cartoon which shows a lawyer reading the will to the family: "Being of sound mind, I spent every penny while I was alive."

During Chico's waning years, when he'd been too ill to work, he was forced to live off the generosity of his brothers. If they resented, just a little, having to shell out money to support a man who by all rights should have been as well-heeled as they, you didn't hear them complain too loudly. They perhaps realized that there might not have been as much to shell out if it hadn't been for Chico's contribution to the Marx Brothers' act. Maybe he wasn't Paderewsky, but nobody, including Paderewsky, has ever been able to duplicate his piano tricks, or to mesmerize an audience with quite the élan of the audacious Chico Marx.

Perhaps that's the legacy he left to everyone who knew him or saw him perform—the memory of him at the piano, in his little green hat, playing "On the Beach at Bali Bali," while fending off Groucho's wisecracks in his atrocious, but also inimitable, Italian dialect.

GROUCHO: (to Chico at the piano) How much do you get an hour to play?
CHICO: Six a-dollars.
GROUCHO: How much would you take not to play?
CHICO: Oh, you-a couldn't afford it.

Audiences ate it up—even complained bitterly when a Marx Brothers film didn't contain at least one Chico Marx number. Father hasn't forgotten that, as much as he'd like to.

So perhaps there was as much gratitude as resentment mixed in with their generosity when the other brothers, after supporting him in his later years, also had to spring for a very expensive funeral, catered by those great throwers of funerals, Forest Lawn.

The morning of the funeral—October 14, 1961—the immediate family was asked to assemble at the bereaved widow's house, there to be picked up in Cadillac limousines and driven to the services at Forest Lawn's Wee Kirk of the Heather chapel.

Lois and I arrived at the house a few minutes before ten, to be greeted solemnly by Mary, Chico's widow; my cousin Maxine, Chico's forty-four-year-old daughter, who had flown out from New York for the occasion; my sister, Miriam, who had moved back to California after an unsuccessful marriage in the East; and my Uncle Gummo and his wife, Helen.

Gummo, who had functioned as his brothers' agent and business manager for the past twenty-five years, remained in that capacity even in death. He had taken care of all the unpleasant details of getting his elder brother buried, from selecting the coffin to ordering the platters of cold cuts from Nate and Al's—for the after the service get-together. When we arrived he was efficiently seeing to it that everyone interested in a snack before the ride to the cemetery was served coffee and danish rolls.

Father and Eden hadn't shown up yet. Neither had Harpo and Zeppo, who, with their wives, had to drive in from Palm Springs, where they were permanently residing.

Father and Eden burst in through the front door shortly after we arrived. Father, looking properly solemn but making no sartorial concessions to the grim reaper, was dressed in a light gray business suit and tie, and could have been going to the Brown Derby to have lunch. His Mormon sidekick, however, was clad in black from the tip of her I. Magnin shoes to the crown of her cloche hat. This outfit, combined with her dead-white complexion, shoulder-length black hair, and tall, willowy figure, gave her the same appearance as the ghoulish lady in the Charles Addams cartoons.

As the two of them stepped into the living room, where the rest of us were sitting around trying to make cheerful small-talk with Chico's widow, Father seemed to notice Eden's sepulchral mien for the first time.

Indicating Eden with a jerk of his thumb, he remarked loudly to the rest of us mourners, "The way my wife's dressed you'd think *I* was the corpse!"

A few minutes later, Harpo and Zeppo arrived with their wives. After paying his respects to Mary, Harpo turned to Father and asked him how *he* felt.

"Better than Chico," answered Father.

Harpo grinned impishly, and said, "Wanna make a bet on which one of us goes next? I'll give you three to one, and take either corner. Zep'll hold the money."

"Oh, no," shot back Father. "I wouldn't trust him with my money any more than I would Chico."

Lois and I rode to Forest Lawn in the same limousine with Harpo and Susan and Father and Eden.

During the slow drive, Father kept our minds off the grimness of the occasion by telling a few of his favorite "death" jokes (including the one about the husband on his deathbed sniffing the aroma of freshly baked coffee cake and requesting a piece. "Don't be silly, Sam—that's for *after* the funeral!"); reciting a little Shakespeare ("Life is short, and the goal is but the grave."); and spouting a few comforting clichés ("It's nothing to feel sad about. Chico had more fun out of life than the rest of us combined.")

At Forest Lawn, a tremendous crowd of fans, mourners and the merely curious swarmed the walks and grassy areas around the chapel as our limousine pulled to a stop at the sidewalk, and the six of us alighted into the warm sunlight.

As we approached the chapel, I heard my name being called, and, turning, was surprised to see my mother standing among the uninvited throng lining the walk.

The temperature was pushing ninety, but Mother was wearing a full length mink coat and gloves. Her once near perfect figure was heavy-set and matronly now, like I remember my grandmother's was before she died, and her face was bloated from thirty years of too much booze, but you could still see vestiges of its former beauty.

Although she and I talked on the phone occasionally, and maybe even had dinner once a year around Christmas time, she and I were practically strangers now—just as she was to the rest of the Marx family. Nevertheless, her presence at the funeral that day was ample indication that she couldn't quite forget that she had once been a Marx, that her own rear end, when it had been small, firm and provocative, had probably been the recipient of some of Chico's affectionate slaps.

I gave her a quick dutiful kiss on her whiskey-smelling lips, but it was Father she was mainly interested in.

"Hello, Grouch," she whispered as he walked by.

He acknowledged her presence with a grim smile, then quickly ducked inside the chapel.

I believe it was the last time they ever saw each other. She died, ironically enough, while I was writing this chapter.

Inside the chapel, which pulsated with soft organ music and reeked of that cloyingly-sweet miasma of too many flowers under one roof, there wasn't an empty seat.

Chico's silver casket rested in the appropriate place before the altar, and as we filed past it in order to reach the cloistered section of seats reserved for "family," I was shocked to see that the lid was open. Father averted his eyes as he walked past the waxen-looking Chico.

We were the first to sit down in the family room, except for a complete stranger who had taken one of the better seats for himself.

I nudged Father and asked him if he knew the fellow. Father studied him for a moment, then shook his head. "He must be left over from the last funeral," he said.

The rabbi who delivered the eulogy had never met Chico. He gave a long, dull, cliché-ridden speech that would have fit just about anybody except the man we were there to remember.

Eventually the torturesome service came to an end with a short prayer, and we rose to leave. At that moment, I heard a commotion in the rear of the chapel and saw three precocious children—about eight years old and all wearing Harpo-type wigs—and a man, who was evidently their manager, rush down the aisle towards the open casket.

The three midget-sized Harpos struck a theatrical-looking pose in front of the casket, while the adult of the group aimed a camera and flash gun at them and took three quick pictures.

"I'm surprised he didn't ask Chico to say 'cheese,'" muttered Father as he looked with contempt at the publicity seekers.

To my relief, Father and Harpo chose to skip the graveside ceremonies, and the six of us piled into the limousine for the long drive back to Beverly Hills from Burbank.

The mood in the car wasn't exactly a gay one now, but there was that relaxed, relieved feeling that comes from being able to say to yourself, "Well, thank God that's over," and the exhilaration of knowing you're still alive and not the unfortunate one in the casket.

As Father leaned back and made himself more comfortable, he suddenly exclaimed, "For Christ's sake, Harpo. Why in hell did Mary have to hire a rabbi who didn't even know Chico? Have you ever heard such a goddamn pack of lies?"

"Nobody could know Chico unless he was a card hustler," Harpo reminded him.

"Or a madame in a whorehouse," added Father.

"I guess Mary didn't know who to get," commented Susan.

"She should have got me," said Father, a little testily. "I should have done the eulogy. I could have told the congregation plenty about Chico that they didn't know."

"You certainly could have," said Harpo. "I could have too."

"Imagine that schmuck getting up there in front of all those people and saying Chico was so generous he'd give you the shirt off his back," exclaimed Father. "Sure, he'd give you the shirt off his back if he had one. Trouble is he never had one."

"The rabbi also said he was charitable," interjected Harpo.

"He was charitable all right," said Father. "I'd like to tell them about the time he stole the bass drum from a Salvation Army band so he could hock it to pay off a debt. I don't think that he gave a penny to charity in his life."

"But he was kind to his family and good to his kids," said Harpo.

"Sure, he was cheating on Betty from the first day he married her."

"And the only time he ever saw Maxine was at dinner time between golf and his bridge game," added Harpo.

"He wouldn't even take her to Europe when I took my kids," said Father. "I'll never forget the picture of Maxine standing on the dock crying as all of us sailed for France on the *Paris*."

"He was especially charitable to his family," said the normally mild Harpo. "Mary tells me he didn't have a dime of life insurance. That's what I call being kind to your family. If you had Chic for a husband, you didn't need an enemy."

"I suppose he was so good to *us*," said Father, really warming to his subject. "Will you ever forget that time we were playing Scranton when we nearly got lynched by a mob of angry coal miners because one of them found Chico in the hay with his daughter?"

"Or about the time in Chicago," chimed in Harpo, "when we had to do the show without him for a week because the son of a bitch was escaping across the Canadian border with a gangster he'd given a bum check to chasing him with a machine gun?"

"Yeah," said Father. "I'll never forget what the manager of the theater told us when we went to collect our salary after the last show Saturday night: 'Not one red cent. I hired *four* Marx Brothers, not three!' Yes, you couldn't help loving Chico after all the charitable things he did for everybody. I still can feel the thrashing I got from Pop when he blamed me for losing Stuckfish's trousers, when actually Chico had hocked them."

"You just got a licking," said Harpo. "But what about poor Mom and Pop? They couldn't come up with the rent because Stuckfish refused to pay them, and we all got evicted from the flat on 92nd Street."

"If you couldn't love him for that, then you just don't know a charitable fellow when you see one," concluded Father with a shake of his head. "Well, it's the old story—the people who are really nice and charitable, like you and me, never get the credit for it."

They panned Chico irreverently all the way back to the house. Then, just as the limousine was pulling to the curb, Harpo said, as though he'd just thought of it, "Yeah, Grouch—you should have done the eulogy."

"At least I wouldn't have been hypocritical," said Father, getting out of the car. "They'd have known what Chic was really like when I got through with him."

That evening, Father took me and Lois to dinner at Chasen's.

For the first time, I saw him completely disregard "moderation" as the governing word in his approach to health and happiness. In rapid succession he had four straight whiskies, and got so loaded we practically had to carry him to the car after dinner.

I guess he felt worse about losing Chico than he let on.

Three years later, on September 28, 1964, Harpo breathed his last, at the age of seventy-six, following open-heart surgery.

According to his wishes, there was no funeral service of any kind —just a quick cremation.

Harpo wasn't taking any chances.

CHAPTER 35

THE
SON
ALSO
RISES

DESPITE the divorce, which wiped out all our savings, including Father's five-thousand-dollar wedding present (which went to pay off Irene's lawyer), we still managed to avoid living over a fish store.

When our lease was up and we no longer had to worry about private detectives spying on us, Lois and I moved down from the hills and into another house in West Los Angeles, so that Linda, my combination niece and stepdaughter, wouldn't have so far to travel to reach University High on the days she felt like attending.

Our new abode was a charming Colonial bungalow which belonged to the actress Mona Freeman. The rent we paid her was more than we could afford, but I didn't care. With Lois as my wife, I was happier than I'd ever been in my life, and I would have been even happier if it hadn't been for two things: (1) I had to live in the same house with a teen-aged girl, and (2) Father still considered me practically a welfare case, in spite of the fact that I was scratching out a fair living as a free-lance writer. One evening at Chasen's I overheard Father remark to a friend, "I still have to support all my kids."

It wasn't true, in spite of the five grand he had given me, but I knew what he meant—I wasn't in the ninety percent bracket as he was, and that was his only yardstick.

Anyway, his remark—plus the many financial obligations I found myself saddled with as a result of my divorce settlement—started me thinking that I'd better commit myself to some business where the pay was steadier and more lucrative than it was free-lancing the magazine market, which was slowly but steadily being eroded by TV.

Every magazine to which I had contributed regularly over the years had folded, or was in the process of folding—*Collier's*, *The Saturday Evening Post*, and *Women's Home Companion*. And two brand new entries in the magazine derby—Hugh Hefner's *Show Business Illustrated* and Huntington Hartford's *Show*—also went under shortly after they had bought articles from me. Which caused Father to remark to me, "What magazines have you put out of business this week?"

"It's not funny," I said.

He shrugged, and said, "I told you to be a director."

Although I had many solo TV writing credits to my name, I had not really taken the medium seriously until shortly after Lois and I were married, when I became friendly with a television writer named Bob Fisher, who wrote with a fellow named Alan Lipscott.

Bob was about my age, but he was a veteran in the television business. He'd written over 500 TV scripts with Lipscott, and the team was responsible for the success of many highly rated series—*The Danny Thomas Show* and *Bachelor Father*, among others.

Bob doesn't like to work alone—he needs company—so when Lipscott died on him in the middle of a script they were writing for the *Pete and Gladys* series, he asked me to team up with him. Ironically, Father had given Bob his first job in the business way back in 1942, when he was doing the Pabst radio show, and Bob was only nineteen.

Bob and I got along well from the start.

After finishing out the *Pete and Gladys* series together, we created

a series for Mickey Rooney and sold it to ABC. We wrote it and produced it, but we will take no responsibility for its quick demise after
seventeen weeks. Tom Moore, who was masterminding ABC at the
time, foolishly slotted us at nine o'clock, Wednesday evenings—opposite the original Dick Van Dyke–Mary Tyler Moore show, at the
peak of its success, and the NBC movie of the week. After six weeks,
you couldn't find the *Mickey Rooney Show* in the first hundred in the
ratings. But that's television—it isn't always what you are, it's where
you are.

Bob Fisher was an incredibly fast writer, and one who didn't believe in wasting time. He couldn't afford to—he had a wife who spent
money faster than he could make it.

One week, when we had three days off between television assignments, my new collaborator said, "Let's write a movie original. Have
you any ideas?"

I told him one I had, it appealed to him, and in three days we had
finished an eighteen page treatment called *Eight on the Lam*. Our
agent told us it was too short to sell, but figuring I had little to lose, I
handed it to Louis Shurr, Bob Hope's agent, one afternoon and asked
him to read it with his famous client in mind, for the leading role.

Two days later Shurr phoned and said Bob Hope wanted to buy
our story, and would give us fifty thousand dollars to do the screenplay.
That surprised me, but not so much as the story of how Hope happened to read *Eight on the Lam* in the first place.

Hope is notorious for his aversion to reading anything—even
scripts that he is already committed to doing. He's too busy flying
around the country making personal appearances, raising funds for
charity, and playing golf with Agnew and other politicians to waste
time on his own business pursuits.

One day he walked into Shurr's office, and said he had a yen to
make a picture but couldn't find a story he liked. "What have you got
that's good, Doc?" he asked Shurr.

Shurr pointed to a stack of thick scripts on his desk. Wedged in
between two of them was our very thin manuscript. Hope's hand
quickly pulled *Eight on the Lam* out of the stack.

"I'll read this one," he said. "It'll take me less time."

That's how we sold our first picture. Following *Eight on the Lam*, we did several more for Hope—none of them Academy Award Winners, but all good money makers—and a picture for Ross Hunter starring Andy Williams, Robert Goulet and Sandra Dee (you should pardon the expression).

It was while we were waiting for a story conference with Ross, who was too busy with his numerous other projects to see us for a few days, that we wrote the first scene of *The Impossible Years*.

Linda, my new step-daughter (formerly my niece), was the main inspiration for our first collaborative play effort. Until I inherited her, I never knew the delights of living with a teen-aged girl who chain-smoked; dressed like a slob; kept her room in a pig-pen condition; never went to bed before two A.M. or rose before one P.M. if she could help it; and was a devotee of the new music—the Beatles, in particular, but in a pinch any group with a loud enough electric guitar to destroy an ear drum, and which didn't play tunes by such squares as George Gershwin or Rodgers & Hammerstein or Cole Porter.

A particularly sharp thorn in Lois's side was Linda's habit of bringing food back to her room to munch on while she was watching television, phoning, or pretending to be doing homework, and never returning a dish, glass, empty Coke bottle or piece of silverware to the kitchen when she was through with it.

Naturally, this infuriated Lois, who is a very neat housekeeper, but neither sharp words nor threats of punishment could persuade Linda to change her ways.

To cope with this problem, I finally suggested that we just let the dirty dishes pile up in Linda's bedroom until she *herself* grew so tired of seeing them there that she would return the crockery to the kitchen of her own accord.

Lois thought this was a brilliant idea, too, and followed my advice for about six weeks. Unfortunately, Linda didn't seem to mind, or even notice, that no one was cleaning up her room. She let the dishes and glasses accumulate there until finally we had none left for our table use. We realized then that we'd either have to break down and retrieve the plates from Linda's room, or buy a new set of china.

Necessity forced us to run up the white flag in this battle of wills between parent and teen-ager. It was cheaper to clean her room ourselves than to buy new table china and flatware.

Besides her annoying personal habits, Linda hated school. Her grades showed it, but since neither Lois nor I had ever cared much for school when we were kids, we tried to be understanding about her lack of application—until one semester in her final year at University High when she received a "flunking" notice in gym. Gym wasn't important, for she got all the exercise she needed doing the watusi until three every morning, but unfortunately she couldn't graduate from high school if she failed Physical Ed.

It seemed incredible to Lois and me that anyone as well-coordinated as Linda on the dance floor could flunk gym. As I pointed out to her, "All you have to do is show up and take a shower."

"The gym teacher hates me," said Linda.

"That's easy to understand," said Lois.

"No, I mean it, Mom. She's always picking on me for no reason."

Convinced by Linda's earnestness that her daughter was the victim of some unwarranted prejudice, Lois, dressed to the teeth, showed up at University High bright and early the following morning, and demanded to see the principal.

The principal, a Mrs. Atterbury, listened very attentively as Lois poured out the story of how her "baby" was being persecuted by a gym teacher who had evidently taken a disliking to her for "no apparent reason."

"And do you believe your daughter?" Mrs. Atterbury asked after the defense had rested its case.

"Of course I do," replied Lois indignantly. "She may have a few faults, but she never lies."

The principal went to the files and pulled out a Manila envelope containing Linda's records.

As she looked them over, a smile creased the corners of her mouth in a way that made Lois fidget uneasily in her chair.

"Did you know Linda has been absent from school eighteen times so far this semester?" asked the principal, removing a letter from the file.

"I don't believe it," answered Lois irately. "I see her leave for school every morning."

"Oh, by the way, this is off the subject," said the principal, casually, "How is Mr. Kahn getting along after his heart attack?"

"What heart attack?" asked Lois.

"The one you mentioned in the excuse you wrote," said the principal, handing Lois a note written on her personal stationery.

Please excuse Linda from school yesterday as her father had a severe heart attack and she has to visit him at the hospital.

Sincerely,

Lois Marx

"I didn't write that," protested Lois. "Linda's father didn't have a heart attack."

"Then your baby must have written it—the one who never lies," said the principal, with a saccharine-sweet smile.

As Lois's face reddened with humiliation, the principal added, riffling through the file, "I have a few more notes here, too, if you'd care to see them."

"No, thanks," said Lois, and she fled from the office in disorderly retreat.

If Linda wasn't making fools of us, she'd be frightening us. One evening she went out on a date, and didn't return until after breakfast the next morning. When we bawled her out for it, she answered, "Don't blame me."

"Who should I blame?" demanded Lois.

"The police."

"The police?"

"Yes, they rounded up a whole bunch of us and kept us in jail all night because they found a little pot in one of our cars."

Every morning, before Bob and I would actually begin work, I'd fill him in on Linda's latest caper. Not having to live through it himself, he found her antics extremely amusing.

After a year of listening to my complaints, Bob said, "Why don't we write a play about teen-agers? There hasn't been a really funny one in years. And you certainly have enough material for one."

If it accomplished nothing else, it seemed like a good way of getting rid of my hostility toward the younger generation, so I agreed to take a crack at it.

Because neither of us could afford to give up our movie and TV assignments, we were forced to write the play in our spare time—on week-ends, holidays, evenings, and when we were waiting for Ross Hunter. But even so we completed the play in a little over six weeks.

We called it *The Impossible Years*, and at the suggestion of a friend, sent it to Brandt and Brandt—a firm of literary agents in New York City.

In a few days the play came back to us with a cryptic note that said, "In our opinion this material is not for Broadway."

Not ones to accept defeat easily, we threw the play in a drawer and left it there for nearly a year, while continuing to knock out scripts for *My Three Sons*, *McHale's Navy*, and a debacle called *The Cara Williams Show*.

As spring, the time for development of new series ideas, approached, Bob and I decided that *The Impossible Years* might be a good bet for a TV series so we dug it out of the file and gave it to Sylvia Hirsch, our television agent, at William Morris.

Sylvia thought it too good to waste as a TV series, and sent it to Helen Harvey, who handled theater for William Morris in New York at the time. Helen thought it was salable, too, and within a few days found us three producers—David Merrick, George George (who produced *Any Wednesday*), and David Black, who hadn't produced much of anything.

On Helen Harvey's advice, we gave *The Impossible Years* to David Black, because he didn't want it rewritten, intended to go into production with it immediately, and was hopeful of getting it on the boards by early fall.

By June, however, we were still having trouble snagging a star to play the leading role of the teenaged girl's father, a psychiatrist.

We wrote the part with John Forsythe in mind, because of Bob's long association with *The Bachelor Father* series. But Forsythe passed on the grounds that playing the part of a father of a teenager might destroy his image of a romantic leading man, which he was trying to re-create.

We were also turned down by Henry Fonda, Art Carney and everyone else who meant anything at the box office.

There were plenty of actors available who didn't mean anything at the box office, but David Black couldn't raise the money on their names.

Which is one of the big things wrong with Broadway today. Most producers won't risk going into production without a name to give them the insurance of a healthy run in spite of what the critics might say; and most stars of that magnitude aren't anxious to go to Broadway, because (1) they don't want to live in New York and be chained to a theater every night, or (2) they can make more money at Las Vegas, in films or on TV without nearly so much risk, or (3) their agents tout them off doing plays because Broadway salaries are comparatively small, and the agent's cut will be less.

So you must either get an older big name who's interested in making a comeback (Katharine Hepburn or a Jimmy Stewart) or a new name who already has a reputation (Barbra Streisand in *Funny Girl* or Alan Arkin in *Luv*), but who is still adventurous enough to try something different, his agent be damned.

Or be Neil Simon, who himself is the star.

For a brief time, we thought we had Paul Ford, who was very hot in 1965, having just finished a three-year run in *Never Too Late*. Ford, in fact, gave David Black a verbal commitment. Black, in turn, was so grateful that he bought the actor a two-hundred-dollar sport jacket. Since Black is the kind of fellow who will call you long distance from a phone booth and reverse the charges because he claims he doesn't have any change, we had to assume that Paul Ford was a sure thing if David would part with that kind of money.

But soon after he accepted the sport jacket, Ford reneged on the handshake deal and went into a play of Jerry Chorodorov's that closed in three weeks. The last I heard, David was still trying to get back custody of the sport jacket.

One day Black called us from New York and didn't reverse the charges, so we had to assume something important was up. It was.

He said that Alan King had read the play and was dying to do it.

We questioned whether Alan was a big enough name or a good enough actor. At the time, his reputation was mainly as a nightclub comic. He appeared sporadically on the *Ed Sullivan Show*, and two or three times a year he played Las Vegas, which was the only place I'd ever seen him.

Black assured us that King was our man, for three reasons: (1) he was a big name with the "theater party ladies," which automatically assured us a long run in spite of what the critics might say, (2) his acting was good. He was at that very moment appearing in the Sam Levene role in *Guys & Dolls* at the City Center Theater and had received "rave notices" from all the papers, and (3) his enthusiasm for the play knew no bounds. (I knew the latter to be true, because King called me up later that afternoon while I was at the tennis club and interrupted me in the middle of a singles match to say *The Impossible Years* was the funniest play he'd ever read, and would we please consider him for the lead?)

So that we would have no doubts, Black flew Bob and me and our wives to New York to catch Alan in *Guys & Dolls* that Saturday night. We thought he was great as Nathan Detroit, but we weren't sure if he'd be believable as a psychiatrist. He sounded more like a truck driver.

We were anxious to get into rehearsals, however, so we reluctantly gave Alan King our approval.

Signing Alan turned out to be a great *coup,* for not only was he hilarious in the role, but he was an unbelievably great attraction at the box office. Before we left New York for our Philadelphia opening, the Playhouse on 48th Street, which was to be the home of *The Impossible Years* for the next two years, had already sold $800,000 worth of tickets in advance.

I have detailed how we signed Alan King to repudiate those critics—and they were legion—who accused Bob and me of "manufacturing" a vehicle just for Alan King, or "stringing together a lot of television jokes." Obviously neither accusation was true, but then a good many things theater critics write are of doubtful validity.

A particular piece of critical insanity that has always galled me came from the pen of Elliot Norton, the acerbic drama critic on the *Boston Globe,* the morning after our pre-Broadway try-out in his home town. In reviewing (or should I say "murdering") *The Impossible Years,* he wrote:

There are a number of very funny jokes in *The Impossible Years*. Possibly they were written by Arthur Marx, who is co-author with Bob Fisher of this new comedy at the Wilbur, and most significantly, a son of Groucho.

There are a great many other jokes in the same show which are not funny at all . . . the son of Groucho couldn't have written these.

In analyzing Norton's blast, I have to ask: In implying that the culprit was my partner and that no son of Groucho could write an unfunny line, which Groucho Marx was Mr. Norton referring to—the Groucho of *A Night at the Opera*, whose dialogue was written for him by George S. Kaufman and Morrie Ryskind (Pulitzer Prize playwrights), or the Groucho who co-authored the play *Time for Elizabeth*, which Mr. Norton panned unmercifully, even with my father appearing in the leading role?

I have exhumed that incident not to defend *The Impossible Years*, but only to illustrate my main theme. Without the Son of Groucho label to peg his review on, perhaps Mr. Norton could have been objective enough not to have to compare every line with something from a Marx Brothers film. Maybe he could have even relaxed enough to enjoy the show.

Fortunately, the major critics spared us any further reviews that petty and obviously resentful of the fact that I was Groucho's son, and thus able to get a play produced when others, more lowly born, might not be able to. But quite a few critics did allude to the fact that we wouldn't have been a hit without Alan King (as though a perfect wedding of material and performer hasn't always been the key to a stage hit).

Even Alan King finally came to believe he was solely responsible for the show's success. One night, after *The Impossible Years* had been running on Broadway for over a year, he confided in me that it certainly wouldn't have been a hit without him.

"I suppose you're up there on the stage ad libbing," I said angrily. "Whose words are getting the laughs? *You* certainly didn't make them up!"

At that moment, I couldn't help remembering the time Alan had phoned me up on the tennis court and said he thought *The Impossible*

Years was the funniest play he'd ever read, and would we *"please* consider me for the part?"

Jack Gaver, the United Press critic, summed up my feelings most eloquently in his book on the 1965–66 Broadway season, *Season In, Season Out,* when he wrote of *The Impossible Years*:

> There have been at least a dozen comedies this season in which King conceivably could have played the leading role. And his presence wouldn't have saved one of them.
>
> It just happened that the collision of King and *The Impossible Years* added up to one of those thousand-and-one happy intangibles that keep the theater going . . . King could make another attempt next season with a far better script—even in one by the currently red-hot Neil Simon—and be a loser. That's show business.

Whether we'd written the great American comedy or not, *The Impossible Years* was a successful play from the start.

During our pre-Broadway tryout, it set a new house record at the Forest Theater in Philadelphia, grossing over sixty thousand dollars in our second week there. At the Colonial Theater in Boston the week following, we also broke the house record (in spite of Elliot Norton). And by the time we were headed for our New York opening, *Variety* was already proclaiming us a solid hit.

Not only were we sold out at the Playhouse until the following March, but just before our New York opening, MGM purchased the film rights for $350,000.

The only person who was curiously unenthusiastic about *The Impossible Years* impending success was Father.

All during our rehearsal period in New York his was the one voice of doom. He didn't come East during that time but his letters kept stressing that "Broadway's the toughest racket there is," "critics are all out to stick knives in any Hollywood writer," and "Don't worry if it's not a hit—we'll love you, anyway."

I didn't receive a telegram from Father before our first opening on the road, and when I called him from Philadelphia to tell him it looked as if we had a hit, he explained that he hadn't sent a wire because he didn't know we had opened yet.

I'd written him the date, of course, but it was quite possible he had forgotten. After all, his memory wasn't what it used to be—especially on dates that weren't important to *him*.

Although many of our close friends and relatives—including Linda—flew in for our New York opening, Father chose to sit it out in California, claiming, "My nerves couldn't take one of your openings."

I guess his nerves couldn't take sending me a telegram either, because there was no word from him among the large stack of Western Union good-luck messages I found waiting for me at the stage door of the Playhouse on opening night.

But as Father explained to me when I mentioned this to him upon my return to California, "You know I was thinking of you, Big Feet. That's all that counts."

I know *I* was thinking of Father, as I sat nervously with Lois and Linda in the orchestra of the Playhouse Theater opening night, and waited with bated breath and the usual butterflies in my stomach, every time Alan King or one of the other actors snapped a punch line, to see if it evoked the proper response. Father had sweated out a few Broadway first nights himself—only from up on the stage.

As I listened gratefully to the waves of laughter and heard the cheers as the cast took one curtain call after another, I knew that no matter what the critics might say, *The Impossible Years* was in for a long run on Broadway. Our advance assured us of that. Father had to be aware of it, too, I felt, for he also read *Variety*. I couldn't help wondering if he wasn't just the least bit proud to know that his son had his name up in lights along Broadway's "gay white way" just as he and his brothers once had theirs there in the past.

I felt proud anyway, as I realized that this Marx had made it to Broadway instead of to that room over a fish store in Boston. The important money I'd be making over the next couple of years was incidental. Bob and I had written a standard. As Cecil Smith, the drama critic for the L.A. *Times,* wrote:

> . . . it's festooned with some very funny jokes at which the chic opening night audience roared with laughter and it is so sturdily assembled that I imagine it will run as long as a 1920 Dodge. And I will bet a thin dime or even a fat dime that sooner or later, wherever you are, you'll be exposed to it. It's one of those comedies that hits every circuit, the road, stock, tents, musical roundhouses, the movies

(MGM has bought it for $350,000), maybe someday, cleaned up a little, TV.

Smith's prediction turned out to be the case. *The Impossible Years* has played everywhere—including Berlin, London, Prague, and Mexico City—and the picture version was a hit, too.

Still, it was a hollow victory if I couldn't get my own father to see the show while it was still on Broadway. He hadn't seen me beat Jack Kramer, either.

But Father finally came through, like the loyal father I'd always hoped he'd be.

Shortly after the first of the year, Father couldn't contain his curiosity any longer. ("What possibly could that upstart have written that was so successful it even sold out Christmas week, the worst week in the theater?") He fabricated a reason for going to New York on business, and told me he expected "good seats, and for nothing" to *The Impossible Years*.

I immediately phoned the box office to make sure they gave him my house seats and charged them to me.

A week later, Father flew back into town.

"How'd you like the show?" I asked.

"It's a hell of a funny evening in the theater," he replied, without a moment's hesitation. "The most laughs I've had in a long time."

I couldn't believe it. There wasn't even a qualifying statement.

"There's just one trouble," he suddenly added, after I thought I was home free. "The management tried to charge me for the tickets."

"Well, I told them not to let you pay," I explained, feeling a little bit embarrassed. "The dumb girl at the box office must have slipped up."

"That's all right," he said. "I finally got in for nothing."

"How?"

"I demanded to see the manager. And when he came out in the lobby, I yelled at him in front of all those people milling around, 'I'm not paying money to see this turkey. You know who I am? I'm Arthur Marx's father!'"

CHAPTER 36

WHERE
HAVE ALL
THE MARXES GONE?

MY status in the Marx family did get a boost with the success of *The Impossible Years*. To my uncles, I was no longer just their nephew the tennis player who was always losing in the finals of a tennis tournament when they were sitting in the grandstand—I was the author of a Broadway hit, to which everybody expected free tickets.

And Father paid me the supreme compliment.

He invited me out to lunch, and insisted that I pay the check (if you're out of work, or he believes you're not doing well, he'll always lift the tab). So I knew he no longer figured I was a candidate for that room over the fish store, and that gave me more satisfaction than beating Kramer.

In addition to the fact that I finally seemed to have an identity of my own, the passing years have seen a few other important changes in the look of the Marx family.

Harpo and Chico are, of course, gone—nearly ten years now. My mother has been dead just a few weeks, dying a lonely death in a convalescent hospital. All that remains of that once beautiful but restless body are a few ashes in an urn somewhere in San Fernando Valley— the same San Fernando Valley about which she once told Father, when he was threatening to settle down there, "I could never live in the Valley permanently. It isn't gay enough!" How ironic that she will be there through eternity.

Gummo and Zeppo are both in excellent health, retired, and living in Palm Springs, in beautiful homes just off one of Tamerisk Country Club's oasis-green fairways. When he isn't hobnobbing with the Sinatra-Agnew crowd, Zeppo keeps active by hustling rich suckers at golf and cards, and giving Gummo tips on what's wrong with his putting.

My sister, Miriam, now forty-four, is living in Hollywood.

My stepdaughter, Linda The Impossible, has finally settled down, is married to a college professor, of all things, and is about to become a mother herself, God help her.

My half-sister, Melinda—that lively little bundle of precocity you might have seen singing duets with Father on *You Bet Your Life* when she was a child—is already on her second marriage at the age of twenty-six.

Her first marriage was to the producer of an ungerground movie in which she was starring. Father spent $8,000 on an extravagant celebrity-attended wedding which he threw at his house. He walked down the aisle with Melinda on his arm, as gravely and sedately as Spencer Tracy did in *Father of the Bride*. Two weeks later Melinda dissolved the marriage by running off with the handsome, long-haired young man who was playing opposite her in the underground movie.

The movie was never completed. Instead of a career, Melinda has a two-year-old son, Miles, to show for her impetuosity. She's never been happier.

Father keeps a picture of Miles in his wallet and, like any proud grandpa, will whip it out at the slightest provocation and say, "Have I shown you the latest picture of my grandson?" Also, like any proud grandpa, he will show you the picture whether you've seen it before or not.

Father's own marital status is once again—single.

In 1969, Eden surprised no one (except Father) by suing him for divorce and asking for a settlement of half of four million dollars, which she accused him of accumulating during the fourteen years of their marriage.

Despite his outward cynicism about women and their predatory motives, Father deep down is a romanticist. He truly believed Eden loved him, and was deeply hurt and surprised by her decision to walk out on him. When he phoned to tell me about it, he sounded on the verge of tears. I felt like shedding a few tears for him myself. The only other time in my life that I had ever seen him cry was when he received the news of Harpo's death.

I was not surprised by Eden's leaving, however.

At a party one night, Eden had once said to me and Lois—in a very frank confession induced by several martinis—"I've waited this long. I might as well stick it out all the way."

•Whatever she meant by "sticking it out all the way," she evidently didn't have the patience, and decided to go for a large settlement instead.

According to Father, Eden didn't come close to getting two million dollars, but I can assure you she's not living over a fish store in Bell, California, either.

Father's never been one to hold grudges, however. He's always remained on friendly terms with his ex-wives, no matter what they accused him of in court or how many pounds of flesh their high-priced attorneys tried to exact. He continued to pay my own mother alimony long after their settlement agreement said he didn't have to, and a few months after Eden divorced him, he was dating her again, and even flew her to the opening of *Minnie's Boys* on Broadway.

"How can you take her out after what she's done to you?" asked Irwin Allen one evening. "What have you two got to talk about?"

"There's a wealth of material," explained Father blithely. "We talk over our old fights."

Father's divorce and the resultant unpleasant headlines in the Los

Angeles papers have not, fortunately for him, sullied his image as a desirable bachelor and a good catch.

Despite his eighty-plus years, Father is constantly being accosted by young women who are interested in sharing his community property with him.

One bold lady that I have in mind showed up on his doorstep soon after the divorce was publicized, bearing gifts of a bottle of wine and honey cake she had baked. "I just thought you might be lonely," she said, introducing herself.

They went steady for eight months, but when the young lady mentioned the word "marriage," Father told her to go peddle her honey cake somewhere else.

If Father's not being accosted, chances are he'll be doing the accosting. If you patronize Nate and Al's Delicatessen in Beverly Hills at lunchtime, you might even be lucky enough to see him in action. If you are a pretty girl, you might even get picked up and have your check paid by him.

Father eats lunch at Nate and Al's a couple of times a week, usually with his long-time friends—Harry Ruby, Arthur Sheekman, and Nunnally Johnson.

Nate and Al's is probably the most popular luncheon spot in chic Beverly Hills. There's always a long wait to get a table, and plenty of good-looking single (and married) women to ogle and strike up acquaintances with before you're seated.

Father has made several notable conquests in this corned-beef-and-pastrami–perfumed ambience. Sometimes he fails, but in true Marxian tradition, he never stops trying.

A year after Dino Martin Junior asked me what it was like to be Groucho's son, I was playing tennis with him again. Between sets Dino complained to me, "Did you know your father tried to pick up my wife in Nate and Al's today?" Dino's wife is the actress Olivia Hussey, who played Juliet in the latest film version of *Romeo and Juliet.*

I told him I didn't know it, but that I wasn't a bit surprised.

"Yeah, Olivia was at a table alone while I was out phoning," explained Dino, "and when I came back she said to me, 'Dino, Groucho Marx came over to the table while you were gone, and you know something—I do believe he tried to pick me up.' "

"Was she very upset?" I asked Dino.

"No, she seemed pleased," replied Dino, with a look of consternation.

When I mentioned the incident to Father and asked him if he knew he'd been fooling around with a married girl, he shrugged and said, "Look, a pretty broad has to expect that kind of thing from me. I'm too old to wait around for her to get divorced."

Recently Nunnally Johnson became so infuriated with Father's girl-watching and girl-picking-up attempts in Nate and Al's that he quit the table in the middle of his meal, complaining indignantly, "Listen, Groucho, I came here to have lunch with you—not to witness your conquests."

If he's not in the mood for love, Father will generally take his noontime repasts at Hillcrest Country Club, where he can trade quips with his fellow comedians—Jack Benny, George Burns and George Jessel.

For many years, a favorite luncheon hangout of Father's was the Friar's Club. But when the club started catering to a gambling crowd, he didn't like the atmosphere and sent in his resignation. By return mail came a letter from the club management insisting on a reason for his resignation. Father swiftly dashed off a reply that has since become a classic. "I don't want to belong to any club that would have me for a member."

Writing funny letters is still one of Father's favorite pastimes. In fact, these days he much prefers the typewriter to the stage as a means of expressing his wit.

In 1971, while rehearsing a strenuous dance number for a television show he was doing in London, Father blacked out on the stage. It was only from exhaustion, but when he returned home, he told me one night, "Tomorrow I'm calling a group of newspapermen to the house and officially announcing my retirement from show business. I'm too old for dancing."

Knowing he could never be happy in complete retirement, I said, "Why do you have to *announce* you're retiring? Why can't you just turn down the jobs you think might be too strenuous, and accept the ones that might be easy and fun?"

"Don't you understand?" he said. "This way I can start collecting my social security benefits."

The rules and regulations of the Social Security Department notwithstanding, the surprising resurgence of the Marx Brothers' popularity today—especially among the anti-establishment on college campuses—has made it virtually impossible for Father to stick to his promise of retirement.

The Marx Brothers' old films—even those that were considered flops in their time—are showing surprising strength as box office attractions in re-run movie houses today. They also turn up regularly on TV, and every now and then are honored at film festivals around the world. The 1972 Cannes Film Festival was the latest to accord them honors.

Because of this, Father is constantly being besieged with offers to lecture at college campuses and to put on one-man shows, such as the one he did in 1972 at Carnegie Hall, which was received with such enthusiasm.

Since the Marx Brothers derived most of their comedy from poking fun at dignity—a formula that dates back to the Greeks—the young people of today, looking for heroes, try to read into their films deeper meaning than was ever intended.

As an example of how this erroneous thinking has proliferated among film students who think they are so hip but in reality are so square, I cite the recent *New Yorker* cartoon that shows a group of hirsute, bespectacled college kids in ernest discussion around a conference table with their professor. The caption reads: "The tautology of their symbolism thus begins to achieve mythic proportions in *A Day at the Races, Duck Soup* and *A Night at the Opera.*"

In Question and Answer sessions on college campuses, Father will frequently be asked to field such erudite Queries as, "In *Duck Soup* how did you arrive at a theme that illustrated so palpably your feelings that the masses are merely pawns of the establishment and big business?" . . . "Was there something symbolic in Chico playing the role of Prime Minister of Sylvania?" . . . "How was the ethnic imbalance of the Marx Brothers as a comedy team arrived at?"

In answer to the latter, I've heard Father reply to a group of film students from UCLA at the Motion Picture Academy one night, "Who knew from ethnic imbalance in our day? We were just struggling vaudevillians trying to be funny. Dialect comics were very popular when we were starting out, so we decided to make Chico a wop."

As for the symbolism of *Duck Soup*, "We just sat down one day and said, 'What can we do a funny picture about next?' And one of us jumped up in the conference room and said, 'Hey, I know—let's do a war picture. Harpo'll look funny in a General's uniform and Groucho'll make a hilarious head of state because he talks fast.' "

When students voice incredulism, disappointment and sometimes even contempt over Father's revelation that the Marx Brothers' only intent was to make audiences laugh so that they would pack customers in at the box office, he is likely to cool them off with, "I suppose you think Herman Melville set out to be symbolic about good and evil when he wrote *Moby Dick*? If you ask me, he just thought he was writing another whaling story. It's the critics who decided he was being symbolic."

If Father's show business career has finally reduced itself to fielding smart-ass questions from over-analytical students, and making occasional appearances on talk shows, it's the world's loss, not his. His mind and tongue are almost as sharp as ever—and probably more uncontrollable.

Among those who see him strolling the sidewalks of Beverly Hills—usually in early afternoon after he has finished casing the girls at Nate and Al's—Father is known as the Elder Statesman. Father is elderly all right. Very few residents of Beverly Hills are any older. But a statesman he still isn't—at least judging from the way he's comported himself in interviews, on talk shows and in private life in recent years.

In *Life with Groucho* I once described Father as having a "tongue that's quicker than his mind." This facility, while of inestimable value when trying to evoke laughter, has also got him into considerable hot water at times.

During President Nixon's first term, a young man phoned Father and represented himself as being a staff writer for *Esquire* with an assignment to do a piece on him. Flattered, Father invited the author and two of his companions to the Bistro to have lunch. They were bearded, and dressed in bell bottoms and a lot of leather, but since that kind of garb isn't unusual today, Father in no way suspected that they might be misrepresenting themselves—that they were actually reporters from a left-wing publication called *The Berkeley Barb*, on specific instructions to goad him into saying something controversial and quotable against the establishment.

Father didn't disappoint them. After two Bloody Marys made his tongue more reckless than it ordinarily was, he remarked that he thought the country might be better off if Richard Nixon were assassinated.

It is, of course, a Federal crime even to suggest such a thing, and Father certainly had no idea that responsible reporters from a magazine like *Esquire* would dream of committing his remark to the public prints—even if they thought he meant it, which he did not. As a matter of fact, he's not even sure that he said it. But publications like *The Berkeley Barb* can never be accused of good taste or restraint, and the editor latched on to what Father allegedly said and printed it in his newspaper.

Within hours, it was picked up by *The New York Times*, and then *Time* and *Newsweek*. Almost before the Elder Statesman of Beverly Hills knew what was happening, he was the center of a furor and being made the subject of a Federal investigation for conspiracy.

Fortunately, Father was able to convince the authorities that he's not only not an advocate of violence, but pro capital punishment, and the charges were dropped.

"Today I'm careful about who I invite to lunch," grins Father. "Just broads with big knockers."

When Pearl Bailey played *Hello Dolly* on the West Coast, Lois and I accompanied Father to the opening at the Shrine Auditorium. Half the audience was black, including the row immediately behind us. As we stood up to go out to the lobby between the acts, Father turned to four nondescript black girls sitting behind us and asked, "Are you the Supremes?"

After a long flight from New York to London, where he went to tape a television show, Father was in a particularly grumpy and ungracious mood when he got off a jet liner at Heathrow Airport. And having to climb thirty-two steps from the field to the arrival terminal didn't improve his disposition. After recovering his breath, he grumbled to the reporters who had come to greet him, "I thought you wanted live tourists over here, but I guess I'm wrong. It must be that your undertakers are having a hard time."

At the Cannes Film Festival in 1972, where the Marx Brothers were being honored for their contributions to comedy, the president of the festival ceremoniously made Father a Commander of the Order of Arts and Letters, and tied around his neck an imposing gold medal pendant hanging from a green and white ribbon.

"All the way from Beverly Hills for this?" cried Father indignantly. "It's not even real gold."

After a week of insulting all the dignitaries at Cannes, Father was approached by an emissary of the British Royal Family, inquiring if he would do his one-man show—the same one he did at Carnegie Hall—as a Command Performance before the Queen.

Father was honored and tempted—until the Britisher informed him that, according to British tradition, all the proceeds from the performance would be given to charity. Upon hearing this shocker, Father shook his head "no," and replied, "Tell the Queen that Groucho doesn't work for nothing."

As I said before, a statesman he isn't.

Occasionally, Father's audaciousness has resulted in his being the recipient of the put-down.

For many years, whenever Father ran into Sam Goldwyn around Hollywood, the producer's opening line would always be, "Hello, Groucho, how's your brother, Harpo?"

It always galled Father that Goldwyn was never interested enough in Groucho to inquire how *he* was, but diplomat that he surprisingly remained in this case, he harbored his resentment for several decades. With his advancing years, he suddenly couldn't take the slight any longer. One night when he bumped into Goldwyn at the Brown Derby, the producer again made an inquiry about Harpo's health. This time Father lashed back with, "For Christ's sake, Sam, why do you always ask me how Harpo is? Why don't you ever ask me how *I* am?"

Goldwyn considered Father's statement for a moment, then said, "I'll do that sometime, Groucho, but right now, how is your brother Harpo?"

On one of his last appearances on the *Dick Cavett Show*, Father showed up sporting a knitted tam, with three large, ball-shaped tassels dangling from it. Because his hair is thinning, and the top of his head was cold in the air-conditioned studio, Father wore the tam during the entire performance.

Sharing a spot with Father that night was Truman Capote, who at one point monopolized the talk with a diatribe against the United States Government for taxing him too heavily.

Father kept trying to interject his opinions, but neither Cavett nor Capote would acknowledge his presence, until finally he said, out of sheer annoyance, "If you were married, Truman, your taxes would be smaller. Why don't you get married?"

"No one has asked me," lisped the quick-thinking Capote.

"I'm available," said Father, with a pert toss of his head that caused the three balls on his tam to bounce around merrily. "Why don't you marry me?"

Piqued that Father wouldn't get off the delicate subject, Capote retorted icily, "Because Groucho, you have three balls!"

If the years haven't very noticeably mellowed Father's approach to the rest of the world, the same can be said of his relations with his family—particularly towards the younger generation. He loves them, but can be just as discouraging to their aspirations as he was when I was growing up.

My son, Andy, is a theater arts major at UCLA, and quite a talented writer and actor. Like many of his generation, he is an ardent fan of the Marx Brothers' old films, and without much provocation will start spouting Grouchoisms, even around the old master.

"Stop already with those old jokes of mine," Father scolded him one day, "and tell me what you're studying in college."

"Writing and acting," answered Andy.

"What makes you think you have any talent?" snapped Father. "Why don't you go into something where you can make a living?"

Andy's not easily discouraged, but he sounded pretty upset when he reported the results of his conversation with his grandfather to me.

"How can he talk that way to me?" complained Andy. "Everyone else thinks I'm pretty good."

"If you think you're going to get any compliments out of him," I said, "you're barking up the wrong grandfather. I'll bet he even told you that hundreds of actors are starving—even those with talent."

"Yeah, how'd you know that?" asked Andy, impressed.

"Remember me?" I said. "I had Groucho for a *father*."

I was annoyed, nevertheless, and the next time I was with Father I told him that I thought it was lousy of him to try to discourage a boy with as much enthusiasm as Andy.

"But he probably hasn't any talent," said Father. "Everyone wants to be an actor."

"You're incorrigible," I said.

"No, I'm not—I'm Groucho!" he replied.

There's never been another one quite like him. And I doubt if there ever will be. He may be retired, but with age, his reputation seems to be growing—also his audacity.

When *Modern Times* was rerun in Beverly Hills not long ago, Father invited Lois and me and his latest girlfriend to see it with him one evening.

It was a week night. There wasn't a soul near the theater, and only about four customers inside, as Father sidled up to the box office and studied the girl behind the cage.

"Can we get in for nothing?" asked Father. "I'm a member of the Academy."

"This isn't an Academy showing," explained the girl.

"You ought to let us in for nothing," remonstrated Father. "I'm Groucho Marx—I'm a Living Legend!"

Nonplussed, the girl hastily summoned the manager.

"I'm Groucho Marx—I'm a Living Legend!" exclaimed Father. "You're not going to make *me* pay."

The manager shrugged helplessly, then waved us through.

Lois and I felt like sinking through the floor with embarrassment. Business wasn't bad enough. The poor guy had to let in four customers on the cuff, besides.

A Living Legend yet!

Well, who but a Living Legend could get away with such outrageous things and still be loved by his friends, fans and family?

"Sure, I'm difficult," admits Father, as he sits back in his hillside home and surveys a legendary show business career that's spanned over sixty years, and the wreckage of three marriages. "Sure I'm difficult. But if I weren't, maybe I'd be a nobody. That's part of my charm."

EPILOGUE

If he was difficult, it's been worth it.

If he inflicted pain (whatever the reason), it might have stung at the time, but it was never intentional.

If it was hard to get out from under his shadow, it wasn't his fault. A giant's shadow often falls a great distance.